Quicken 2000
for the Mac:
THE OFFICIAL GUIDE

Quicken 2000
for the Mac:
THE OFFICIAL GUIDE

Maria LANGER

Osborne **McGraw-Hill**

BerkeleyNew YorkSt. LouisSan Francisco
AucklandBogotáHamburgLondonMadrid
Mexico CityMilanMontrealNewDelhiPanama City
ParisSão PauloSingaporeSydneyTokyoToronto

Osborne/**McGraw-Hill**
2600 Tenth Street
Berkeley, California 94710
U.S.A.

For information on translations or book distributors outside the U.S.A., or to arrange bulk purchase discounts for sales promotions, premiums, or fund-raisers, please contact Osborne/**McGraw-Hill** at the above address.

Quicken 2000 for the Mac: The Official Guide

1234567890 AGM AGM 019876543210

ISBN 0-07-212141-6

Publisher
  Brandon A. Nordin
Associate Publisher and
Editor-in-Chief
  Scott Rogers
Acquisitions Editor
  Joanne Cuthbertson
Project Editor
  Ron Hull
Editorial Assistant
  Stephane Thomas
Technical Editor
  Mark Budzyn

Copy Editor
  Claire Splan
Proofreader
  Linda Medoff
Indexer
  Jack Lewis
Computer Designers
  Roberta Steele
  Gary Corrigan
Illustrators
  Beth Young
  Brian Wells
Series Designers
  Jill Weil, Peter F. Hancik

This book was composed with Corel VENTURA ™ Publisher.

To Leigh Chapman

Contents At A Glance

▍Part V   Saving Money and Achieving Your Goals

Contents

Part II Organizing Your Finances

▌ Part III   Managing Your Financial Records

Acknowledgments

This book, like any other, is the end product of a lot of imagination and hard work by many people. I'd like to take a moment to thank the people who were involved with the creation of this book.

First, thanks to Joanne Cuthbertson at Osborne/McGraw-Hill, for developing the concept of the Quicken Official Guide books and for letting me write the Macintosh version. (I proudly admit that I'm a Mac person at heart!) Joanne worked with me, Osborne, and Intuit to make sure the book's content and design were what everyone wanted. She worked hard, worried only slightly less than she did for the Windows book, and did a great job. She should be proud of the entire Quicken Press series.

Next, thanks to the folks at Intuit, starting with Adam Samuels, Mike Barden, and Rod Cherkas. These guys made sure I had everything I needed to write the book, and then made sure everything I wrote was correct. A special thanks goes to Leigh Chapman, author of the Quicken documentation, for his help and his dedication to making sure terminology falls within Apple's guidelines. (Your name's in this book twice, Leigh; hope you spot the other occurrence!) I'd also like to thank the Quicken 2000 development team for bringing the Mac version of Quicken into the next millennium. We Mac users are glad you didn't desert us after all! Finally, a big thanks to the Quicken 2000 beta support team for giving me quick answers to quick questions when I had them.

More thanks go to the production and editorial folks, including Ron Hull, the project editor; Claire Splan, the copy editor; Mark Budzyn, yet another technical editor; and all the production people who laid out pages and painstakingly positioned all those callouts and callout lines.

Another thanks to Stephane Thomas, the editorial assistant who managed the FedEx packages and e-mails between me, Joanne, Ron, and Mark. Stephane's cheerful e-mails were always the first I read when I checked for messages.

Finally, a huge thanks to Jeremy Judson at Osborne/McGraw-Hill for suggesting me for the Quicken Press projects. Last year was great; this year will be even better!

The last thanks goes to Mike, for putting up with my crazy moods while working on this project and letting yet another summer go by without a vacation. One of these days, we'll squeeze a vacation in . . . I promise!

Introduction

Choosing Quicken to organize your finances was a great decision. Quicken has all the tools you need to manage your personal finances. Its well-designed, intuitive interface makes it easy to use. And its online and automation features make entering transactions and paying bills a snap. But if that isn't enough, Quicken also offers features that can help you learn more about financial opportunities that can save you time and money—two things there never seems to be enough of.

Choosing this book to learn Quicken was also a good decision. As the Official Guide, it has Intuit Corporation's "seal of approval"—which means that Intuit, the developer of Quicken, was involved throughout the book's planning, writing, and production stages. The book was even reviewed for accuracy by the folks at Intuit's Technical Support Department.

This Introduction tells you a little about the book and a little about me—so you know what to expect in the chapters to come.

About This Book

Throughout this book, I tell you how to get the most out of Quicken. I start by explaining the basics—the common, everyday tasks that you need to know just to use the program. Then I go beyond the basics to show you how to use Quicken to save time, save money, and make smart financial decisions. Along the way, I'll show you all of Quicken's features, including a bunch that you probably didn't even know existed. You'll find yourself using Quicken for far more than you ever dreamed you would.

Every book is based on certain assumptions, presents information in a certain order, and uses certain conventions to communicate information. This book is no different. Knowing the book's assumptions, organization, and conventions can help you understand how to use this book as a learning tool.

Assumptions

In writing this book, I had to make a few assumptions about your knowledge of your computer, Mac OS, Quicken, and financial management. These assumptions give me a starting point, making it possible for me to skip over the things that I assume you already know.

What You Should Know About Your Computer and Mac OS

To use this book (or Quicken 2000, for that matter), you should have a general understanding of how to use your computer and Mac OS. You don't need to be an expert. As you'll see, Quicken uses many standard and intuitive interface elements, making it easy to use—even if you're a complete computer novice.

At a bare minimum, you should know how to turn your computer on and off and how to use your mouse. You should also know how to perform basic Mac OS tasks, such as launching and quitting programs, using menus and dialog boxes, and entering and editing text.

If you're not sure how to do these things, check the manual that came with your computer or consult the Mac OS Help Center (choose Help Center from the Help menu). These two resources can provide all the information you need to get started.

What You Should Know About Quicken and Financial Management

You don't need to know much about either Quicken or financial management to get the most out of this book; I assume that both are new to you.

This doesn't mean that this book is just for raw beginners. I provide plenty of useful information for seasoned Quicken users—especially those of you who have used previous versions of Quicken—and for people who have been managing their finances with other tools, such as other software (welcome to Quicken!) or pencil and paper (welcome to the new millennium!).

Because I assume that all this is new to you, I make a special effort to explain Quicken procedures, as well as the financial concepts and terms on which they depend. New concepts and terms first appear in italic type. By understanding these things, not only can you better understand how to use Quicken, you can communicate more effectively with finance professionals such as bankers, stock brokers, and financial advisors.

Organization

This book is logically organized into five parts, each with at least three chapters. It starts with the most basic concepts and procedures, most of which involve specific Quicken tasks, and then works its way up to more advanced topics, many of which are based on finance-related concepts that Quicken makes easy to master.

I want to stress one point here: it is not necessary to read this book from beginning to end. Skip around as desired. Although the book is organized for cover-to-cover reading, not all of its information may apply to you. For example, if you're not in the least bit interested in investing, skip the chapters related to investing. It's as simple as that. When you're ready for the information that you skipped, it'll be waiting for you.

Now here's a brief summary of the book's organization and contents.

Part One: Quicken Setup and Basics

This part of the book introduces Quicken's interface and features and helps you set up Quicken for managing your finances. It also provides the information you need to set up and test Quicken's online features. If you're brand-new to Quicken, I highly recommend reading at least the first two chapters in this part of the book.

Part One has three chapters:

- Chapter 1: Getting to Know Quicken
- Chapter 2: Setting Up Accounts and Categories
- Chapter 3: Online Setup

Part Two: Organizing Your Finances

This part of the book is primarily how-to information about using Quicken to record financial transactions. Because not all Quicken users take advantage of its online features, this section provides details about features you can use without connecting to the Internet, an online service, or a financial institution. But as you read through the chapters in this section, you'll learn some of the ways Quicken's online features can make organizing your finances quicker or easier to do.

There are four chapters in Part Two:

- Chapter 4: Recording Bank and Credit Card Transactions
- Chapter 5: Tracking Investments
- Chapter 6: Monitoring Assets and Loans
- Chapter 7: Automating Transactions

Part Three: Managing Your Financial Records

Once you've entered data into Quicken, you can use that information to manage and analyze your finances. That's what this part of the book is all about. It explains how to reconcile accounts, generate reports and graphs, and develop budgets and forecasts.

There are three chapters in Part Three:

- Chapter 8: Reconciling Accounts
- Chapter 9: Insights, Reports, and Graphs
- Chapter 10: Budgeting and Forecasting

Part Four: Saving Time with Online Features

While Part Two only mentions Quicken's online features, Part Four provides the details you need to use them to their fullest. In its chapters, you'll learn about the Quicken.com Web site and how to take advantage of the convenience of online financial services and investing.

Part Four has three chapters:

- Chapter 11: Introducing Quicken.com
- Chapter 12: Using Online Account Access and Payment
- Chapter 13: Updating Your Portfolio's Value with Quicken Quotes

Part Five: Saving Money and Achieving Your Goals

This part of the book helps you to save money where savings are needed most: on big-ticket items such as income taxes, insurance, and the purchase of a home or car. Although Quicken can't pay for these things, it can help you gather the information you need—or organize the information you already have—to make smart, money-saving decisions. This part also shows you how you can use Quicken to help achieve your goals. Whether you want to make the most of your invested funds; have financial security in your retirement years; or save up for the down payment on a house or college education for your children, Quicken can help you.

Part Five has four chapters:

- Chapter 14: Saving Money at Tax Time
- Chapter 15: Minimizing Home, Car, and Insurance Expenses
- Chapter 16: Maximizing Investment Returns
- Chapter 17: Planning for the Future

Conventions

All how-to books—especially computer books—have certain conventions for communicating information. The following sections outline the conventions I use throughout this book.

Menu Commands

Quicken, like other Mac OS programs, makes commands accessible on the menu bar at the top of screen. Throughout this book, I tell you which menu commands to choose to open a window or dialog box or to complete a task. I use the following format to indicate menu commands: Menu | Submenu (if applicable) | Command.

So, for example, if I wanted you to choose the QuickReport command under the Activities menu, I'd tell you to choose Activities | QuickReport. If I wanted you to choose the Find command from the Find/Replace submenu under the Edit menu, I'd tell you to choose Edit | Find/Replace | Find.

Keystrokes

Keystrokes are the keys you must press to complete a task. There are two kinds of keystrokes.

Keyboard Shortcuts   Keyboard shortcuts are combinations of keys you press to complete a task more quickly. For example, the shortcut for "clicking" a Cancel button may be to press the Esc key. When instructing you to press a key, I provide the name of the key in small caps, like this: ESC. If you must press two or more keys simultaneously, I separate them with a dash, like this: COMMAND-P.

Literal Text   Literal text is text that you must type in exactly as it appears in the book. Although there aren't many instances of literal text in this book, there are a few. I display literal text in bold type, like this: **Checking Acct**. If literal text includes a variable—text you must substitute when you type—I include the variable in bold italic type, like this: ***Payee Name.***

Icons

I use icons to indicate a wide variety of useful information.

Shortcut | *Like most other Mac OS programs, Quicken often offers more than one way to complete a task. The Shortcut icon identifies a method for completing a Quicken task more quickly than other methods.*

Tip   *A Tip is a little something extra that you don't really need to know. Tips can help you get more out of Quicken when you're ready to go beyond the basics.*

Caution   *A Caution is vitally important information that can protect you from data loss or other serious consequences. Don't skip the Cautions!*

 SAVE TIME   The Save Time icon identifies Quicken features that can save you time. Don't confuse these with Shortcuts—although Shortcuts can save you time when working with a specific feature, a Save Time icon identifies specific features that can save you time. For example, as you'll see in Part Four of this book, online credit-card tracking can save lots of time spent entering transactions.

 SAVE MONEY   The Save Money icon identifies Quicken features that can save you money.

 GET SMARTER   The Get Smarter icon identifies Quicken features that can help you learn more about a concept. You'll find that the Get Smarter icons can help you make better, more informed decisions.

 New in Quicken 2000
In addition to extensive interface changes, the folks at Intuit made plenty of changes to Quicken's feature set. The New in Quicken 2000 icon identifies many new features.

About the Author

Finally, let me tell you a little bit about me.

I graduated from Hofstra University with a BBA in Accounting in—well, you don't really need to know *when*. I worked as an accountant, auditor, and financial analyst over the next eight years. Then I realized that I really didn't like what I was doing every day and took the necessary steps to change careers. I've written two dozen computer books since the change, many of which are about business and productivity software such as Word, Excel, and FileMaker Pro. Although some of my books are for Windows users, I'm a Mac person at heart, so most of my books are for the Mac OS platform.

I use Quicken. I've been using it for years. I use it to manage four bank accounts and three credit card accounts, to track two mortgages, and to pay all my bills (online, of course). I also use its investment features to track my portfolio and research the companies in which I invest. While I don't use all Quicken features regularly, I've used them all at least once to save time, save money, make important financial decisions, or help me plan for my future.

Frankly, I can't imagine not using Quicken. And I'm glad to have the opportunity to show you why you would agree.

Quicken Setup and Basics

This part of the book introduces Quicken's interface and features. It begins by explaining how to install Quicken and showing you the elements of its user interface. It tells you all about Quicken's accounts and categories, and explains how you can modify the default setup to add your own accounts and categories. Finally, it tells you why you should be interested in online access and tells you how you can set up your computer to access the Internet and Quicken.com. The three chapters are:

Getting to Know Quicken

In This Chapter:

- *An Overview of Quicken*

- *Installing Quicken*

- *Launching Quicken*

- *The Quicken Interface*

- *Online Help*

- *Quitting Quicken*

If you're brand-new to Quicken, get your relationship with Quicken off to a good start by properly installing it and learning a little more about how you can interact with it.

In this chapter, I provide a brief overview of Quicken, explain how to install and launch it, take you on a tour of its interface, and show you how to use its extensive onscreen Help features. Although the information I provide in this chapter is especially useful to new Quicken users, some of it also applies to upgrading users.

What Is Quicken?

On the surface, Quicken is a computerized checkbook. It enables you to balance your accounts, and organize, manage, and generate reports for your finances. But as you explore Quicken, you'll learn that it's much more than just a computerized checkbook. It's a complete personal finance software package—a tool for taking control of your finances and making your money work harder for you.

What Quicken Can Help You Do

At the very least, Quicken can help you manage your bank and credit card accounts. You can enter transactions and have Quicken generate reports and graphs that show where your money went and how much is left.

Quicken can also help you manage investment accounts. You can enter transactions and have Quicken tell you the market value of your investments. Quicken can also help you organize other data, such as the purchase price and current worth information for your possessions, and vital information you may need in the event of an emergency.

With all financial information stored in Quicken's database, you can generate net worth reports to see where you stand today. You can also use a variety of planning calculators to make financial decisions for the future. And Quicken's Deduction Finder helps you find deductible expenses for tax time.

With Quicken's online features, you can automate much of your data entry. Online banking enables you to keep track of bank account transactions and balances and to pay bills without writing checks or sticking on stamps. You can also explore a whole world of up-to-date information that you can use to shop for the best bank accounts, credit card accounts, loans, and insurance. You can read news and information about investment opportunities and advice offered by financial experts. You can get in touch with other Quicken users to see how they use Quicken to manage their money.

Now tell me, can the paper check register that came with your checks do all that?

Save Time, Save Money, Get Smarter

This book has an underlying theme: save time, save money, and make informed financial decisions. You'll see plenty of examples of how Quicken can do this throughout this book, but here are a few simple examples to whet your appetite:

 SAVE TIME   Entering transactions into registers can be tedious. But Quicken offers several features for speeding up this process, including memorized transactions, QuickFill, and the ability to download transactions from a financial institution.

 SAVE MONEY   Many of the organizations you pay every month—credit card companies, banks, and utilities—charge a late fee when payment is received after the due date. Quicken's Billminder feature helps you remember when payments are due. Its online payment and scheduling features can work together to automatically pay bills when they are due. Making timely payments saves money.

 GET SMARTER   Buying a home is a big purchase decision that is based on many smaller decisions. How much can you afford to spend on a home? What are the current interest rates and other loan terms? What will your monthly payments be? Which loan is right for you? Quicken can help answer all of these questions by providing access to up-to-date information via QuickenMortgage and a variety of planning tools such as the Loan Calculator.

These are just a few examples. Quicken is full of smart features like these. It takes the drudgery out of organizing and managing your finances and rewards you by helping you make the most of your money.

Getting Started

Ready to get started? In this section, I explain how to install, launch, and register Quicken. I also explain how to prepare a new data file or update an existing data file for use with Quicken 2000.

Installing Quicken

Quicken uses a basic Mac OS installer that should be familiar to you if you've installed other Mac programs. It installs the software on your hard disk and prompts you to restart your computer.

Insert the Quicken 2000 CD into your CD-ROM drive. If necessary, double-click the Quicken Deluxe 2000 CD icon that appears on your Desktop to open its window. Double-click the icon named "Install Quicken 2000." The installer's splash screen with general information about Quicken appears. Click the Continue button.

The installer displays a software license agreement. Read the agreement. To continue the installation, you'll have to click the Accept button.

Next, the installer displays some important information about installing Quicken. Read the information and click Continue.

Finally, the installer's main installation window appears:

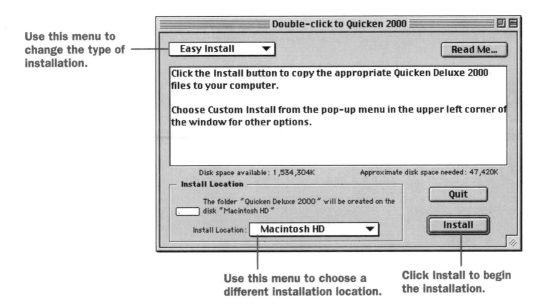

Use this menu to change the type of installation.

Use this menu to choose a different installation location.

Click Install to begin the installation.

This window offers two options for changing the default installation:

Changing the Type of Installation   By default, the installer uses Easy Install to perform a basic installation of all Quicken Deluxe 2000 features. To specify which Quicken features should be installed, choose Custom Install from the pop-up menu at the top of the window. The window's contents change to list different installation options, as shown on the next page. Turn on the check boxes for the options you want to install.

Changing the Installation Location   By default, the installer installs Quicken's files on your startup disk, which is normally your internal hard disk. You can select a different location from the Install Location pop-up menu at the bottom of the window. If you choose Select Folder, a standard open dialog box

Click an "I" icon to learn more about a feature.

Turn on check boxes for the features you want to install.

Click this triangle to display or hide specific applications.

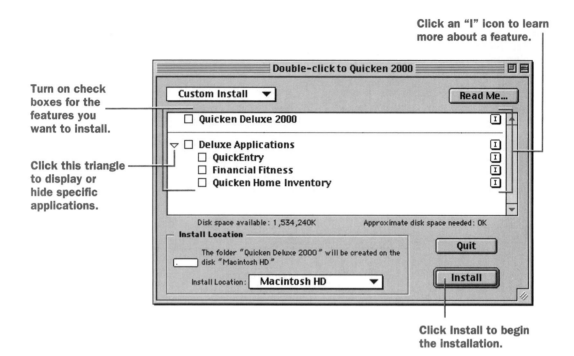

Click Install to begin the installation.

appears. Use it to locate and select the folder you want to install the Quicken Deluxe 2000 folder into, for example, your Applications folder. Then click the Select button.

To begin the installation, click the Install button. A dialog box tells you that you'll have to restart your computer after installation. Click Continue.

The installer begins the installation process. It displays a progress dialog box while it works. If you're upgrading from a previous version of Quicken, a dialog box appears, asking if you want to move your existing Quicken data into the new Quicken 2000 folder. Click the Don't Move or Move button as desired.

When the installer has finished, a dialog box appears, telling you that you must restart your computer. Click Restart.

Tip   *If you're upgrading from a previous version of Quicken, you can delete the old Quicken folder once you've begun using your data file with Quicken 2000. Make sure your Quicken data file is not in the old Quicken folder, and then drag the folder to the Trash and empty the Trash.*

Quicken Deluxe 2000 Components

A default installation of Quicken places the Quicken Deluxe 2000 folder on your hard disk. Open the folder to access Quicken's files:

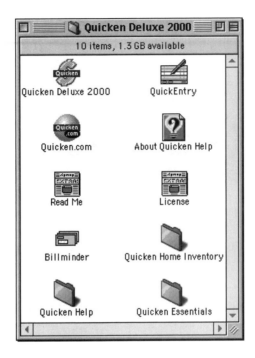

- **Quicken Deluxe 2000** is the main Quicken program I discuss throughout this book.
- **QuickEntry** is a program that enables you to enter transactions into Quicken without opening Quicken itself. I explain how to use QuickEntry in Chapter 4.
- **Quicken.com** is a program that launches your default Web browser and connects you to Quicken.com on the Internet. I tell you about Quicken.com throughout this book.
- **Billminder** is a program that reminds you when it's time to pay bills. I discuss Billminder in Chapter 7.

Other items in the Quicken Deluxe 2000 folder include information and support files that work with Quicken.

Launching Quicken

You can launch Quicken components three different ways.

Opening a Quicken Application Icon   To open a Quicken component in the Quicken Deluxe 2000 folder window, simply double-click its icon.

Opening a Quicken Data File Icon   You can launch Quicken and open a specific Quicken data file by double-clicking the data file icon. I tell you more about data documents later in this chapter.

Using the Apple Menu   Choose the item you want to launch—Quicken.com or QuickEntry—from the Apple menu:

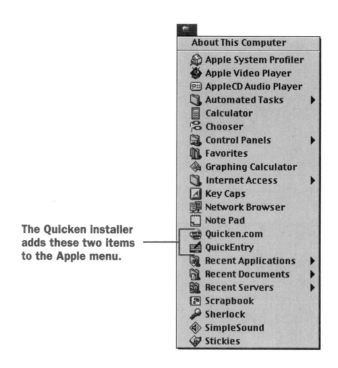

The Quicken installer adds these two items to the Apple menu.

Personalizing and Registering Quicken

The first time you launch Quicken, a personalization dialog box appears. Enter your name in the edit box and click OK.

Next, a registration dialog box appears. You have three options:

- **Remind Later** tells Quicken to remind you to register the next time you launch Quicken. Quicken will keep reminding you until you register.
- **Don't Register** dismisses the dialog box without giving you a chance to register. The dialog box will not appear again.
- **Register Online** uses your Internet connection to exchange information with the folks at Intuit and obtain your Customer Number. When you click this button, a dialog box with an information form appears. Use it to enter information about yourself, and then click the Connect button. Quicken connects and exchanges data. When it's done, Quicken will be registered.

Preparing a Data File

Quicken stores all of your financial information in a Quicken data file. Before you can use Quicken, you must either create a new data file or convert an existing data file for use with Quicken 2000.

The first time you launch Quicken 2000, a dialog box asks whether you are an Upgrading User or a New User. Click the appropriate button.

Upgrading User

When you click the Upgrading User button, Quicken displays a series of dialog boxes with information about Quicken's new features. Click the Continue button in each dialog box to learn about these features.

Next, Quicken updates your existing Quicken data file for use with Quicken 2000. If your data file is in the Quicken Deluxe 2000 folder, Quicken does the update automatically. But if your data file is elsewhere on your hard disk or Quicken can't find it, it displays a standard Open dialog box you can use to locate, select, and open the data file. Quicken makes a copy of the data file and puts it into a folder called Old Quicken® Data. It then updates the data file, opens it, and displays Quicken's Banking tab.

New User Setup

When you click the New User button, Quicken displays a series of dialog boxes you can use to set up a new Quicken data file. The Category Selection dialog box appears first:

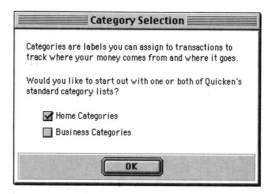

Turn on the check box beside each type of category you want. You have two options:

- **Home Categories**, the default, are income and expense categories related to your home and family.
- **Business Categories** are income and expense categories appropriate for use by a small business, including one you run out of your home.

I tell you more about categories in Chapter 2, so don't worry if the term doesn't mean much to you now. When you've finished setting options, click OK to continue.

Next, Quicken displays the Set Up Account dialog box, which I discuss in greater detail in Chapter 2:

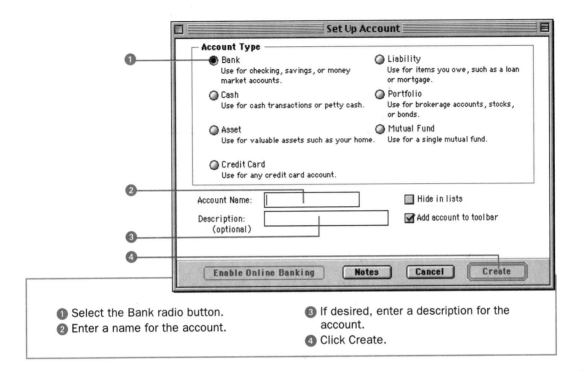

1 Select the Bank radio button.
2 Enter a name for the account.

3 If desired, enter a description for the account.
4 Click Create.

Make sure that Bank is selected under Account Type; then enter a name for your checking account in the Account Name edit box. If desired, you can also enter a description for the account in the edit box below it. For example, my personal checking account's name is "Checking" and its description is "Maria's Checking Account." When you've finished, click Create.

Quicken creates a data file for your financial information. It names the file "Quicken Data" and places it in the Quicken Deluxe 2000 folder. Then it displays Quicken's Banking tab with the Checking Register and Accounts list window open.

Note   *Throughout the New User Setup process, Quicken displays Help windows with additional information and instructions. You can dismiss any of these dialog boxes by clicking its Close box.*

The Quicken Interface

Quicken's interface is designed to be intuitive and easy to use. It puts the tools you need to manage your finances right within mouse pointer reach. You never have to dig through multiple dialog boxes and menus to get to the commands you need most.

In this section, I tell you about the components of the Quicken interface and explain how you can use them to make your work with Quicken easy.

Quicken Desktop and Controls

Quicken windows and controls appear on the Quicken Desktop, which is illustrated in Figure 1-1. Here's a quick overview of the Desktop and controls, with several Quicken windows open.

The Quicken Desktop

The Quicken Desktop is like an electronic desk blotter. It covers your entire screen with a customizable background pattern, except for a triangular tab in the bottom-right corner. You can click in that corner to quickly switch to the Finder. When Quicken is not the active application, the Quicken Desktop disappears, although any open Quicken windows remain on screen.

Menu Bar

Like all other Mac OS programs, Quicken displays a number of menus in a menu bar at the top of the screen. You can choose commands from the menus in two ways:

- Click the menu name to display the menu. If necessary, click the name of the submenu you want (as shown next), and then click the name of the command that you want.
- Press the shortcut key combination for the menu command that you want. A command's shortcut key, if it has one, is displayed to the right of the command name on the menu, as shown here:

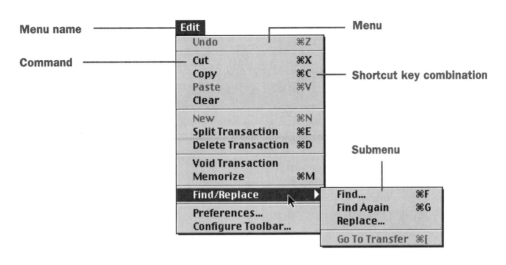

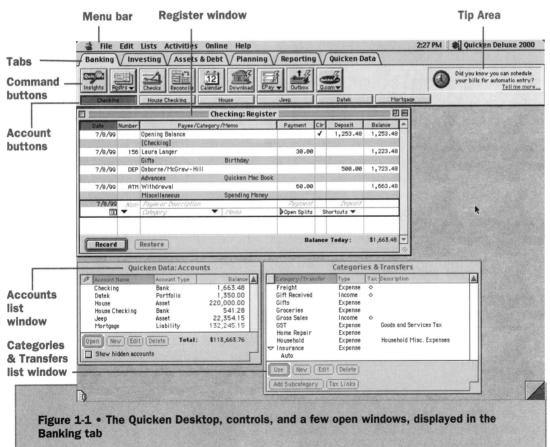

Figure 1-1 • The Quicken Desktop, controls, and a few open windows, displayed in the Banking tab

Tabs

Tabs are used to switch from one set of command buttons and open Quicken windows to another. (This feature was available in Quicken 98, but the tabs appeared as buttons along the left side of the screen.) When you switch to a different tab, Quicken saves the open windows in the current tab. Thus, when you return to that tab, the windows appear just as you left them, enabling you to continue working where you left off.

Here's an example. You can use the Banking tab to pay some bills, then click the Investing tab to check your investments, and then click the Reporting tab to create a report. When you click the Banking tab, the windows are exactly the same as they were when you left them—set up for your banking tasks.

> **Tip** *You can create new tabs for additional custom window configurations. I tell you how in the section titled "Customizing the Toolbar," later in this chapter.*

Command Buttons

Command buttons offer access to frequently used Quicken features. The command buttons that appear in the toolbar vary depending on the currently displayed tab. For example, the Banking tab displays command buttons for banking features while the Investing tab displays command buttons for investing features. Buttons that include tiny black triangles (such as the Rgstrs button in Figure 1-1) are menus; choose an option from the button's menu to access its feature.

> **Tip** *You can customize each set of command buttons by adding or removing buttons as desired. I tell you how in the section titled "Customizing the Toolbar," later in this chapter.*

Account Buttons

Account buttons offer one-click access to frequently used account registers. This feature was also in Quicken 98, but the buttons appeared as tiny tabs at the bottom of the Quicken Desktop.

> **Tip** *You can specify which account buttons appear in each tab. I explain how later in this chapter.*

Tip Area

The Tip Area offers tips and other information about getting the most out of Quicken. Click an underlined link to learn more about a tip topic.

Windows

Quicken displays information in windows. It has different types of windows for the different types of information it displays. Here are some of the windows you'll work with as you use Quicken.

Insights

The Quicken Insights window (see Figure 1-2) provides information about your financial status, as well as clickable links to work with Quicken features and get information from the Internet.

Tip *You can customize the Insights window so it shows the things that interest you most. I tell you how in Chapter 9.*

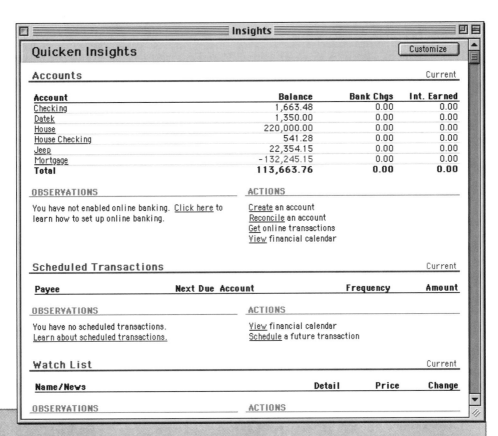

Figure 1-2 • **The Quicken Insights window provides information about your Quicken data.**

List Windows

A list window shows a list of information about related things, such as accounts, categories, classes, or scheduled transactions. You can use a list window to perform tasks with items in the list. The Quicken Data: Accounts window and the Categories & Transfers window shown in Figure 1-1 are two examples of list windows.

Register Windows

You use a register window to enter and edit transactions for a specific account. Each account has its own register. The Checking: Register window shown in Figure 1-1 is an example of a register window. I tell you more about using registers in Chapter 4.

Dialog Boxes

Like other Mac OS applications, Quicken uses dialog boxes to communicate with you. Some dialog boxes display a simple message, while others include edit boxes, radio buttons, check boxes, and pop-up menus you can use to enter information. When a dialog box appears, you must dismiss it before you can continue working with Quicken.

Customizing Quicken

There are two main ways to customize Quicken so it works—and looks—the way you want it to: by setting preferences and by customizing the toolbar. I cover both topics in this section.

Setting Quicken Preferences

Quicken's Preferences window offers a number of preference categories you can set to change Quicken's appearance and functionality. To open the window, choose Edit | Preferences. When you first open it, it displays the General options and looks like this:

Click an icon to view its options.

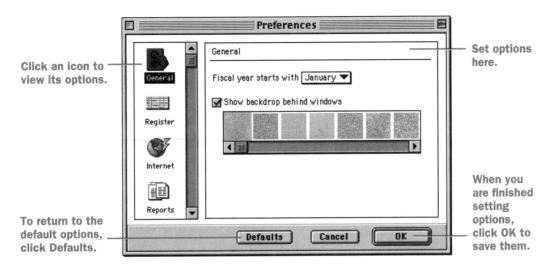

Set options here.

To return to the default options, click Defaults.

When you are finished setting options, click OK to save them.

You can click icons in the scrolling list along the left side of the window to display the various categories of options. Here's a summary of the options you can set.

General Preferences

General preferences control the fiscal year starting month and Quicken Desktop pattern.

- **Fiscal year starts with** enables you to select a month from the pop-up menu. The month you select becomes the starting month of your fiscal year. By default, this option is set to January.
- **Show backdrop behind windows** enables you to toggle the setting for the Desktop's background. Turning off this check box removes the background so other applications' windows and the Finder Desktop appear behind Quicken windows. This option is turned on by default.
- You can change the background pattern of the Quicken Desktop by clicking one of the pattern samples in the middle of the window.

Register Preferences

Register preferences control the way account registers work. As you can see in the following illustration, there are quite a few options!

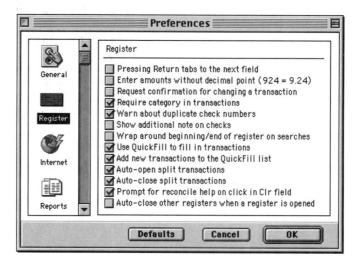

- **Pressing Return tabs to the next field** tells Quicken to move from field to field when you press either the TAB or RETURN key. With this option turned off, Quicken moves to the next field when you press the TAB key only. This option is turned off by default.

- **Enter amounts without decimal point** instructs Quicken to automatically insert a decimal point two places from the right when you enter a number. For example, with this option enabled, if you enter **924**, Quicken accepts it as 9.24. This option is turned off by default.

- **Request confirmation for changing a transaction** tells Quicken to display a confirmation dialog box each time you make a change to a previously entered transaction. By default, this option is turned off.

- **Require category in transactions** tells Quicken to remind you to include a category when you attempt to record a transaction without one. By default, this option is turned on.

- **Warn about duplicate check numbers** tells Quicken to warn you if you attempt to record a transaction with the same check number as an existing transaction. This option is turned on by default.

- **Show additional note on checks** tells Quicken to provide an additional note field in the Write Checks window. By default, this option is turned off.

- **Wrap around beginning/end of register on searches** tells Quicken to continue searches after reaching the beginning or end of a register when the search began in the middle. This option works with the Find and Find and Replace commands. By default, this option is turned off.

- **Use QuickFill to fill in transactions** tells Quicken to automatically enter a transaction from the QuickFill list when you enter the beginning of the QuickFill entry in a register. This feature can save a lot of time, as I explain in Chapter 7. By default, this option is turned on.
- **Add new transactions to the QuickFill list** tells Quicken to automatically add each new register transaction to the QuickFill list. This option is turned on by default.
- **Auto-open split transactions** tells Quicken to automatically display all line items in a split transaction when you select it. This option is turned on by default.
- **Auto-close split transactions** tells Quicken to automatically hide all line items in a split transaction when you have finished working with it. This option is turned on by default.
- **Prompt for reconcile help on click in Clr field** tells Quicken to ask if you want to reconcile a transaction when you click the Clr field for a transaction. This option is turned on by default.
- **Auto-close other registers when a register is open** tells Quicken to automatically close open register windows when you open a different register window. This option can prevent screen clutter by keeping too many windows from being open at once, but it also prevents you from looking at more than one register at a time. By default, this option is turned off.

Note *I provide detailed instructions for using account registers in Chapter 4.*

Internet Preferences

The Internet preferences enable you to configure Quicken for accessing the Internet. There are two options:

- **Internet Service Provider** refers to the service you use to connect to the Internet. Your options are America Online and Other Internet Service Provider. If you have a direct connection to the Internet, you can click the Select Proxy button, if necessary, to enter information about your proxy server.

Caution *Do not set proxy information unless instructed by your network administrator. Doing so could prevent you from connecting to the Internet.*

- **Current Browser** enables you to select a Web browser for use with Quicken. Click the Select Browser button and use the dialog box that appears to locate and open your preferred Web browser.

Note | *I discuss connecting to the Internet in Chapters 3 and 11 and elsewhere in this book.*

Reports Preferences

Reports preferences, which are illustrated next, enable you to specify default settings for creating reports. Here are your options:

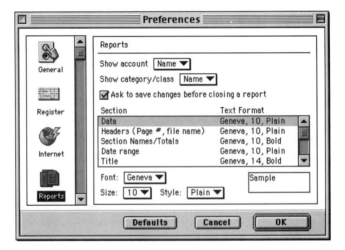

- **Show account** enables you to choose the information that should show for each account in the report. Your options are Name and Description, Name (the default setting), and Description.
- **Show category/class** enables you to choose the information that should show for each category and class in the report. Your options are also Name and Description, Name (the default setting), and Description.
- **Ask to save changes before closing a report** tells Quicken to display a dialog box asking if you want to save changes you made to a report when you close the report. By default, this option is turned on.
- Formatting options can be set for each section of a report. Select the section for which you want to set formatting options, then choose options from the pop-up menus near the bottom of the window. The sample area shows what the changes look like. Do this for each report section that you want to change.

Note   *I cover creating reports in Chapter 9.*

Graphs Preferences

Graphs preferences look and work a lot like report preferences. Use radio buttons to select whether you want 2-dimensional or 3-dimensional styles (3-D is selected by default). Then set formatting options for graph sections the same way you do for report sections.

 Note   *I tell you how to create graphs in Chapter 9.*

Print Checks Preferences

Print Checks preferences enable you to set up Quicken for printing checks. To use this feature, you must obtain Quicken-compatible check stock from Intuit or another supplier. The options vary slightly based on the type of printer you have. Here's what they look like for a LaserWriter printer:

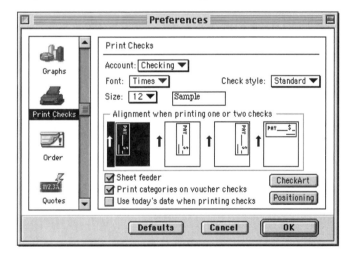

- **Account** enables you to select the account for which you will print checks.
- **Font** and **Size** enable you to set the typeface and typeface size to appear on checks.
- **Check style** enables you to select one of the compatible check styles: Standard (the default selection), Voucher, or Wallet.
- **Alignment when printing one or two checks** enables you to select one of four alignment options for feeding checks. Look carefully at the pictures to determine which one is correct for your printer. This option is not available

when you select the Voucher check style or have a pin-feed printer (such as an ImageWriter).

- **Sheet feeder** tells Quicken you're using a printer with a sheet feeder.
- **Print categories on voucher checks** tells Quicken to print transaction category information on the voucher portion of checks.
- **Use today's date when printing checks** tells Quicken to print the current date on checks. With this option turned off, Quicken prints the transaction date on checks.
- **CheckArt** enables you to include a graphic on your checks. Use the Copy command in your graphics program to copy an image to the Clipboard. Then switch back to Quicken, click the CheckArt button, and use the Paste command to paste the image in.

Caution | *CheckArt images may print over other check information, such as your name and address, depending on the style and layout of your checks.*

- **Positioning** enables you to fine-tune the positioning of check information on check stock. If a sample printed check indicates that adjustments are necessary, click the Positioning button to display the Adjust Positioning dialog box, which is shown next. Enter values to adjust the vertical and horizontal position of various check elements and click OK to save your settings. Print another sample check to see how your adjustments affected the check printout and make additional adjustments if necessary.

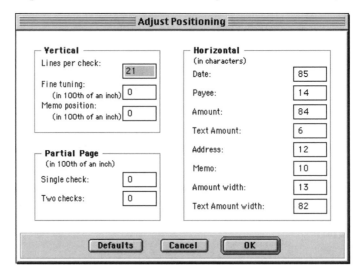

Caution *Under normal circumstances, it should not be necessary to make position adjustments. Do not make changes in this dialog box unless a sample check printout indicates that an adjustment is necessary.*

Note *I tell you how to print checks from within Quicken in Chapter 4.*

Order Preferences

If you print checks with Quicken, you'll probably want to set up order reminders. This tells Quicken to remind you to order checks when you get to a certain check number. You do this in the Order Checks preferences:

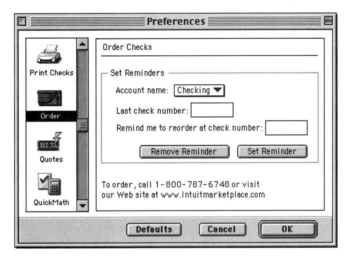

Set three options:

- **Account name** is the name of the account for which you want to be reminded to order checks.
- **Last check number** is the check number on the last check in your box of checks.
- **Remind me to reorder at check number** is the check number at which Quicken should remind you to order checks.

Here's how it works. Suppose you have a box of checks numbered 501 to 700. You write about five checks a week and you want to be reminded to order checks at least three weeks in advance. You'd enter **700** in the "Last check number" edit box and **685** in the "Remind me to reorder at check number" edit box.

To save the reminder, click the Set Reminder button. If you want to remove the reminder—perhaps because you bought checks before Quicken reminded you to—click the Remove Reminder button.

Note | *I explain how to print checks in Chapter 4.*

Quotes Preferences

There's only one Quotes preference: a check box to specify the percent at which you should be notified of a portfolio account's change when you download security prices into Quicken. By default, the value is 2%—this means if an account's value changes by 2% or more (either gain or loss) when you download security prices, Quicken tells you about it.

 Note | *I tell you about downloading stock quotes in Chapter 13.*

QuickMath Preferences

QuickMath preferences enable you to configure the QuickMath feature. This feature can automatically perform calculations when you enter values followed by a non-numeric keyboard key. For example, to multiply the value 5 by 0.01, you'd enter 5%. This is a predefined value for QuickMath, as shown here:

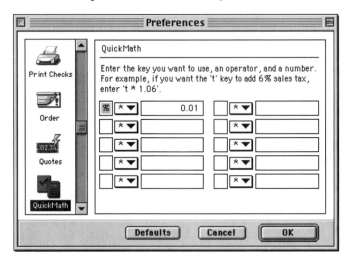

You can create up to ten QuickMath functions by entering a key, operator, and value for each one.

Passwords Preferences

Passwords preferences enable you to set up two different passwords for the Quicken data file:

- **To open a file** is the password that is required to open the data file. You might find this feature useful if the computer on which your Quicken data file resides is shared by others.
- **To modify transactions** is the password that is required to modify transactions made on or before a specific date. To use this option, you must enter a password and a date.

When you enter a password into each of these edit boxes, the password appears as bullet (•) characters. When you click OK or attempt to view another preferences category, Quicken prompts you to re-enter the same password. The passwords you enter each time must match for the feature to be enabled.

Caution   *If you use either of these two features, don't forget your password! If you do, you could be locked out of your data files or prevented from modifying transactions!*

File Backup Preferences

The Data File Backup preferences enable you to set options for Quicken to either automatically back up your data or remind you to back up your data:

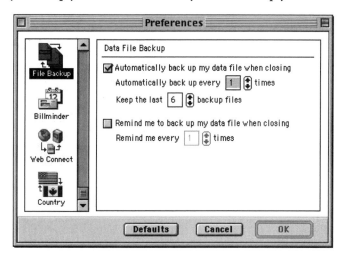

- **Automatically back up my data file when closing** tells Quicken to back up your data file when you close it. If you turn on this check box, you can enter values in the two edit boxes below it. The first tells Quicken how often to back up the data file. The default value is 1, or every time you close your data file. The second value specifies how many backup files Quicken should keep. The default value is 6, or the last six versions of the data file. Backup files are stored with your Quicken data file.

- **Remind me to back up my data file when closing** tells Quicken to display a backup reminder dialog box when you close the data file. If you turn on this check box, you can specify how often Quicken should remind you. The default value is 1, or every single time you close the data file. (A bit annoying, don't you think?)

Tip   *Use the automatic backup feature to prevent data loss in the event of a corrupted data file. Although it doesn't happen often, it could happen. It's a lot better to have a backup copy handy than to have to rebuild a data file from scratch.*

Billminder Preferences

Billminder preferences determine how the Billminder feature works. There are three options to set:

- **Days in advance** enables you to specify how many days in advance Billminder should remind you about postdated checks and scheduled transactions. You can enter a value from 0 to 30 in this edit box.
- **When you turn on your computer** tells Quicken to remind you about postdated checks and scheduled transactions when you turn on your computer.
- **When you start Quicken** tells Quicken to remind you about postdated checks and scheduled transactions when you launch Quicken.

Note   *I tell you about the Billminder feature in Chapter 7.*

Web Connect Preferences

Web Connect preferences includes only one option: "Verify that Quicken is the default Web Connect application when it is launched." With this check box turned on, Quicken will check to see if your Web browser is set up to download bank statements to Quicken. If it is not, Quicken will offer to correct the problem.

Note *The Web Connect feature is offered by some banks that do not directly support Quicken's online banking or bill pay features. If you need to use this feature to download transactions from your bank, your bank can explain how it works. I discuss Quicken's online banking and bill pay features in Chapter 12.*

Country Preferences

Country preferences enable you to specify whether you want to use the U.S. or Canadian version of Quicken. Select the appropriate radio button to make your selection. To complete the switch from one version to another, you'll have to click OK, and then quit and relaunch Quicken.

Customizing the Toolbar

You can also customize the appearance and functionality of Quicken by making changes to the toolbar. You can show or hide any of the toolbar's elements (tabs, command buttons, and account buttons), specify which command buttons should appear on a tab, and even create your own custom tabs.

You do all this with the Configure Toolbar dialog box, shown next. To display it, choose Edit | Configure Toolbar.

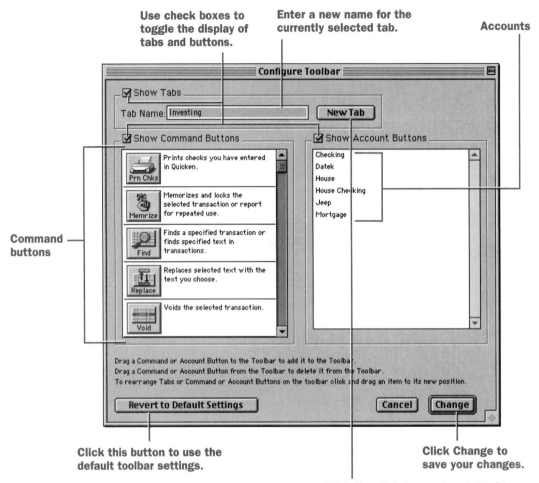

Use check boxes to toggle the display of tabs and buttons.

Enter a new name for the currently selected tab.

Accounts

Command buttons

Click this button to use the default toolbar settings.

Click Change to save your changes.

Click New Tab to create a tab with the name in the Tab Name edit box.

Shortcut *Customizing the toolbar for each Quicken tab enables you to set up your own shortcuts for the features you use most.*

Toggling the Display of Toolbar Elements

Three check boxes within the Configure Toolbar dialog box enable you to toggle the display of toolbar elements: Show Tabs, Show Command Buttons, and Show Account Buttons. Turn off a check box to hide the element; turn on a check box to display the element.

Modifying Tabs

You can modify tabs in a number of ways:

- To change the name of a tab, begin by clicking the tab you want to change to make it active. Then enter a new name in the Tab Name edit box. When you click the Change button, the tab name changes.
- To remove a tab, drag it off the toolbar. When you release the mouse button, the tab disappears.
- To create a new tab, enter a name for the tab in the Tab Name edit box, and then click the New Tab button. The tab appears at the top of the toolbar, beside the other tabs. Follow the instructions earlier in this section to customize the tab's toolbar as desired.
- To change the position of tabs, drag a tab to a new position on the toolbar. When you release the mouse button, the tab moves.

Modifying Command Buttons

Start by clicking the tab for which you want to modify command buttons. Then use one of the following techniques to make the change:

- To remove a command button from the toolbar, drag it off the toolbar. When you release the mouse button, the command button is removed.
- To add a command button to the toolbar, locate the button you want to add in the scrolling list within the Configure Toolbar dialog box. Then drag the button from the list into position on the toolbar. When you release the mouse button, the command button is added.

Modifying Account Buttons

Although Quicken can automatically add account buttons to the toolbar of the tab in which you open the account, you can also specify which account buttons should appear on a tab's toolbar. First, click the tab for which you want to modify account buttons. Then use one of the following techniques to make the change:

- To remove an account button from the toolbar, drag it off the toolbar. When you release the mouse button, the account button is removed and appears in the list of accounts in the Configure Toolbar dialog box.
- To add an account button to the toolbar, locate the account you want to add in the scrolling list within the Configure Toolbar dialog box. Then drag the

account name from the list into position on the toolbar. When you release the mouse button, the account button is added and its name is removed from the list.

- To change the position of account buttons on the toolbar, drag an account button to a new position on the toolbar. When you release the mouse button, the account button moves.

Note   *If all accounts already appear as buttons on the toolbar, the account scrolling list will be empty.*

Restoring all Toolbars to Quicken Defaults

If you decide you don't like your changes to the toolbar, you can restore them to "factory defaults" by clicking the Revert to Default Settings button.

Saving Your Changes

To save your changes, be sure to click the Change button at the bottom of the Configure Toolbar dialog box.

Onscreen Help

Quicken includes an onscreen Help system to provide more information about using Quicken while you work. Onscreen Help includes a variety of Help features, each designed for a specific purpose. In this section, I describe your options and explain how to use Quicken Help.

Using the Help Menu

All components of Quicken's onscreen Help system can be accessed by commands on the Help menu:

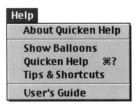

Here's a quick rundown of the kinds of help you can get.

About Quicken Help   The About Quicken Help option displays a window with buttons you can click to learn all about Quicken's onscreen Help features.

Balloon Help   Choosing Help | Show Balloons turns on the Mac OS Balloon Help feature, which is implemented within Quicken. With this feature turned on, you can point to an item onscreen to see a cartoon balloon with information about the item. Although this is a great way to learn about screen elements, those balloons can get annoying. Turn the feature off by choosing Help | Hide Balloons.

Quicken Help   Choosing the Quicken Help command (or pressing COMMAND-?) displays Quicken Help. I explain how to use it in the next section.

Tips & Shortcuts   The Tips & Shortcuts command displays a window with buttons you can click to get tips in a variety of categories: Data Entry, Investments, Planning, Reports & Graphs, Saving Time, Customizing, and Miscellaneous. Click a button to start displaying tips in a Help window. Each time you click the right arrow button, a new tip appears.

Shortcut   *Once you're familiar with using Quicken, be sure to explore the Tips & Shortcuts feature to learn how you can save time performing Quicken tasks.*

User's Guide   The User's Guide command launches the Adobe Acrobat Reader to display Quicken's onscreen *User's Guide* in Acrobat PDF file format (see Figure 1-3). You can use the page navigation buttons at the top of the screen to move from one page to another. If desired, you can even use the Print command (File | Print, or COMMAND-P) to print all 600+ pages of the manual for reference.

Note   *Adobe Acrobat Reader must be installed on your computer to use this feature. The Quicken Deluxe 2000 CD includes the Acrobat Reader 4.0 Installer; if Acrobat is not already installed on your computer, you can use this installer to install it.*

Quicken Help

Quicken's onscreen Help uses the same Help viewer as most Mac OS programs. You can use it to browse or search Help topics.

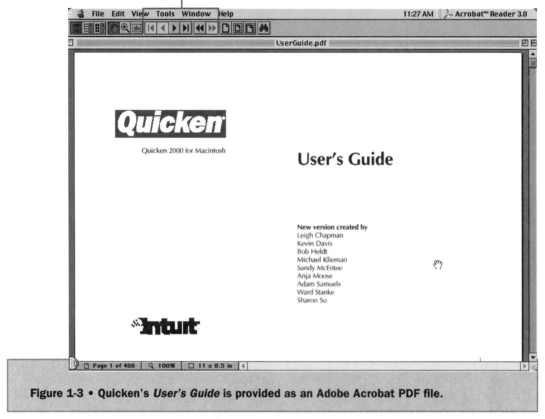

Figure 1-3 • Quicken's *User's Guide* is provided as an Adobe Acrobat PDF file.

Browsing Help Topics

Start by choosing Help | Quicken Help, or pressing COMMAND-? or HELP. The
Quicken Help window appears. Click its Topics button to display Help Topics
and select a topic that interests you. You can then select a phrase related to the
topic, as shown here:

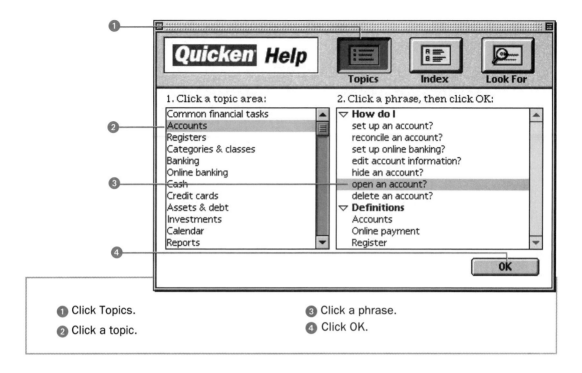

1 Click Topics.
2 Click a topic.
3 Click a phrase.
4 Click OK.

If you select one of the How Do I? phrases in the Quicken Help window, when you click OK, a window containing the first step of step-by-step instructions appears:

These step-by-step instructions utilize Apple Guide technology—this means that while the window provides written instructions, onscreen prompts such as red circles and red, underlined menu commands may also appear to guide you. You click the right arrow in the window to advance to the next step.

If you select one of the Definitions phrases in the Quicken Help window, a definition window like the one illustrated next appears. It defines the term you selected.

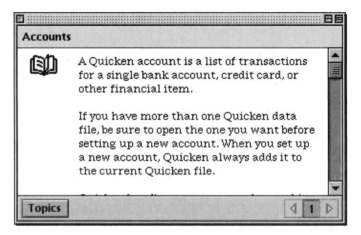

When you've finished using either of these Help windows, you can click its Close box to dismiss Help or click the Topics button to return to the Quicken Help window.

Browsing the Help Index

Start by choosing Help | Quicken Help or pressing COMMAND-? or HELP to display the Quicken Help window. Click its Index button to display an alphabetical index. Use the slider at the top of the index to choose the first letter of the topic that interests you, and then select a topic in the index below it. You can then select a phrase related to the topic, as shown here:

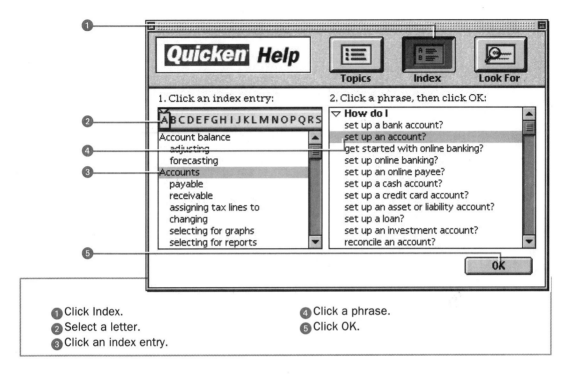

1. Click Index.
2. Select a letter.
3. Click an index entry.
4. Click a phrase.
5. Click OK.

The Help windows that appear when you click OK are the same as the ones that appear when you browse Help, as discussed in the previous section.

Searching Help

Choose Help | Quicken Help or press COMMAND-? to display the Quicken Help window. Click its Look For button to display a search window. Click in the edit box to activate it and enter search words, then click the Search button. A list of matches appears on the right side of the window. You can then select a topic, as shown next:

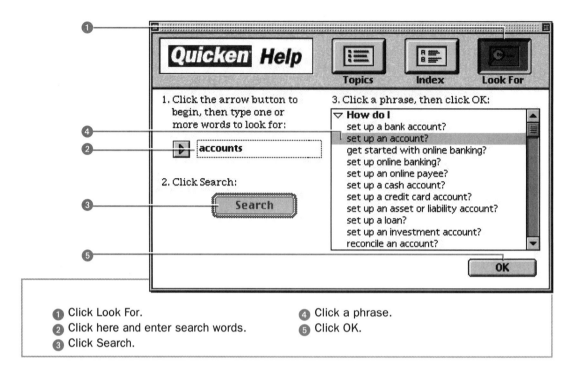

- ❶ Click Look For.
- ❷ Click here and enter search words.
- ❸ Click Search.
- ❹ Click a phrase.
- ❺ Click OK.

The Help windows that appear when you click OK are the same as the ones that appear when you browse Help, as discussed earlier in this section.

Quitting Quicken

When you've finished using Quicken, choose File | Quit or press COMMAND-Q. This saves your data file and closes the Quicken application.

Setting Up Accounts and Categories

Chapter 2

In This Chapter:

- *Overview of Data Files, Accounts, and Categories*

- *Creating a New Data File*

- *Setting Up Accounts*

- *Working with the Accounts List*

- *Setting Up Categories and Subcategories*

- *Working with the Categories & Transfers List*

To make the most of Quicken, you must properly set it up for your particular financial situation. This means adding accounts and categories as necessary to meet your specific needs. It takes only a minute or two to add each account or category. You'll probably want to do this when you first start using Quicken, but you can do it anytime you like.

In this chapter, I explain how to set up the Quicken accounts and categories you'll use to organize your finances.

Before You Begin

Before you start the setup process, it's a good idea to have an understanding of how data files, accounts, and categories work. You should also gather together a few documents to help you properly set up your accounts.

Data Files

All the transactions you record with Quicken are stored in a *data file* on your hard disk. This file includes all the components—accounts, categories, and transactions—that make up your Quicken accounting system.

Although it's possible to have more than one Quicken data file, it isn't usually necessary. One file can hold all of your data. In fact, it's difficult (if not downright impossible) to use more than one Quicken file to track a single account, like a checking or credit card account. And splitting your financial records among multiple data files makes it impossible to generate reports that consolidate all the information.

When would you want more than one data file? Well, you could use two data files if you wanted to use Quicken to organize your personal finances and the finances of your business, which has entirely separate bank, credit, and asset accounts—or if you're using Quicken to track the separate finances of multiple individuals.

Accounts and Categories

There are two primary components to every transaction you record in Quicken: account and category.

An *account* is a record of what you either own or owe. For example, your checking account is a record of cash on deposit in the bank that is available for writing checks. A credit card account is a record of money you owe to the credit card company or bank for the use of your credit card. All transactions either increase or decrease the balance in one or more accounts.

A *category* is a record of where your money comes from or goes. For example, salary is an income category for recording the money you earn from your job. Dining is an expense category you might use to record the cost of eating out. Categories make it possible to track how you earn and spend money.

If you know anything about accounting, these concepts should sound familiar, even if the names don't match what you learned in school or on the job. Accounts are what you'd find on a *balance sheet;* categories are what you'd find on an *income statement.* Quicken can produce reports like these; I tell you how in Chapter 9.

What You Need

To properly set up accounts, you should have balance information for the accounts that you want to monitor with Quicken. You can get this information from your most recent bank, investment, and credit card statements. It's a good idea to gather these documents before you start the setup process so they're on hand when you need them.

If you plan to use Quicken to replace an existing accounting system—whether it's paper-based or prepared with a different computer program—you may also find it helpful to have a *chart of accounts* (a list of account names) or a recent income statement. This way, when you set up Quicken accounts and categories, you can use familiar names.

Creating a Quicken Data File

To use Quicken, you must have at least one data file. If you followed the instructions in Chapter 1 for installing and setting up Quicken, you already have a data file and can skip this section. But if, for some reason, you decide you need additional data files, here's how you can create them.

Start by choosing File | New File. A dialog box appears, asking if you're sure you want to create a new file. Click OK. Quicken displays the Save: Quicken Deluxe 2000 dialog box:

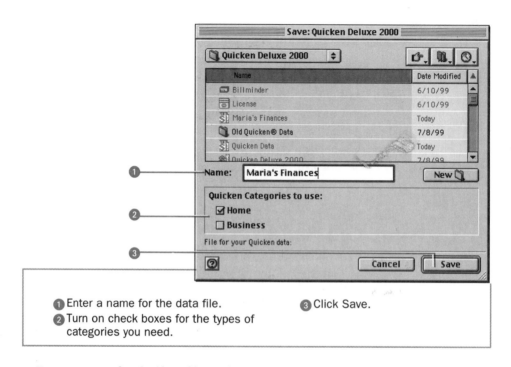

① Enter a name for the data file.
② Turn on check boxes for the types of categories you need.
③ Click Save.

Enter a name for the data file in the Name edit box and turn on the check boxes for the types of Quicken categories you want to use. Although you can also change the folder location for the file, it's easier to find the data file if it's in the Quicken Deluxe 2000 directory with other Quicken data files. Click Save to create the file.

Quicken then displays the Set Up Account dialog box, which you can use to create an account. Every Quicken file must have at least one account—normally, the first account you create is a checking account. I explain how to use this dialog box to create accounts in the section titled "Setting Up Accounts," a little later in this chapter. When the account has been created, you can begin working with the new Quicken data file.

Tip   *If you have more than one Quicken data file, you can see which one is open by looking at the tabs in the toolbar— the name of the active file should appear on the last tab. To open a different data file, choose File | Open File and use the dialog box that appears to select and open a different file. Only one Quicken data file can be opened at a time.*

Accounts

While the majority of your expenditures may come from your checking account, you probably have more than one account that Quicken can track for you. By setting up all your accounts in Quicken, you can keep track of balances and activity to get a full picture of what you own and what you owe.

Types of Accounts

Quicken Deluxe offers seven different kinds of accounts for tracking what you own and what you owe:

What You Own

In accounting jargon, what you own are *assets*. In Quicken, an asset is one type of account, but there are several others:

Bank   Bank accounts are for tracking money in the bank. You can use bank accounts for checking, savings, and money market accounts.

Cash   Cash is for tracking cash inflows and expenditures—pocket money, so to speak.

Asset   Asset accounts are for tracking items that you own, such as your home, car, or recreational vehicle.

Portfolio   Portfolio accounts are for tracking the stocks, bonds, and groups of mutual funds in your portfolio.

Mutual Fund   Mutual fund accounts are for tracking individual mutual funds.

What You Owe

The accounting term for what you owe is *liabilities*. Quicken offers two kinds of accounts for amounts you owe:

Credit Card   Credit Card is for tracking credit card transactions and balances.

Liability   Liability is for tracking loans, such as a mortgage or car loan, and other liabilities.

Displaying the Accounts List Window

You can view a list of your accounts at any time. Choose Lists | Accounts, or press COMMAND-A. The Accounts list window (shown next) appears. For each account, it displays the account name, account type, and balance.

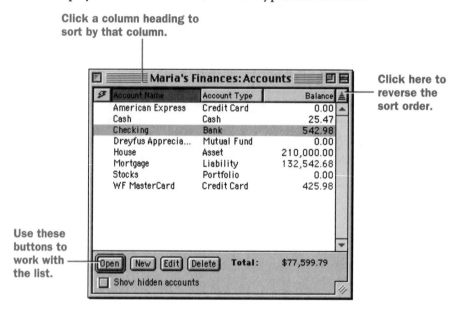

Click a column heading to sort by that column.

Click here to reverse the sort order.

Use these buttons to work with the list.

Setting Up Accounts

You create new accounts by entering basic information into the Set Up Account dialog box, and then entering starting balances for most types of accounts in the account's register.

Entering Account Information

Click the New button at the bottom of the Accounts list window or, with the Accounts list window active, choose Edit | New Account, or press COMMAND-N. The Set Up Account dialog box appears:

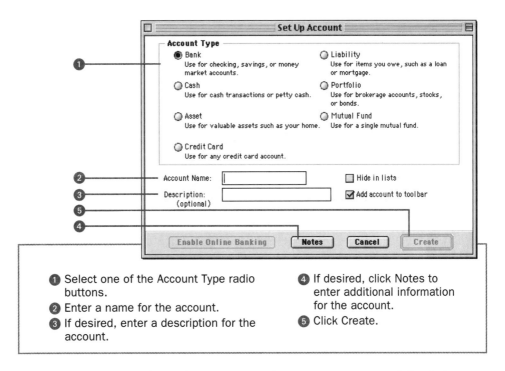

① Select one of the Account Type radio buttons.
② Enter a name for the account.
③ If desired, enter a description for the account.
④ If desired, click Notes to enter additional information for the account.
⑤ Click Create.

Enter information about the account in the appropriate areas of the dialog box. Here's the information you'll have to provide:

Account Type   The account type is one of the seven account types. Select a radio button to specify the type.

Account Name   The account name is the name of the account. Account names should be short yet descriptive, so they're not confused with other accounts. For example, rather than name your two checking accounts Checking 1 and Checking 2, give them names that are based on their purposes, like Primary Checking and House Checking.

Description Although a description is optional, you may want to use it to provide additional information about the account, such as the financial institution name or the account number.

Credit Limit For credit card accounts, Quicken also prompts you to enter the credit limit for the account. This is the amount of credit you're allowed to accumulate on the credit card.

Add Account to Toolbar You can turn on the "Add account to toolbar" check box to automatically add an account button for the account to the toolbar of the currently displayed tab.

Taxable For portfolio and mutual fund accounts, Quicken provides a check box you can use to specify whether the account is taxable. For example, the account for an IRA would not be taxable, so you can turn off the check box for this type of account.

To enter more information about the account, such as the contact information for the financial institution or a complete description of the account's purpose, click the Notes button. Enter information in the Notes dialog box (shown next) and click OK.

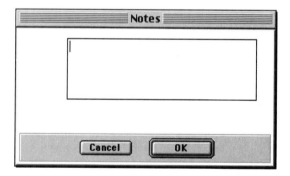

When you've finished entering account information, click the Create button to create the account.

Entering Account Balances

When you click Create in the Set Up Account dialog box, the account is created and its register window, which is shown next, appears. If you created any account other than a portfolio or mutual fund account, you can enter opening balance information for the account right in the register window. The best place to get

opening balance information is from your most recent account statement—
a bank statement, credit card bill, or similar document for the account.

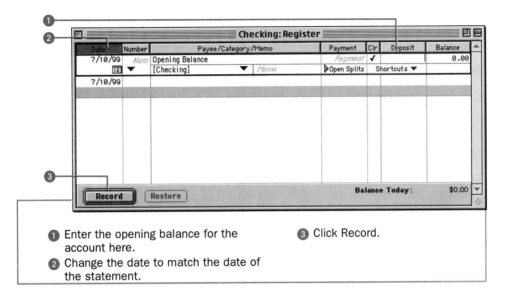

① Enter the opening balance for the account here.

② Change the date to match the date of the statement.

③ Click Record.

Note   *I tell you more about using register windows in Part II of this book.*

Where you enter the opening balance depends on the type of account:

Type of Account	Enter Opening Balance in First Row of This Column
Bank	Deposit
Cash	Receive
Asset	Increase
Credit Card	Charge
Liability	Increase

You should also enter the statement date for the account. This defines your starting date—you will only enter new transactions for the account if they occurred *after* that date.

After entering the opening balance and date, click Record to save the entry.

Note   *You enter balances for portfolio and mutual fund accounts by entering security transactions. I explain how to do this in Chapter 5.*

Managing Accounts

The Accounts list window offers a quick and easy way to manage your accounts. You can use buttons at the bottom of the window to open, add, remove, or modify accounts and you can edit accounts to hide or display them in lists. Here's a quick rundown of the things you can do.

Working with Accounts

The buttons at the bottom of the Accounts list window perform specific account management tasks:

Open Open opens the register for the selected account. I explain how to use registers in Part II of this book.

Shortcut *You can also open an account by double-clicking its name in the Accounts list window or by clicking its button in the toolbar.*

New New displays the Set Up Account dialog box (illustrated earlier in this chapter) so you can create a new account.

Edit Edit displays the Edit Account dialog box for the selected account. This dialog box looks and works just like the Set Up Account dialog box. You can use it to change the name and description of the account or hide the account. For some types of accounts, you can also change the account type. Just make the desired changes and click the Change button.

Delete Delete enables you to delete the selected account. It displays a dialog box you can use to confirm that you want to delete the account. You must click Yes in the dialog box to delete the account.

Caution *When you delete an account, you permanently remove all of its transactions from your Quicken data file. To get the account out of sight without actually deleting it and its data, consider hiding it instead. I tell you how next.*

Hiding Accounts

You can use the Hide option to remove an account from view so it does not appear in lists and cannot be used in transactions. This is a good way to get an inactive account out of the way without deleting it and its transactions.

In the Set Up Account or Edit Account dialog box, turn on the Hide in Lists check box. When you click Create or Change, the account is hidden.

You can display hidden accounts in the Accounts list window by turning on the "Show hidden accounts" check box. The information for a hidden account appears in italics, like this:

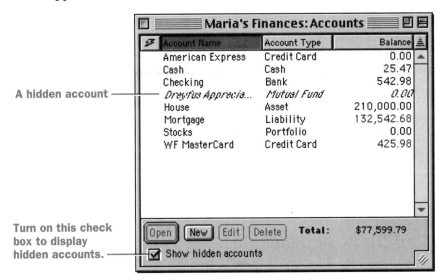

A hidden account ————

Turn on this check
box to display
hidden accounts. ————

To unhide an account, turn off the check box for the account in the Edit Account dialog box. The account appears in lists and can be used in transactions again.

Categories

When you create a data file, Quicken automatically creates dozens of commonly used categories based on options you set. Although these categories might completely meet your needs, there may be times when you'll want to add, remove, or modify a category to fine-tune Quicken for your use.

Types of Categories

There are basically two types of categories: income and expense.

Income

Income is incoming money. It includes things such as your salary, commissions, interest income, dividend income, child support, gifts received, and tips.

Expense

An *expense* is outgoing money. It includes things such as insurance, groceries, rent, interest expense, bank fees, finance charges, charitable donations, and clothing.

Subcategories

A *subcategory* is a subset or part of a category. It must be the same type of category as its primary category. For example, the Auto category may be used to track expenses to operate your car. Within that category, however, you may want subcategories to record specific expenses, such as fuel and repairs. Subcategories make it easy to keep income and expenses organized into manageable categories, while providing the transaction detail you might want or need.

Displaying the Categories & Transfers List Window

You can view a list of your categories at any time. Choose Lists | Categories & Transfers or press COMMAND-L. The Categories & Transfers list window appears. For each category, it displays the category name, type, tax status, and description:

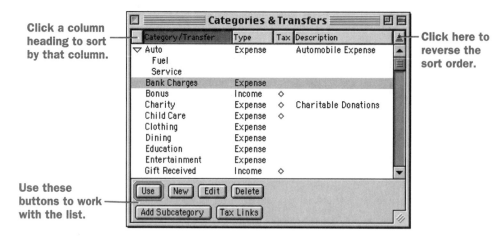

Creating a New Category

Click the New button at the bottom of the Categories & Transfers list window or, with the Categories & Transfers list window active, choose

Edit | New Category, or press COMMAND-N. The Set Up Category dialog box appears:.

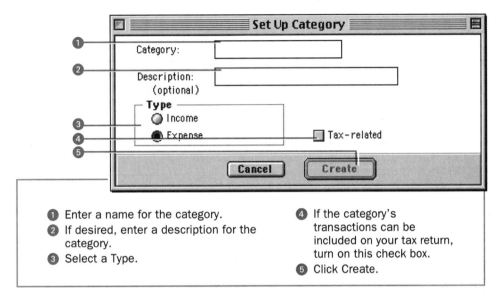

① Enter a name for the category.
② If desired, enter a description for the category.
③ Select a Type.

④ If the category's transactions can be included on your tax return, turn on this check box.
⑤ Click Create.

Enter information about the category in the appropriate areas of the dialog box. Here's the information you'll have to provide:

Category Name   The Category Name is the name of the category. Make sure it's descriptive enough that you won't confuse it with other categories.

Description   The Description is an optional description for the category.

Type   Type is the type of category: Income or Expense. Select one of the radio buttons.

Tax-Related   If the category can be included on your tax returns, turn on the Tax-related check box. It will then appear on tax reports you generate with Quicken. I tell you how to create reports in Chapter 9 and how to use Quicken's tax features in Chapter 14.

When you've finished entering information in the Set Up Category dialog box, click Create. The category is added to the list.

Creating a Subcategory

You create a subcategory almost the same way you create a category. Start by selecting the category under which you want to create the subcategory. Then click the Add Subcategory button. The Set Up Category dialog box that appears looks and works just like the one shown previously, but you cannot select a category type—remember, a subcategory must be the same type as its parent category. Enter information about the subcategory and click Create. It's added to the Categories & Transfers list window, indented beneath the parent category, like this:

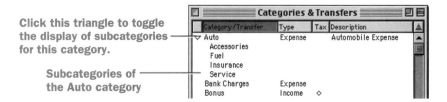

Click this triangle to toggle the display of subcategories for this category.

Subcategories of the Auto category

> **Tip**   *You can turn a category into a subcategory by dragging its name onto the name of another category. When you release the mouse button, the category you dragged becomes a subcategory. Likewise, you can "promote" a subcategory to a category by dragging its name to the left. When a tiny box appears to the left of the subcategory name, release the mouse button. The subcategory turns into a category.*

Managing Categories

You can use buttons at the bottom of the Categories & Transfers list window to work with the list.

Use   The Use button enables you to use the selected category in a transaction. I explain how to enter transactions in Part II of this book.

New   The New button displays the Set Up Category dialog box illustrated earlier in this chapter. Use it to create a new category.

Edit   The Edit button displays the Edit Category dialog box for the selected category or subcategory. This dialog box looks and works just like the Set Up Category dialog box. You can use it to make just about any change to a category.

Delete   The Delete button enables you to delete the selected category or subcategory. If you click this button, a dialog box appears, asking you to confirm that you really do want to delete the category. You must click Yes to delete it. If the category is referenced by transactions, the category is removed from those transactions, thus resulting in uncategorized transactions.

Caution   *If you delete a category that has subcategories, the category and all of its subcategories are removed.*

Add Subcategory   The Add Subcategory button enables you to create a subcategory for the selected category.

Tax Links   The Tax Links button enables you to link categories and subcategories to specific income tax schedules and lines. I tell you how to use this feature to help you prepare for tax time in Chapter 14.

Online Setup

In This Chapter:

- *Benefits of Going Online with Quicken*

- *What You Need to Connect to the Internet*

- *Setting Up an Internet Connection*

- *Testing Your Connection*

- *Troubleshooting Connection Problems*

Many of Quicken's features work seamlessly with the Internet. If you have access to the Internet, either through a connection to an Internet Service Provider (ISP) or through a connection to an online service such as America Online or CompuServe, you can take advantage of these online features to get up-to-date information, automate data entry, pay bills, and obtain Quicken maintenance updates.

In this chapter, I tell you why you might want to take advantage of Quicken's online features. Then I explain how to set up Quicken to go online.

What? You don't currently have Internet access? No problem! I tell you what you need to know to sign up with an ISP, too.

Why Go Online?

Before I go any further, I want to remind you that you don't *have* to go online to use Quicken. Quicken is a good financial management software package, even without its online features. But Quicken's online features make it a *great* financial management software package. As you'll see in this section and throughout this book, Quicken 2000 uses the Internet to help you make better financial decisions by bringing you information and resources relevant to your personal financial situation.

The best way to explain the benefits of going online is to list a few of the features online users can take advantage of.

If You Have a Bank Account, You Can Benefit

Throughout the month, you write checks and mail them to individuals and organizations. You enter these transactions in your checking account register. At month's end, you reconcile the account. You can do all this without going online. I tell you how in Chapters 4 and 8.

But if you register for Online Account Access with your bank, you can download all bank account activity on a daily basis so you know exactly when the transactions hit your account—even the ATM and debit card transactions you always forget to enter. If you register for Online Payment, you can pay your bills without licking another envelope or pasting on another stamp. I explain how all this works in Chapter 12.

If You Have Credit Cards, You Can Benefit

Do you have credit cards? Then you may take advantage of Quicken's credit card tracking features, which I cover in Chapter 4, to keep track of your charges, payments, and balances. You don't need to go online.

But if you sign up for Online Account Access, all your credit card charges can be downloaded directly into Quicken, eliminating the need for time-consuming data entry, while giving you an up-to-date summary of your debt and how you spent your money. Online Account Access can even tell you when your bills are due and prepare the transactions for payment. I tell you more about this in Chapter 12.

If You Invest, You Can Benefit

Quicken can keep track of your investments, whether they are 401(k) accounts, mutual funds, or stocks. You can enter share, price, and transaction information into Quicken and it will summarize portfolio value, gains, and losses. It'll even keep track of securities by lot. You don't need to go online to track your investments. I explain how in Chapter 5.

But with Online Investment Tracking, Quicken can automatically obtain quotes on all the securities in your portfolio and update its market value. You can use its online features to obtain valuable, up-to-date research information about securities that interest you. You can "chat" with other investors to see what's hot—and what's not. These online features help you make informed investment decisions. I tell you about all this in Chapters 13 and 17.

If You Want to Save Money, You Can Benefit

Car insurance. Mortgages. Car loans. Bank accounts. All of these things have one thing in common: their rates vary from one provider to another. Shopping for the best deal can be a lot of time-consuming work—wading through newspaper and magazine ads, making calls, visiting banks. Quicken's planners can help you evaluate the deals you learn about, without going online.

But with the help of Quicken's built-in Internet links, you can shop for the best deal online, without leaving the comfort of your desk, getting newspaper ink all over your hands, or spending an afternoon listening to music while on hold. Up-to-date rates are only a mouse click away with an Internet connection and Quicken to guide you.

Enough Already!

If all this doesn't convince you that going online with Quicken can help you save time, save money, and get smarter, stop reading and move on to the next chapter. You'll probably never be convinced. I will say one more thing, however: after using Quicken's online features for more than four years now, I can't imagine using Quicken any other way.

Security Features

Perhaps you're already convinced that the online features can benefit you. Maybe you're worried about security, concerned that a stranger will be able to access your accounts or steal your credit card numbers.

You can stop worrying. The folks at Intuit and the participating banks, credit card companies, and brokerage firms have done all the worrying for you. They've come up with a secure system that protects your information and accounts.

PINs

A *PIN,* or *Personal Identification Number,* is a secret password you must use to access your accounts online. If you have an ATM card or cash advance capabilities through your credit card, you probably already have at least one PIN, so the idea shouldn't be new to you. It simply prevents anyone from accessing the account for any reason without first entering the correct PIN.

An account's PIN is initially assigned by the bank, credit card company, or brokerage firm. Some companies, like American Express, require that your PIN consist of a mixture of letters and numbers for additional security. You can change your PINs to make them easier to remember—just don't use something obvious like your birthday or telephone number. And don't write it on a sticky note and attach it to your monitor! If you think someone might have guessed your PIN, you can change it.

> **Tip**   *It's a good idea to regularly change all your PINs and passwords— not just the ones you use in Quicken.*

Encryption

Once you've correctly entered your PIN, the instructions that flow from your computer to the bank, credit card company, or brokerage firm are encrypted.

This means they are encoded in such a way that anyone able to "tap in" to the transactions would "hear" only gibberish. Quicken does the encryption using, at a minimum, the 56-bit single Data Encryption Standard (DES). Quicken is also capable of encrypting data with stronger methods, including the 128-bit RC4 or 168-bit triple DES. Once the encrypted information reaches the computer at the bank, credit card company, or brokerage firm, it is unencrypted, and then validated and processed.

Encryption makes it virtually impossible for any unauthorized party to "listen in" on your transaction. It also makes it impossible for someone to alter a transaction between the moment it leaves your computer and the moment it arrives at your bank, credit card company, or brokerage firm for processing.

Other Security Methods

Quicken also takes advantage of other security methods for online communications, including Secure Sockets Layer (SSL) encryption, digital signatures, and digital certificates. Together, all of these security methods make online financial transactions secure—even more secure than telephone banking, which you may already use!

What You Need

To take advantage of Quicken's online features, you need a connection to the Internet. There are different ways to connect and different organizations that can provide the connection. In this section, I explain your options.

> **Tip** | *If you already have a connection to the Internet or online service, you may already have everything you need. Read on to make sure.*

Internet Service Provider (ISP)

An *ISP* is an organization that provides access to the Internet, usually for a monthly fee. These days, there are literally thousands of ISPs that can provide the access you need for Quicken's online features. Here's a partial list:

- America Online (version 3.0 or higher)
- AT&T WorldNet
- CompuServe
- Concentric Network (CNC)

- Earthlink/Sprint
- GTE
- Internet MCI
- Microsoft Network
- Mindspring
- Netcom
- Prodigy

If you don't already have an account with an ISP, you must set one up before you can configure Quicken to use its online features. Consult the information that came with your copy of Quicken for special deals on Internet accounts through Quicken-preferred ISPs. Or check your local phone book for an ISP near you.

Internet Connection Methods

You can connect to the Internet in either of two ways: with a direct connection or a dial-up connection.

Direct Connection   A *direct* or *network* connection directly connects your computer to the ISP, usually via a network. This is common in office environments these days, but it is still uncommon for households because it's expensive and can be difficult to set up.

Dial-Up Connection   A *dial-up* or *modem* connection uses a modem to connect to an ISP via a telephone line. The modem dials a telephone number, connects to your ISP's computer, exchanges some ID and protocol information, and connects to the Internet. This is the most common connection method for households because it's inexpensive and easy to set up.

Keep two things in mind if you use a dial-up connection:

- If you have only one phone line, that phone line will be in use while you are accessing Quicken's online features (or any other Internet feature). That means you can't accept incoming calls. And if someone picks up an extension while you're online, there's a good chance you'll be disconnected. If you spend a lot of time online, whether using Quicken or just "surfing the Net," you might want to consider adding a second line to your house. It's not as expensive as you might think. Just don't let the phone company talk you into a special data phone line for modem connections. You don't need a special line, and you certainly don't need to pay for one.

- If you have call waiting, you must disable it when you connect to the Internet. Otherwise, the call waiting tone that sounds when there's an incoming call can disconnect you. You can automatically disable call waiting by entering specific digits—usually *70—before dialing the phone. If you have call waiting, check with the phone company to see what the codes in your area are.

More About Modems

If you know that modem stands for *mo*dulator/*dem*odulator, I'm impressed! But do you need to know that? No. Modem connections are so easy to set up and use that you don't need to know the geeky terminology for the things that make it work.

Anyway, a dial-up connection requires a modem. Here are some things to consider when shopping for a modem:

- If you have a 9,600 bps modem lying around, give it away (if you can find someone to take it). Although it will be fast enough to exchange data for Online Account Access, Online Payment, and Online Quotes, you'll fall asleep if you try to use it to view Web pages. A 14.4 Kbps modem is (barely) okay; a 28.8 Kbps modem is better. If you buy a new modem, don't buy anything slower than 56 Kbps if you expect it to last more than a few years. These numbers, in case you haven't caught on, refer to speeds; the higher the number the better.
- Modem prices are way down these days—you should be able to get a good 56 Kbps fax-modem for well under $200. And yes, I did say fax-modem. That means you can use it to send and receive faxes, too. (It isn't worth buying a modem that can't handle faxes, even if you could find one.)
- Modems can be internal or external. If internal, the modem plugs into a slot on your computer's main circuit board. That means you (or your friendly neighborhood computer guru) must open the computer's case and install it. If external, the modem plugs into your computer's serial or USB port. That means you must have an available port.

Modems really are easy to set up. Read the manual that comes with yours. It'll tell you everything you need to know—and more.

Fringe Benefits

One more thought I'd like to share with you here: If you set up an Internet account, you can use it for a wide variety of things—not just Quicken. Use it to exchange e-mail with friends and family members. Use it to search the Internet for information about your hobbies and interests, your next vacation, or the local weather. Shop online. Chat. Download shareware, freeware, or the latest updates to commercial software products.

Heck, if you have it, you may as well use it. Just remember to turn off your computer and go outside once in a while.

Setting Up an Internet Connection

To use Quicken's online features, you need to set up Quicken for your Internet connection. This means using Apple's Internet Setup Assistant to set up your Internet connection and then setting two options in Quicken's Preferences window.

Using the Internet Setup Assistant

Apple's Internet Setup Assistant, which is part of the Mac OS system software, walks you, step by step, through the process of setting up an Internet connection. It prompts you for information you should have received from your ISP or network administrator when you opened your Internet access account. When it's finished, it sets all TCP/IP and Remote Access (if applicable) control panel options and offers to connect you to the Internet so you can test your setup. You can learn more about using Apple's Internet Setup Assistant in the documentation that came with your computer or with Mac OS.

Tip   *If you've already gone through the process of setting up an Internet connection and can successfully connect to the Internet, you can skip this step.*

Setting Internet Preferences

Quicken's Preferences window, which I discuss in detail in Chapter 1, offers two Internet options that must be properly set before you can use Quicken to access Internet features.

Choose Edit | Preferences to display the Preferences window. Then click the Internet icon on the left side of the window to display Internet options.

① Click Internet.

② Select the appropriate option for your ISP.

③ If necessary, click the Select Proxy button to enter information about your proxy server.

④ Click the Select Browser button to locate and select your preferred Web browser.

⑤ Click OK.

If you are connecting to the Internet via America Online 3.0 or later, select the America Online option. (Quicken 2000's Internet features are not compatible with versions of America Online prior to 3.0.) Otherwise, select Other Internet Service Provider. If you have a direct connection to the Internet and are accessing the Internet from behind a firewall, click the Select Proxy button to enter information about your proxy server. You can get this information from your Network Administrator.

Caution   *Do not set proxy information unless instructed by your network administrator. Doing so could prevent you from connecting to the Internet.*

Finally, click the Select Browser button and use the standard Open dialog box that appears to locate and select your preferred Web browser application. To benefit from all of Quicken's Web-based features, this should be Netscape Navigator (or Communicator) version 4.0 or later or Microsoft Internet Explorer version 4.0 or later. (Both of these Web browsers come with Mac OS 8.0 or later.)

After selecting a Web browser, Quicken may display a dialog box like the one shown next, telling you that Quicken is not currently the application configured for handling Web Connect data. For now, click the No button. I tell you about the Web Connect feature in Chapter 11.

Back in the Preferences window, click OK to save your settings and continue working with Quicken.

Testing Your Connection

Once you've set up Quicken for an Internet connection, you're ready to test it. Here are three simple tasks to get you started.

Tip   *I show you how to set up and connect for Online Account Access and other features in Part IV of this book.*

Visiting Quicken.com

A good connection test is a visit to Quicken.com, Intuit's feature-packed financial Web site for Quicken users and other visitors. I tell you more about Quicken.com in Chapter 11 and in Part V of this book; but for now, let's just connect to it to make sure your Internet connection works.

Choose Online | To the Web | Quicken Home Page. Quicken launches your Web browser and attempts to connect to the Internet. What you see during the connection process will vary depending on your ISP. If you use an online service such as America Online, CompuServe, or Prodigy, the service's access software may start automatically to make the connection. You may be prompted to enter a username or password. Other dialog boxes may appear. Provide any requested information.

When the connection is complete, your Web browser requests the Quicken.com home page. After a few moments, it appears in the Web browser window (see Figure 3-1).

Tip *If you were already connected to the Internet when you accessed one of Quicken's online features or you have a direct connection to the Internet, you won't see the connection happening. Instead, the Quicken.com page will simply appear in your Web browser window.*

Switching Back to Quicken

When you accessed the Quicken.com home page from within Quicken, the Quicken application remained open but moved to the background. You can

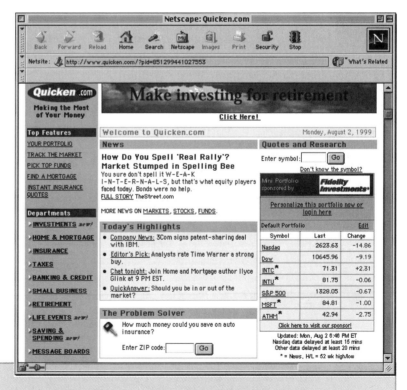

Figure 3-1 • Quicken.com's home page changes daily to offer new information and features.

switch back to Quicken at any time by choosing Quicken Deluxe 2000 from the Application menu in the top-right corner of the screen:

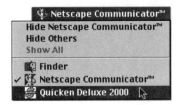

Quicken 2000 moves back into the foreground so you can continue working with it.

Disconnecting from the Internet

If you are using a dial-up connection to the Internet, it's a good idea to disconnect from the Internet when you have finished using Quicken's online features. How you do this depends on your Internet Service Provider:

- If you are connected via an online service such as America Online, CompuServe, or Prodigy, switch to the online service's access software by choosing its name from the Application menu. Then choose File | Quit to quit the online service's software, thus disconnecting from the Internet.
- If you are connected via another ISP, choose Remote Access Status from the Apple menu. Then click the Disconnect button in the Remote Access window that appears:

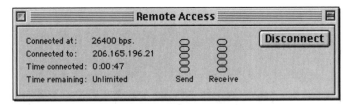

 Note   *If you have a direct connection to the Internet, you can't disconnect.*

Troubleshooting

If you followed the instructions I provided throughout the chapter, you shouldn't have any trouble connecting to the Internet from Quicken. But things aren't always as easy as they should be. Sometimes even the tiniest problems can prevent you from successfully connecting and exchanging data.

In this section, I provide some troubleshooting advice to help you with connection problems you may experience. Check this section before you start pulling out your hair and cursing the day computers were invented.

Setup Problems

To determine whether the problem is a Quicken setup problem or a general Internet setup problem, quit Quicken and try connecting to the Internet from another program, such as your Web browser or e-mail program.

- If you can connect to the Internet from another program but not from within Quicken, the problem may be with Quicken's Internet preferences. Go back to the section titled "Setting Internet Preferences," earlier in this chapter, and check your settings.
- If you can't connect to the Internet from any other program or with Remote Access (for dial-up connections), the problem is with your TCP/IP control panel settings, your Remote Access control panel settings (for dial-up connections), your modem (for dial-up connections), or your network (for direct connections). You must fix any problem you find before you can successfully set up and connect with Quicken. Use Apple's Internet Setup Assistant to run through the setup process again.

Modem Problems

Problems with a dial-up connection may be related to your modem. Try each of the following, attempting a connection after each one.

- Check all cables between your computer and your modem (if you have an external modem), and between your modem and the telephone outlet.
- Check the telephone line to make sure it has a dial tone and that it is not being used by someone else or another program.
- Turn off your modem, and then turn it back on. Or, if you have an internal modem, restart your computer. This resets the modem and may resolve the problem.

If you can connect but have trouble staying connected, try the following:

- Make sure no one is picking up an extension of the phone line while you are online.
- Make sure call waiting is disabled by entering the appropriate codes for the dial-up connection.
- Have the phone company check the line for noise. If noise is detected, ask the phone company to fix the problem. (It shouldn't cost you anything if the line noise is the result of a problem outside your premises.)

Network Problems

Problems with a direct connection may be related to your network. Try these things, attempting a connection after each one:

- Check all cables between your computer and the network hub or router.
- Check to make sure the correct Proxy Server information was entered for Quicken's Internet Preferences, which I discuss earlier in this chapter.
- Restart your computer. Sometimes resetting your computer's system software can clear network problems.
- Ask your system administrator to check your network setup.

Organizing Your Finances

This part of the book explains how to use Quicken to organize your finances—manage your checkbook and other bank and credit card accounts, track investment transactions and performance, and monitor asset values and loan balances. It also tells you how you can take advantage of Quicken's time-saving automation features to perform many entry tasks. It has four chapters:

Part Two

Recording Bank and Credit Card Transactions

In This Chapter:

- *Entering Payments and Other Transactions*

- *Writing and Printing Checks*

- *Entering Credit Card Transactions*

- *Transferring Money*

- *Working with Existing Transactions*

- *Using QuickEntry*

- *Using Splits and Classes*

At Quicken's core is its ability to manage your bank accounts. This is probably Quicken's most-used feature. You enter the transactions and Quicken keeps track of account balances and the source and destination of the money you spend. You can even have Quicken print checks for you.

Using similar transaction entry techniques, Quicken can also keep track of credit card accounts. You enter transactions as you make them or at month's end when you receive your statement and pay your bill. Quicken keeps track of balances and offers you an easy way to monitor what you used your credit card to buy. It also enables you to keep an eye on how much your credit cards cost you in terms of finance charges and other fees.

Tip   *Quicken's Online Account Access and Online Payment features can save you time and money. Once you understand the basics of entering transactions as discussed in this chapter, be sure to consult Chapter 12 to see how Quicken's online features can make transaction entry easier.*

Overview of Accounts and Transactions

Most of the transactions you track with Quicken will involve one or more of its bank, cash, or credit card accounts. Before you can use Quicken to track bank and credit card transactions, you should prepare by creating the necessary accounts and having a good idea of how recording transactions works. Here's a closer look at each account type, along with some transaction examples. As you read about these accounts, imagine how they might apply to your financial situation.

Note   *I explain how to use the Set Up Account window to create new Quicken accounts in Chapter 2.*

Bank Accounts

Bank accounts are for tracking the money you have in checking, savings, or money market accounts in a bank or similar financial institution. Generally speaking, bank account transactions can be broken down into three broad categories: payments, deposits, and transfers.

Payments   *Payments* are cash outflows. Here are some examples:

- You write a check to pay your electric bill.
- You withdraw money from your savings account to buy a gift for your mother.
- You use your ATM card to withdraw spending money from a bank account.
- You use your debit card to buy groceries.
- You pay a monthly checking account fee.

Tip   *Quicken's Online Payment feature enables you to send a check to anyone, without actually writing or mailing the check. I tell you about this feature in Chapter 12.*

Deposits   *Deposits* are cash inflows. Here are some examples:

- You deposit your paycheck in your checking account.
- You sell your old computer and deposit the proceeds in your savings account.
- Your paycheck or social security check is deposited into your bank account as a direct deposit.
- You earn interest on your savings account.

Transfers   A *transfer* is a movement of funds from one account to another. Here are some examples:

- You transfer money from an interest-bearing savings account to your checking account when you're ready to pay your bills.
- You transfer money from a money market account to your home equity line of credit account to reduce its balance.

Cash Accounts

Quicken offers cash accounts for tracking cash expenditures. For example, you might create an account called My Wallet or Spending Money and use it to keep track of the cash you have on hand. Cash accounts are like bank accounts, but there's no bank. The money is in your wallet or your pocket or the old coffee can on the windowsill.

Cash accounts have two types of transactions: receive and spend.

Receive When you *receive* cash, you increase the amount of cash you have on hand. Here are some examples:

- You withdraw cash from the bank for weekly spending money.
- You sell your *National Geographic* magazine collection for cash at a garage sale.
- You get a twenty-dollar bill in a birthday card from your grandmother.

Spend When you *spend* cash, you reduce your cash balance. Here are some examples:

- You buy coffee and a newspaper and pay a bridge toll on your way to work.
- You give your son his allowance.
- You put a twenty-dollar bill in the birthday card you send to your granddaughter.

Tip *Tracking every penny you spend, from the cup of coffee you buy at work in the morning to the quart of milk you pick up on your way home that evening, isn't for everyone. You may prefer to track only large cash inflows or outflows and record the rest as Misc (miscellaneous) expenses.*

Credit Card Accounts

Credit card accounts track money you owe, not money you own. Some credit cards, such as MasterCard, Visa, American Express, and Discover, can be used in most stores that accept credit cards. Other credit cards, such as Macy's, Dillard's, and Texaco, can only be used in certain stores. But they all have one thing in common: if there's a balance, it's usually because you owe the credit card company money.

Credit card account transactions can also be broken down into two categories: charges and payments.

Charges *Charges* result when you use your credit card to buy something or the credit card company charges a fee for services. Here are some examples:

- You use your Visa card to buy a new computer.
- You use your Discover card to pay for a hotel stay.
- You use your Texaco card to fill the gas tank on your boat at the marina.
- A finance charge based on your account balance is added to your Macy's bill at month's end.

- A late fee is added to your MasterCard bill because you didn't pay the previous month's bill on time.
- A fee is added to your American Express bill for annual membership dues.

The opposite of a charge is a *credit*. Think of it as a negative charge; don't confuse it with a payment. Here are two examples:

- You return the sweater you bought with your American Express card to the store you bought it from.
- In reviewing your MasterCard bill, you discover that a merchant charged you in error and you arrange to have the incorrect charge removed.

Payments   *Payments* are amounts you send to a credit card company to reduce your balance. Here are three examples:

- You pay the minimum amount due on your Visa card.
- You pay $150 toward the balance on your Macy's card.
- You pay the balance on your American Express card.

Credit Card Tracking Techniques

You can use either of two techniques for paying credit card bills and monitoring credit card balances:

- Simply record amounts paid to each credit card company in your checking account. Although this does track the amounts you pay, it doesn't track how much you owe or the individual charges.
- Record each individual credit card expenditure and payment in the appropriate credit card account. This takes a bit more effort on your part, but it tracks how much you owe and what you bought.

Tip   *Knowing how much you owe on your credit cards helps you maintain a clear picture of your financial situation. In my opinion, it's worth the extra effort to track your credit card expenditures and balances in individual credit card accounts.*

Credit Card Transaction Recording Strategies

There are two strategies you can use to record transactions in credit card accounts. Choosing the strategy that's right for you makes the job easier to handle.

Ente ... actions as you spend. To do th ... ıt are handed to you when you ı ... ; you already do. Don't forge ... line shopping you do. Ther ... cken or QuickEntry and ente ...

W ... hings, it offers two main ben ...

- ... te what you owe to credit ... ses at month's end, or at the check-out ... ıed your limit.

- At month's end, you don't have to spend a ıoı of time entering big batches of transactions. All (or at least most) of them should already be entered.

I'll be the first to admit that I never was able to use this strategy. I just don't like holding onto all those pieces of paper. (Of course, since signing up for Online Financial Services, all this information is entered regularly for me.)

Enter When You Pay   The other strategy, which you may find better for you, is to enter transactions when you get your monthly statement. With this strategy, when you open your credit card statement, you'll spend some time sitting in front of your computer with Quicken to enter each and every transaction. If there aren't many, this isn't a big deal. But if there are many transactions, this could take some time.

Of course, the main benefit of this strategy is that you don't have to collect credit card receipts and spend time throughout the month entering your transactions. But you still have to enter them! This is the method I use for the one credit card I have that I cannot access online yet.

Entering Transactions

To make the most of Quicken, you must be willing to spend a little time entering transactions for the accounts you want to track. There are different ways to enter transactions, based on the type of transaction you want to enter:

- Use *registers* to record virtually any type of transaction, including checks, bank account payments and deposits, credit card charges and payments, and cash receipts and spending.
- Use the *Write Checks window* to record checks to be printed by Quicken.
- Enter *transfers* to transfer money from one account to another.

In this section, I cover all of these techniques.

Tip   *You may prefer to work with bank, cash, and credit card accounts while in the Banking tab's work environment. By default, this tab has buttons commonly used for banking-related transactions. I tell you how to switch to and customize Quicken's tabs in Chapter 1.*

Using Account Registers

Quicken's account registers offer a standard way to enter all kinds of transactions. As the name suggests, these electronic account registers are very similar to the paper checking account register that comes with your checks.

Tip   *You can customize the way the account register window looks and works by setting Register options in the Preferences window. I tell you how in Chapter 1.*

There are several ways to open an account register. Here are three of them:

- Choose Lists | Accounts or press COMMAND-A to display the Accounts list window, shown next. Then double-click the name of the account for which you want to use the register.

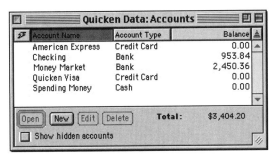

- Choose the name of the register from the Rgstrs button menu at the top of the Banking tab:

Tip   *The Current Register is the register in the active window or, if no register windows are open, the register window that was open last.*

- Click the button for the account near the top of the Banking tab:

The account's register window appears (see Figure 4-1). Use it to enter and record transactions.

Basic Entry Techniques

Figure 4-1 provides basic step-by-step instructions for using the account register window. Here are a few additional things to consider when entering transactions.

Advancing from Field to Field   To move from one edit box to another when entering transactions, you can either click in the edit box or press the TAB key. Pressing TAB is usually quicker.

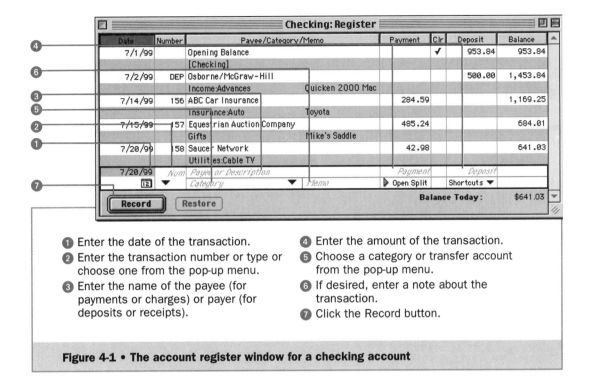

1. Enter the date of the transaction.
2. Enter the transaction number or type or choose one from the pop-up menu.
3. Enter the name of the payee (for payments or charges) or payer (for deposits or receipts).
4. Enter the amount of the transaction.
5. Choose a category or transfer account from the pop-up menu.
6. If desired, enter a note about the transaction.
7. Click the Record button.

Figure 4-1 • The account register window for a checking account

Using the Calendar Button   If you click the calendar icon in the Date field, a tiny calendar like the one shown next appears. You can click the arrow buttons at the top of the calendar to change the month displayed. Then click a date to select and enter it in the Date field.

Using the Number Menu   The Number field is where you enter a transaction number or type. You can enter any number you like or use the pop-up menu to display a list of standard entries:

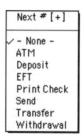

- **Next # (+)** automatically increments the most recently entered check number and enters the resulting number in the Number field.
- **– None –** leaves the Number field blank. This is the default selection.
- **ATM** is for ATM transactions.
- **Deposit** is for deposits.
- **EFT**, which stands for Electronic Funds Transfer, is for direct deposits and similar transactions.
- **Print Check** is for transactions for which you want Quicken to print a check. Quicken automatically records the check number when the check is printed.
- **Send** is for online payments. This option is only available when Online Payment is enabled for the account. I tell you about paying bills online in Chapter 12.
- **Transfer** is for a transfer of funds from one account to another.
- **Withdrawal** is for withdrawals and direct debit transactions.

Tip   *You can press the + or – key on the keyboard to increment or decrement the check number while the Number field is active.*

QuickFill   As you start to enter the name of a payee or payer that is already in Quicken's data file, Quicken may fill in the entire name and most recent transaction for you. This is Quicken's QuickFill feature, which I tell you more about in Chapter 7.

Using a Calculator   When an Amount field is active, you can display a calculator (like the one shown next) by entering a number and then pressing any standard mathematical operator—such as +, –, * (for multiplication), or / (for division). Complete the calculation and click the Total button to enter the result in the field.

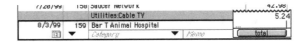

Entering New Categories   If you enter a category that does not exist in the Categories & Transfers List, Quicken displays a dialog box, like the one shown next, that offers to create the category for you. I explain how to create categories in Chapter 2.

Click Cancel to return to the register window and enter a different category.

Click Select to display the Categories & Transfers List window and select a category.

Click Set Up to create a new category.

Entering Multiple Categories   To enter more than one category for a transaction, click the triangle beside *Open Split*. This enables you to enter multiple categories for the transaction. I tell you about splits later in this chapter.

Entering Cash Transactions

Although Quicken enables you to keep track of cash transactions through the use of a cash account, not everyone does. The reason: Most people make many small cash transactions every day. Is it worth tracking every penny you spend? That's something you need to decide.

Personally, I don't track all cash transactions. I only track expenditures that are large or tax deductible. You may want to do the same. If so, you still need to set up a cash account, but you don't need to record every transaction. That's what I do; Figure 4-2 shows an example.

Cash Receipts   Cash receipts may come from using your ATM card, cashing a check, or getting cash from some other source. If the cash comes from one of

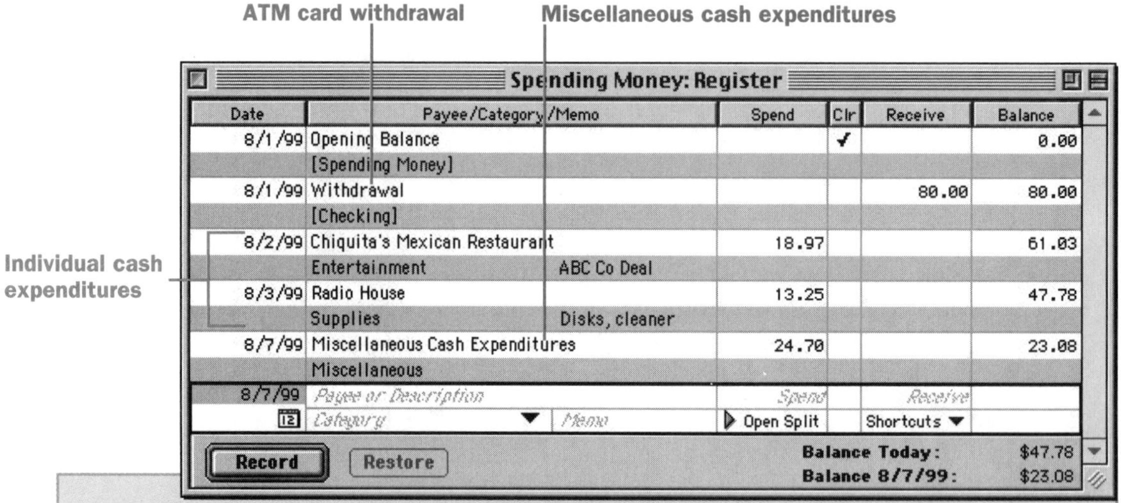

ATM card withdrawal   Miscellaneous cash expenditures

Date	Payee/Category/Memo		Spend	Clr	Receive	Balance
8/1/99	Opening Balance			✓		0.00
	[Spending Money]					
8/1/99	Withdrawal				80.00	80.00
	[Checking]					
8/2/99	Chiquita's Mexican Restaurant		18.97			61.03
	Entertainment	ABC Co Deal				
8/3/99	Radio House		13.25			47.78
	Supplies	Disks, cleaner				
8/7/99	Miscellaneous Cash Expenditures		24.70			23.08
	Miscellaneous					
8/7/99	*Payee or Description*		*Spend*		*Receive*	
📅	*Category* ▼	*Memo*	▶ Open Split	Shortcuts ▼		

Individual cash expenditures

Spending Money: Register

(Record) (Restore)   **Balance Today:** $47.78
                                 Balance 8/7/99: $23.08

Figure 4-2 • Typical cash account transactions

your other accounts through an ATM or check transaction, when you record that transaction, use your cash account as the transfer in the Category edit box. That increases your cash balance. Here's what the transaction might look like in your checking account:

8/1/99	ATM	Withdrawal		80.00	*Deposit*	461.03
📅	▼	[Spending Money] ▼	*Memo*	▶ Open Split	Shortcuts ▼	

Important Cash Expenditures   In your cash account, record large, tax-deductible, or other important cash expenditures like any other transaction. Be sure to assign the correct category.

Other Cash Expenditures   Throughout the week, you may spend fifty cents for a newspaper, a dollar for a cup of coffee, and about seven dollars for lunch at your favorite sushi restaurant. Recording transactions like these can be tedious, so don't bother if you don't want to. Instead, at the end of the week, compare your cash on hand to the balance in your cash account register. Then enter a transaction to record the difference as an expenditure. You can use the Miscellaneous category—it's for miscellaneous expenditures—and put anything you like in the Payee or Description edit box.

Entering Credit Card Transactions

Entering credit card transactions works very much like entering banking transactions. Check Figure 4-1 for step-by-step instructions. Here are a few additional tips; Figure 4-3 illustrates some examples.

Entering Individual Charges Open the account register for the credit card account. Then enter the charge transaction, using the name of the merchant that accepted the charge as the payee name. You can leave the Ref edit box empty.

Entering Credits Enter the transaction just as if it were a charge, but put the amount of the credit in the Payment edit box. This subtracts it from your account balance.

Entering Finance Charges In the credit card account register, enter the name of the credit card company as the payee and the amount of the finance charge as a charge.

Entering Payments In the account register for your checking account or in the Write Checks window, enter a payment transaction with the credit card company name in the Payee or Description edit box. Enter the credit card account name in the Category edit box; you should find it as a transfer account at the bottom of the Category pop-up menu that appears when you activate the field. The checking

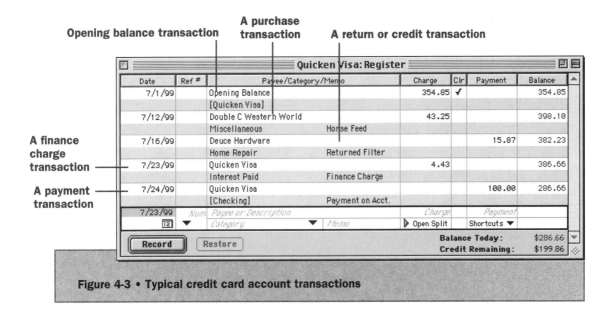

Figure 4-3 • Typical credit card account transactions

account register transaction should look like the one shown next; Figure 4-3 shows what this transaction looks like in the credit card account register.

7/24/99	160	Quicken Visa		100.00	*Deposit*	541.03
📅	▼	[Quicken Visa] ▼	Payment on Acct.	▶ Open Split	Shortcuts ▼	

> **Tip**   *You can also enter a payment transaction for your credit card account at the end of the credit card account reconciliation process, which I discuss in Chapter 8.*

Writing Checks

Quicken's Write Checks window uses a basic check-like interface to record checks. You enter the same information that you would write on an actual check. You then tell Quicken to print the check based on the information you entered.

> **Tip**   *You can customize the way the Write Checks window looks and works by setting Register options in the Preferences window. I explain how in Chapter 1.*

> **Note**   *To use this feature, you must order compatible check stock from Intuit or another check printer. I tell you how and explain how to print checks later in this chapter.*

To begin, open or activate the register window for the account from which you want to write checks. Then open the Write Checks window using one of these techniques:

- Choose Activities | Write Checks or press COMMAND-J.
- Click the Checks button near the top of the Banking tab.

The Write Checks window, which is shown in Figure 4-4, appears. Use it to enter the necessary information for a check and record the transaction.

Figure 4-4 provides basic step-by-step instructions for using the Write Checks window. As you can imagine, it works a lot like the account register window discussed earlier in this chapter—consult that section for more information. Here are a few additional things to consider when entering transactions in the Write Checks window.

Addresses on Checks   If you enter an address on the check, you can mail the check using a window envelope. Quicken will remember the address and automatically enter it in the Write Checks window the next time you enter the payee's name.

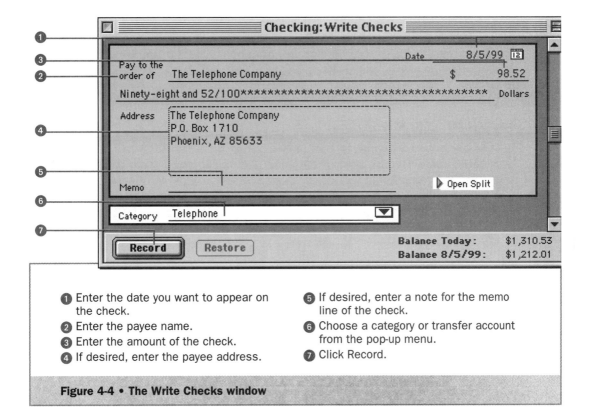

Figure 4-4 • The Write Checks window

Within the figure:

Checking: Write Checks

Date 8/5/99

Pay to the order of The Telephone Company $ 98.52

Ninety-eight and 52/100*************************************** Dollars

Address The Telephone Company
P.O. Box 1710
Phoenix, AZ 85633

▶ Open Split

Memo

Category Telephone   ▼

Record   Restore

Balance Today : $1,310.53
Balance 8/5/99 : $1,212.01

1 Enter the date you want to appear on the check.
2 Enter the payee name.
3 Enter the amount of the check.
4 If desired, enter the payee address.
5 If desired, enter a note for the memo line of the check.
6 Choose a category or transfer account from the pop-up menu.
7 Click Record.

Check Memos   If you enter a note on the memo line of a check, it might be visible if you mail the check in a window envelope.

Recording a Check   When you click the Record button to accept the information entered for a check, Quicken automatically displays a blank Write Checks window so you can record another check.

Viewing Other Checks   You can use the scroll bar along the right side of the Write Checks window to scroll through checks you have written. Click the up arrow to see the previous check; click the down arrow to see the next check. In addition, the checks you write with the Write Checks window appear in the account's register window. As shown next, the word "PRINT" appears in the Number edit box until the check is printed.

8/5/99	PRINT	The Telephone Company		98.52	*Deposit*	1,212.01
	▼	Telephone	▼ *Memo*	▶ Open Split	Shortcuts ▼	

Transferring Money

You can also record the transfer of funds from one account to another. You might find this feature especially useful for recording telephone or ATM transfers.

SAVE TIME   Online Account Access enables you to transfer money from one account to another by simply entering the transaction and sending it to your bank via the Internet. There's no need to call or visit your bank or submit any paper forms. I tell you more about this feature in Chapter 12.

Using the Transfer Window

One way to record a transfer is with the Transfer window. Choose Activities | Transfer Money. The Transfer Money Between Quicken Registers window, which is illustrated next, appears. Use it to enter information about the transfer and click OK.

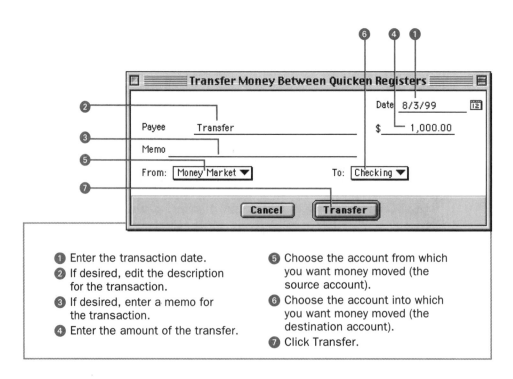

1. Enter the transaction date.
2. If desired, edit the description for the transaction.
3. If desired, enter a memo for the transaction.
4. Enter the amount of the transfer.
5. Choose the account from which you want money moved (the source account).
6. Choose the account into which you want money moved (the destination account).
7. Click Transfer.

Recording a Transfer in the Account Register Window

The Transfer window isn't the only way to record a transfer. You can also record a transfer in the account register window of either the source or destination account. Choose Transfer (TXFR) from the Number pop-up menu, choose the other transfer account from the pop-up menu in the Category field, and click Record to complete the transaction.

The following illustrations show a transfer of money from a money market account to a checking account. Here's what the money market account transaction looks like:

8/3/99	TXFR	Transfer			1,000.00	*Deposit*	1,450.36
📅	▼	[Checking]	▼	*Memo*	▶ Open Split	Shortcuts ▼	

And here's what the corresponding checking account transaction looks like:

8/3/99	*Num*	Transfer			*Payment*	1,000.00	1,410.53
📅	▼	[Money Market]	▼	*Memo*	▶ Open Split	Shortcuts ▼	

Working with Existing Transactions

So far, this chapter has concentrated on entering transactions. What do you do when you need to modify a transaction you already recorded? That's what this section is all about.

Searching for Transactions

Quicken includes two commands to help you locate and work with transactions:

- **Find** enables you to search for transactions in the current account based on any field.
- **Replace** enables you to find transactions based on any field and replace that field in the found transactions.

Tip *You might also find it helpful to sort a register window's transactions by clicking the Date or Number column heading. For example, clicking the Number heading to sort by check number groups the transactions by the Number field, making it easy to find transactions by number or type. You can quickly move to a specific date or transaction number by dragging the register window's scroll box; the QuickScroll feature displays the date and number of the transaction that will appear when you release the mouse button.*

Using the Find Command

To use the Find command, begin by opening the account register or Write Checks window for the account that you want to search. Then choose Edit | Find/Replace | Find, or press COMMAND-F. The Find window, which is illustrated next, appears. Use it to search for transactions that match the criteria you enter.

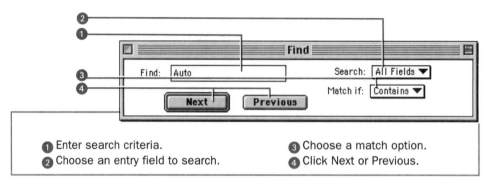

① Enter search criteria.   ③ Choose a match option.
② Choose an entry field to search.   ④ Click Next or Previous.

After setting up the search, when you click the Next button, Quicken activates the first match it finds in the register window. You can then click the Next button again to find the next match. If you click the Previous button, Quicken displays the previous match.

When Quicken's search reaches the end of the transactions in the register, it may display a dialog box like the one shown next, offering to continue the search at the beginning of the account register. Click Yes to continue searching; click No to stop searching.

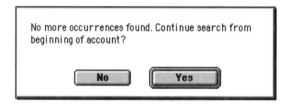

Using the Replace Command

The Replace command also works with a specific account, so you'll have to open the account's register or Write Checks window before you use it. Then choose Edit | Find/Replace | Replace. The Replace window, shown next, appears. It looks and works very much like the Find window, but it includes a With edit box you can use to enter replacement information.

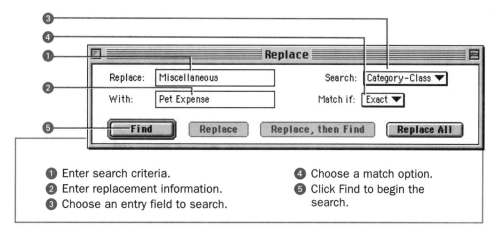

① Enter search criteria.
② Enter replacement information.
③ Choose an entry field to search.
④ Choose a match option.
⑤ Click Find to begin the search.

When you set up the search and click the Find button, Quicken displays the first match for the search criteria. You can then click one of the four buttons at the bottom of the window to continue:

- **Find** finds the next occurrence without changing the currently found occurrence.
- **Replace** replaces the currently found occurrence. You'll have to click the Find button again to continue searching for other occurrences.
- **Replace, then Find** replaces the currently found occurrence and finds the next occurrence.
- **Replace All** replaces all occurrences.

Caution *Use the Replace All option with care! You will not get a chance to review each change before you make it.*

Changing Transactions

Quicken enables you to change a transaction at any time—even after it has been reconciled. This makes it possible to correct errors in any transaction you have entered.

Making Minor Changes

If all you want to do is change one of the fields in the transaction—such as the category, date, or number—simply find the transaction in the appropriate account register, make changes as desired, and click the Record button to record them.

Using Edit Menu Commands

The Edit menu offers other options for working with a selected transaction:

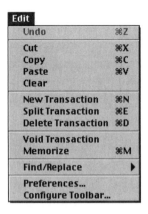

- **New Transaction** (COMMAND-N) enables you to create a new transaction for the account. This does not affect the currently selected transaction.
- **Split Transaction** (COMMAND-E) enables you to enter multiple categories for an account. I tell you more about using splits a little later in this chapter.
- **Delete Transaction** (COMMAND-D) deletes the selected transaction.

Caution | *Deleting a transaction removes the transaction from the Quicken data file, thus changing the account balance and category activity.*

- **Void Transaction** marks the selected transaction as void. This reverses the effect of the transaction on the account balance and category activity without actually deleting the transaction.
- **Memorize** tells Quicken to add the selected transaction to its list of memorized transactions. I tell you more about memorized transactions in Chapter 7.

Moving Transactions

Occasionally, after entering a transaction into a register, you may realize that you entered it in the wrong register. The Move this Transaction command makes it possible to move the transaction to another register. This is a lot quicker and often more practical than deleting the transaction and re-entering it in another register.

In the account register window, click anywhere in the transaction you want to move to select it. Then choose Move this Transaction from the Shortcuts pop-up menu in the second line of the transaction, as shown next:

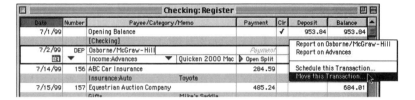

The Move Transaction dialog box, which is shown next, appears. Choose the correct account from the pop-up menu at the top of the dialog box, make any other necessary changes to the transaction, and click Move. The transaction is removed from the original account and appears in the account you selected.

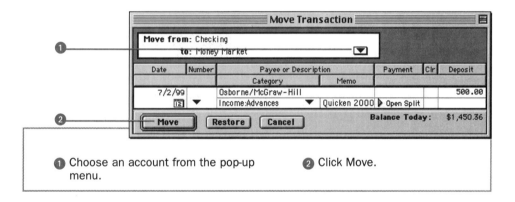

① Choose an account from the pop-up menu.   ② Click Move.

Using Splits and Classes

Up to this point, all I've covered is basic transaction entry and editing techniques. Now I'll go beyond the basics to show you how you can use splits and classes to fine-tune your classification of transactions.

Splits

A *split* is a transaction with more than one category. For example, suppose you pay one utility bill for two categories of utilities—electric and water. If you want to track each of these two expenses separately, you can use a split to record each category's portion of the payment you make. This enables you to keep good records without writing multiple checks to the same payee.

To record a transaction with a split, click the triangle beside *Open Split* in the account register (see Figure 4-1) or Write Checks (see Figure 4-4) window when entering the transaction. The entry area expands to include multiple category lines. Figure 4-5 shows what it might look like for an account register window with two categories entered.

Enter the category name and amount for each category that you want to include in the transaction, one per line. Quicken automatically totals the amounts you enter for the transaction. You can use buttons beneath the split area to work with the split:

- **Close Split** closes the split.
- **Clear Split** clears all lines from the split, permanently removing them.
- **Adjust Total** adjusts the transaction total, if necessary, to match the total of all amounts entered for the split.

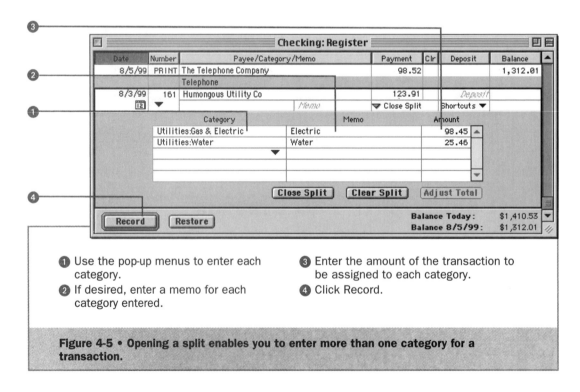

❶ Use the pop-up menus to enter each category.
❷ If desired, enter a memo for each category entered.
❸ Enter the amount of the transaction to be assigned to each category.
❹ Click Record.

Figure 4-5 • Opening a split enables you to enter more than one category for a transaction.

When you click Record, the transaction is recorded. When the split is closed, the word "split" appears in the Category field of the transaction:

8/3/99	161	Humongous Utility Co		123.91	*Deposit*	1,286.62
📅 ▼		*split*	*Memo*	▷ Open Split	Shortcuts ▼	

Classes

A *class* is an optional identifier for specifying what a transaction applies to. For example, if you have two cars for which you track expenses, you can create a class for each car—say, *Jeep* and *Toyota*. Then, when you record a transaction for one of the cars, you can include the appropriate class with the category for the transaction. Because Quicken can produce reports based on categories, classes, or both, classes offer an additional dimension for tracking and reporting information.

Working with the Class List Window

Quicken maintains a list of all the classes you create. You can display the Classes list by choosing Lists | Classes, or by pressing COMMAND-K. Here's an example with some classes I created:

You can use buttons in the Classes list window to work with the class list or a selected class:

- **Use** uses the class in the current transaction.
- **New** enables you to create a new class.
- **Edit** enables you to modify the currently selected class name or other information.

- **Delete** enables you to delete the currently selected class.
- **Add Subclass** enables you to create a subclass for the currently selected class.
- **Tax Copies** enables you to enter tax copy information for the class. I explain this feature in the section titled "Setting Tax Copies," later in this chapter.

Creating a New Class

Click the New button in the Classes list window. The Set Up Class window appears. Use it to enter a name and description for the class and click Create:

Only one piece of information is really necessary: the class name. You may want to make it short so it's easy to remember and enter. The description can be used to provide additional information on what the class is used for. When you click Create, the new class is added to the Classes list.

Setting Tax Copies

If you use the Tax Links feature of Quicken, which I discuss in Chapter 14, you may want to set tax copies for some of the classes you use. This helps identify tax-related items for specific tax schedule copies.

Here's how it works. Say you have two businesses and have a separate vehicle for each one. Because you'll report the income and expenses for these businesses on two separate copies of Schedule C (or other schedule, depending on the type of business), you may want to set up one car's class for the first copy and the other car's class for the second copy. This way, when you create reports in preparation for paying your taxes, Quicken will automatically separate and subtotal the costs related to each of the two cars.

This feature is entirely optional and, in reality, is only useful for tax-related classes when you prepare multiple copies of the same form or schedule. So if you don't think this feature will benefit you, it probably won't. You can skip it.

To set tax copy numbers, click the Tax Copies button in the Classes list window. The Assign Copies dialog box appears. Select the class for which you want to set a copy number and click one of the tiny arrows beside the word

"Copy" to change the number. Here's what the previous example might look like set up for personal expenses (Copy 1) and two separate businesses (Copies 2 and 3):

Click these arrows to change the copy number of a selected class.

Assign Copies

For tax categories with multi-copy schedules and forms, select a class, and enter its copy

Class	Copy
Condo	2
House	1
Jeep	2
Toyota	3

Cancel   OK

Including a Class in a Transaction

To include a class in a transaction, enter a slash (/) followed by the class name after the category. Here's an example in the register window:

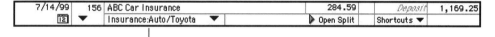

7/14/99	156	ABC Car Insurance		284.59		*Deposit*	1,169.25
🗓	▼	Insurance:Auto/Toyota ▼		▶ Open Split	Shortcuts ▼		

Enter a slash and the class name after the category.

> **Tip**   *If you enter a class name that is not on the Classes list, Quicken displays a dialog box offering to set up or select the class.*

Using QuickEntry

Quicken Deluxe users can also enter transactions with QuickEntry. This program, which works just like the account register feature of Quicken, makes it possible to enter transaction information without opening Quicken. Then, the next time you open Quicken, you can review and either accept or reject the QuickEntry transactions.

> **Tip**   *You might find QuickEntry useful if both you and your spouse want to track payments and deposits, but only you know how to use Quicken. This prevents your spouse from accidentally changing the financial records, while enabling him or her to help you enter transactions.*

Entering Transactions in QuickEntry

To enter transactions in QuickEntry, open it by double-clicking its icon in the Quicken Deluxe 2000 folder window or choosing it from the Apple menu. (If a Welcome window appears, click OK to dismiss it.) As shown in Figure 4-6, QuickEntry looks and works very much like the account register shown in Figure 4-1.

When you've finished entering information in QuickEntry, choose File | Quit or press COMMAND-Q. The transactions you entered are automatically saved for entry the next time you use Quicken.

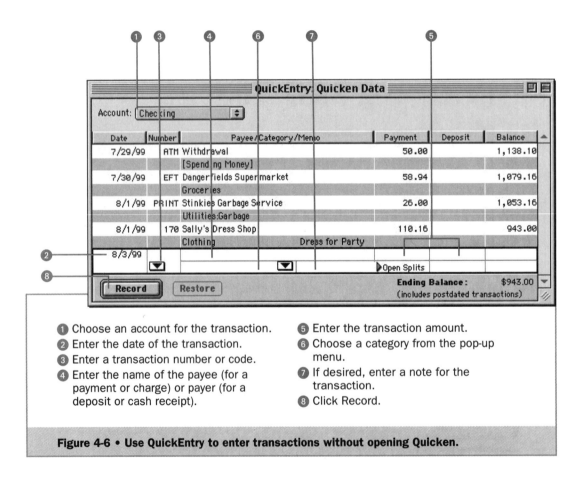

① Choose an account for the transaction.
② Enter the date of the transaction.
③ Enter a transaction number or code.
④ Enter the name of the payee (for a payment or charge) or payer (for a deposit or cash receipt).
⑤ Enter the transaction amount.
⑥ Choose a category from the pop-up menu.
⑦ If desired, enter a note for the transaction.
⑧ Click Record.

Figure 4-6 • Use QuickEntry to enter transactions without opening Quicken.

Adding QuickEntry Transactions to Your Data File

After you use QuickEntry to enter one or more transactions, the next time you open Quicken, the QuickEntry Transactions window, shown next, automatically appears. It lists the transactions and informs you that they have been added to your Quicken data file. Click OK to continue working with Quicken.

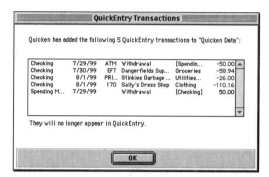

Printing Checks

Quicken's ability to print checks enables you to create accurate, legible, professional-looking checks without picking up a pen. In this section, I explain how to print the checks you enter in the Write Checks window discussed earlier in this chapter.

Getting the Right Checks

Before you can print checks from Quicken, you must obtain compatible check stock. Intuit offers checks in a number of different styles:

- **Standard** checks print just checks. There's no voucher or stub.
- **Voucher** checks pair each check with a similarly sized voucher form. When you print on a voucher check, the transaction category information, including splits and classes, can be printed on the voucher part.
- **Wallet** checks pair each check with a stub. When you print on a wallet check, the transaction information is printed on the stub.

In addition to these styles, you can get the checks in two different formats for your printer:

- **Sheet-fed** or **page-oriented** checks are for laser and inkjet printers.
- **Continuous** checks are for pin-feed printers.

A catalog and order form for checks came with your copy of Quicken. You can use it to order checks. If you have an Internet connection, you can order checks from Intuit by visiting **http://www.intuitmarketplace.com/**. Or you can order checks by phone by calling (800) 787-6748.

Setting Up

Quicken must also be set up to print the kind of checks you purchased. You do this once and Quicken remembers the settings.

Choose Edit | Preferences to display the Preferences window. Click the Print Checks icon on the left side of the window (you may have to scroll down to see it) to display Print Checks options:

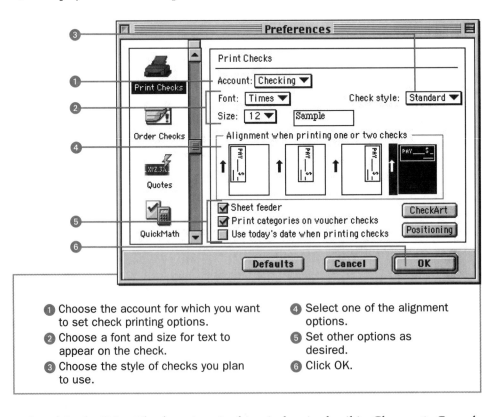

❶ Choose the account for which you want to set check printing options.

❷ Choose a font and size for text to appear on the check.

❸ Choose the style of checks you plan to use.

❹ Select one of the alignment options.

❺ Set other options as desired.

❻ Click OK.

I explain the Print Check options in this window in detail in Chapter 1. Consult that chapter if you need additional information about any of these options.

Printing Checks

Once setup is complete, you're ready to print checks. Insert the check stock in your printer. Then choose File | Print Checks or press COMMAND-P. The Print Checks dialog box, which is shown next, appears. Use it to set printing options.

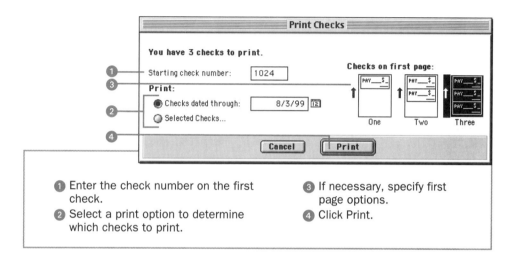

1 Enter the check number on the first check.
2 Select a print option to determine which checks to print.
3 If necessary, specify first page options.
4 Click Print.

Note   *The options in the Print Checks dialog box can vary depending on your printer and the type of checks you selected in the Preferences window.*

In the Starting Check Number edit box, enter the number that appears on the first check you inserted in your printer. Then select a Print option. If you select the Selected Checks option, the Select Checks to Print dialog box, shown next, appears. Click to place a check mark beside each check you want to print and click OK to return to the Print Checks dialog box.

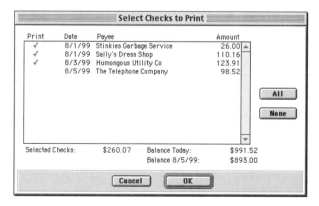

When you click Print, a standard Mac OS Print dialog box appears. Check settings in the dialog box and click Print to send the print job to your printer. Quicken then displays a dialog box asking if the checks printed correctly. You have two options:

- If all checks printed fine, click Yes.
- If there was a problem printing the checks, click No. You can then use the Incorrectly Printed Checks dialog box, shown next, to enter the number of the first incorrectly printed check. Click OK and then use the Print Checks command to try printing the incorrectly printed checks again.

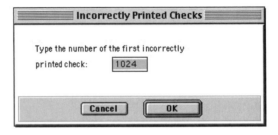

Tracking Investments

In This Chapter:

- *Investment Basics*

- *Working with Investment Accounts*

- *Adding and Editing Securities*

- *Recording Investment Transactions*

- *Viewing Investment Information*

- *Tracking the Market Value of Investments*

Chapter 5

Investments offer individuals a way to make their money grow. Although more risky than deposits made to an FDIC-insured bank, stocks, bonds, mutual funds, and other types of investments have the potential to earn more. That's why many people build investment portfolios as a way to save for future goals or retirement.

In this chapter, I tell you a little about investments and portfolio management, and then explain how you can use Quicken to keep track of the money you invest.

Investment Basics

Quicken enables you to record your investment transactions and track your portfolio value. With the information about your investments that you enter into Quicken, you can see how various investments perform, generate reports for tax time, and get a clear picture of what your investments are worth.

Before learning how to use Quicken to track your investments, here's a review of what investments and portfolios are.

Tip   *You may prefer to work with investment accounts and securities while in the Investing tab's work environment. By default, this tab has buttons and menus commonly used for investing-related transactions. I tell you how to switch to and customize Quicken's tabs in Chapter 1.*

Types of Investments

An *investment* is a security or asset that you expect to increase in value and/or generate income. There are many types of investments:

- **A certificate of deposit, or CD,** is an account with a bank or other financial institution. It earns a fixed rate of return and has a predetermined maturity date. Withdrawals before the maturity date normally result in penalty fees, which can exceed earned interest. CDs on deposit with a bank are normally FDIC-insured against loss.
- **A money market fund** is an account with a bank or other financial institution that earns interest based on short-term cash values. Money market funds are not FDIC-insured against loss.
- **Stocks** represent part ownership of an organization. Stock investments can earn you money by paying dividends or appreciating in value.
- **Bonds** represent loans to an organization. Bonds can earn you money by paying interest either during the bond's term or at its maturity date.

- **Treasury bills** represent loans to the U.S. government. They are issued at a discount and redeemed at face value; the difference between the two prices are the earnings.
- **Mutual funds** consist of multiple investments owned by many people. When you buy into a mutual fund, you pool your money with other investors to buy stocks, bonds, or other securities. Mutual funds can earn you money by paying dividends and interest and appreciating in value.
- **Annuities** are regularly funded accounts that earn interest or dividends paid in the future.
- **401(k) and 403(b) plans** are employer-funded retirement investments. They can consist of stocks, bonds, mutual funds, or any other type of investment.
- **IRAs, SEPs, and Keogh accounts** are employee-funded retirement investments. They have special tax implications and rules for funding. They can consist of stocks, bonds, mutual funds, or any other type of investment.
- **Real estate** is land or buildings. Real estate investments can earn money from rental or lease income and by appreciating in value.

Most investments can also earn you money if you sell them for more than you paid for them. I provide more specifics about investments and retirement planning in Chapters 16 and 17, respectively.

The Importance of Portfolio Management

The term *portfolio* refers to the total of all of your investments. For example, if you have shares of one company's stock, shares in two mutual funds, and a 401(k) plan account, these are the items that make up your portfolio.

At this point, you may be wondering why you should bother including investment information in your Quicken data file. After all, you may already get quarterly (or even monthly) statements from your broker or investment firm. What you may not realize, however, is how you can benefit from keeping a close eye on your investments. Take a look at what portfolio management with Quicken can do for you.

Centralizing Your Investment Records

Unless you have only one brokerage account for all your investments, you probably get multiple statements for the stocks, bonds, mutual funds, and other investments in your portfolio. No single statement can provide a complete picture of your portfolio's worth. Quicken can, however. By entering the transactions and values on each statement within Quicken, you can see the details of your entire portfolio in one place.

Knowing the Value of Your Portfolio on Any Day

Brokerage statements can tell you the value of your investments on the statement's ending date, but not what they're worth today. Or what they were worth on August 15, 1999. Quicken, however, can tell you what your portfolio is worth on any day for which you have entered security prices. And it can estimate values for dates without exact pricing information.

SAVE TIME If you like to keep your portfolio's value up-to-date with the latest security prices, retrieve prices online. I show you how to take advantage of this feature in Chapter 13.

Keeping Track of Performance History

Manually compiling a complete pricing and performance history for an investment is no small task, especially for periods spanning multiple statements. If you consistently enter investment information in your Quicken data file, however, preparing performance charts and reports is as easy as choosing a menu command or clicking a button.

Calculating Your Return on Investment

Return on investment varies from one investment to another. Quicken enables you to see the return on investment for each security you hold—all in one place!

GET SMARTER Use this feature to make better financial decisions. When you're ready to invest more money in your portfolio, it's easy to see which holding is doing the best—and may deserve more funding.

Calculating Capital Gains Quickly and Easily

Calculating the gain on the sale of an investment isn't always easy. Considerations include not only the purchase and selling prices, but commissions, fees, stock splits, and purchase lots. Quicken can take all the work out of calculating capital gains—even if you're just considering the sale and want to know what its impact will be. This is extremely helpful at tax time, as I discuss in Chapter 14.

Setting Up Accounts

In Quicken, you track investments in special investment accounts. These accounts store all information about investment transactions.

In this section, I tell you about the types of investment accounts Quicken offers and provide information about three methods for setting up account balances.

Investment Accounts

Quicken offers two types of investment accounts to track the balances and values of your investments: portfolio and mutual fund.

Portfolio Accounts   A *portfolio* account is used to track a variety of investment types, including brokerage accounts, stocks, bonds, and multiple mutual funds.

Mutual Fund Accounts   A *mutual fund* account is used to track a single mutual fund.

Tip   *There are all kinds of investments. Sometimes it's not clear what kind of Quicken account is best for a specific investment. Table 5-1 offers some guidance.*

Type of Investment	Type of Account
CD	Bank or Portfolio
Money market fund	Bank
Stocks in your possession	Portfolio
Brokerage account with one or more securities	Portfolio
Bonds	Portfolio
Treasury bills	Portfolio or Asset
Mutual fund	Portfolio (for multiple mutual funds) or Mutual Fund (for a single mutual fund)
Variable or fixed annuities	Portfolio or Asset
Retirement Plans including 401(k), 403(b), IRA, SEP, or Keogh	Portfolio (for stocks, bonds, or multiple mutual funds) or Mutual Fund (for a single mutual fund)
Real estate and real estate investment trusts (REITs) or partnerships	Asset

Table 5-1 • Quicken Accounts for Various Investment Types

I explain how to set up accounts in Chapter 2. You can have as many investment accounts as you need to properly represent the investments that make up your portfolio.

Account Setup Options

When you set up your Quicken investment accounts, you have three options for setting up account balances: entering all historical information, entering data for this year, and entering data as of your Quicken start date.

Entering All Historical Information

Entering all historical information means entering all transactions for the securities you currently have on hand. This option can be time consuming, but I think it's worth the extra effort. It has several benefits:

- You will have exact cost information for all securities you purchased. This enables you to distinguish between purchase lots within Quicken, so you can create accurate reports of capital gains and losses. That'll come in handy when it's time to fill out Schedule D of your tax return.
- You will have complete dividend and interest income information for the current year. This means you can use Quicken's investment income and losses reports to get the information you'll need for Schedule B of your tax return.
- You can accurately track security performance for the full amount of time you've owned each security.
- All of your investment records are centralized in one place, making it easy to find data and compare investment performance.

To enter all historical information, gather together all of your investment records for the securities you currently own and enter each transaction into Quicken as discussed later in this chapter.

Entering Data for This Year

A quicker but less accurate way to set up investments in Quicken is to enter only data for the current year. Some pros and cons of this method include:

- Since you don't have to go back as far for transaction and balance information, your records should be easier to find.
- Since there are less transactions to enter, you can enter them more quickly.

- You will have complete dividend and interest income information for the current year, so you can use Quicken's investment income and losses reports to get the information you'll need for Schedule B of your tax return.
- You will not be able to generate accurate capital gains and losses reports for securities purchased prior to the current year.
- You will not be able to track security performance for the entire time you've owned a security purchased prior to the current year.

To enter current year data, begin by entering share balances for all securities you owned as of January 1 using the Move Shares In investment action. Use security prices as of December 31 of the previous year. Then enter all new transactions since the beginning of the year as discussed later in this chapter.

Entering Data as of Your Quicken Start Date

The quickest but least accurate way to set up investments in Quicken is to enter share balances as of the date you set up your Quicken data file. Unless that date happens to be January 1, you won't be able to generate accurate reports of investment income or losses. You also won't be able to generate accurate reports of capital gains or losses for any security you owned as of your Quicken start date.

To enter current year data, begin by entering share balances for all securities you owned as of the current date using the Move Shares In investment action. Use security prices for the same date.

Setting Up Securities

Before you can start recording investment transactions and tracking your portfolio's worth, you need to set up the securities that you own or want to track. The easiest way to do this is with the Securities list window.

Note   *If you created a Mutual Fund account, that account is automatically listed as a security, too. You can edit its security information to provide additional details not entered when you created the account. I explain how later in this section.*

Working with the Securities List Window

The Securities list window (see Figure 5-1) simply lists the securities in Quicken's data file. You can use this window to add, edit, or delete securities, including *WatchList securities*—securities you don't own but want to monitor. To open this window, choose Lists | Securities.

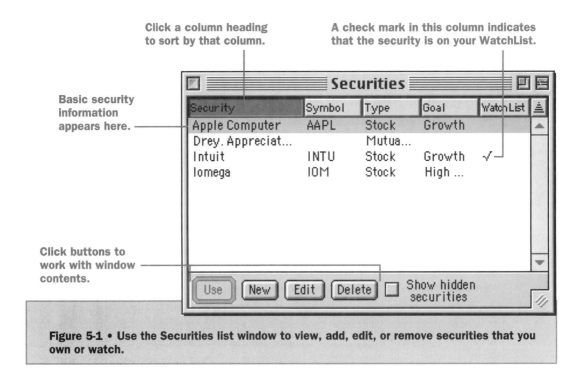

Click a column heading to sort by that column.

A check mark in this column indicates that the security is on your WatchList.

Basic security information appears here.

Click buttons to work with window contents.

Figure 5-1 • Use the Securities list window to view, add, edit, or remove securities that you own or watch.

Buttons at the bottom of the window enable you to work with list items:

- **Use** enables you to use the currently selected security in a transaction. This option is only available when you are entering a transaction.
- **New** enables you to create a new security.
- **Edit** enables you to modify the currently selected security.
- **Delete** removes the currently selected security. Clicking this button displays a confirmation dialog box. You must click Yes in that dialog box to delete the security from your data file.

Caution *Do not delete a security for which you want to maintain historical information, even if you no longer own it. Deleting a security removes all record of the security from your Quicken data file. If you want to keep the information but don't want to see the security in lists, hide the security instead. I tell you how later in this chapter.*

Adding a New Security

To add a new security to your Quicken data file—either as a holding or a
WatchList item—click the New button in the Securities window (see Figure 5-1).
The Set Up Security window, which is shown next, appears. Use it to enter
information about the security and click Create.

Here's a quick rundown of the information you can provide about each
security you enter:

- **Security** is the name of the security.
- **Symbol** is the security's ticker symbol. This information is not required
  unless you plan to use Quicken's Quotes feature to download security prices
  from the Internet. (I tell you more about downloading stock prices in
  Chapter 13.)
- **Type** is the type of security. You can use the pop-up menu to select one of
  four predefined types: Bond, CD, Mutual Fund, or Stock. You can also
  choose Edit from the pop-up menu to display the Types window, shown
  next, and add or remove security types.

- **Goal** is your intended investment goal for the security. You can use the pop-up menu to select one of five predefined types: College Fund, Growth, High Risk, Income, and Low Risk. You can also choose Edit from the pop-up menu to display the Goals window, shown next, and add or remove investment goals.

- **Notify if price is** options enable you to set a high and low price for the security. When the security price reaches either of the values you enter, Quicken notifies you. This feature is especially useful when you use the Quotes feature to download security prices from the Internet, as I discuss in Chapter 13.

- **Taxable** indicates whether the security is taxable. For example, although most investments are taxable, investments such as municipal bonds may not be. You click to toggle this check box on or off as necessary for the security.
- **Hide in lists** indicates whether the security should appear in lists such as the Securities list. You can turn on this check box to hide a security you don't need to use in transactions but want to keep historical information for.

Tip   *You can display hidden securities in the Securities list window (see Figure 5-1) by turning on the "Show hidden securities" check box in the bottom of the window. Hidden securities will appear in italics.*

Editing a Security

You can edit a security to add or change information you previously entered for it. Select the security's name in the Securities window (see Figure 5-1) and click the Edit button. The Edit Security window, which looks and works just like the Set Up Security window shown earlier, appears. Enter or edit information in the window and click Change to save your changes.

Recording Investment Transactions

The most important part of properly tracking investments is recording all investment transactions. This includes purchases, sales, dividends, and other activity affecting your portfolio's value.

In this section, I provide instructions for entering most common investment transactions using Quicken's Investment Actions feature.

Before You Start

Before you enter a transaction, you must have all of its details. In most cases, you can find the information you need on a confirmation form or receipt you receive from your broker or investment firm. The information varies depending on the transaction, but it should include the security name, transaction date, number of shares, price per share, and commissions or fees.

Working with an Investment Register

You can enter security transactions into the account register window for the investment account (see Figure 5-2) that the transaction affects. To open an investment register, use one of the following techniques:

- Choose Lists | Accounts or press COMMAND-A to display the Accounts list window. Then double-click the name of the account for which you want to use the register.
- Choose the name of the register from the Rgstrs button menu at the top of the Investing tab.

> **Tip**   *The Current Register is the register in the active window or, if no register windows are open, the register window that was open last.*

- Click the button for the account near the top of the Investing tab.
- Double-click the name of the account in the Portfolio window (see Figure 5-4, later in this chapter).

As shown in Figure 5-2, an investment account register looks similar to the account register for a banking or credit account window. It enables you to view, enter, and edit transactions for an investment account.

The buttons at the bottom of the register window enable you to enter investments and open other windows:

- **Record** saves the transaction you are currently entering.
- **Restore** reverts the current transaction back to the way it was before you began changing it.
- **Actions** displays the Investment Actions window, shown in Figure 5-3, which lists common transactions for investment accounts. Double-clicking an option displays a form for entering the transaction.
- **Portfolio** opens the Portfolio window (see Figure 5-4), which I discuss later in this chapter.

Using Investment Actions

The easiest way to enter an investment transaction is with Investment Actions, a Quicken feature that displays a custom form for many kinds of investment transactions. To display a list of investment actions, click the Actions button at the bottom of the register window (see Figure 5-2), choose Activities |

A sale transaction

A dividend transaction

Purchase transactions

Use these buttons to work with
transactions and open other windows.

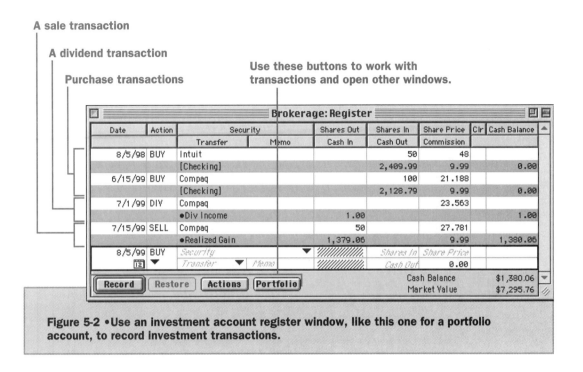

Date	Action	Security		Shares Out	Shares In	Share Price	Clr	Cash Balance
		Transfer	Memo	Cash In	Cash Out	Commission		
8/5/98	BUY	Intuit			50	48		
		[Checking]			2,409.99	9.99		0.00
6/15/99	BUY	Compaq			100	21.188		
		[Checking]			2,128.79	9.99		0.00
7/1/99	DIV	Compaq				23.563		
		•Div Income		1.00				1.00
7/15/99	SELL	Compaq		50		27.781		
		•Realized Gain		1,379.06		9.99		1,380.06
8/5/99	BUY	*Security*	▼	/////////	*Shares In*	*Share Price*		
📅 ▼		*Transfer* ▼	*Memo*	/////////	*Cash Out*	0.00		

Brokerage: Register

[Record] [Restore] [Actions] [Portfolio]

Cash Balance $1,380.06
Market Value $7,295.76

Figure 5-2 •**Use an investment account register window, like this one for a portfolio
account, to record investment transactions.**

Investment Actions, or press COMMAND-J. The Investment Actions window,
which is shown in Figure 5-3, appears.

Shortcut *Experienced Quicken users may prefer to enter transactions
directly into the account register for an investment account. A pop-up menu
in the transaction's entry area offers appropriate transaction codes for all
kinds of transactions. You can explore this feature on your own once you're
accustomed to entering transactions with Investment Actions.*

Here's a quick overview of the transactions you can enter with
Investment Actions:

- **Buy** adds shares to an investment account with an exchange of cash. Use this
  option for purchase transactions.
- **Move Shares In** adds shares to an investment account without an exchange
  of cash. Use this option for securities obtained as a result of a gift or
  inheritance.
- **Sell Shares** removes shares from an investment account with an exchange of
  cash. Use this option for sale transactions.

Click a triangle to display or
hide transactions in a group.

Double-click an action
to enter a transaction.

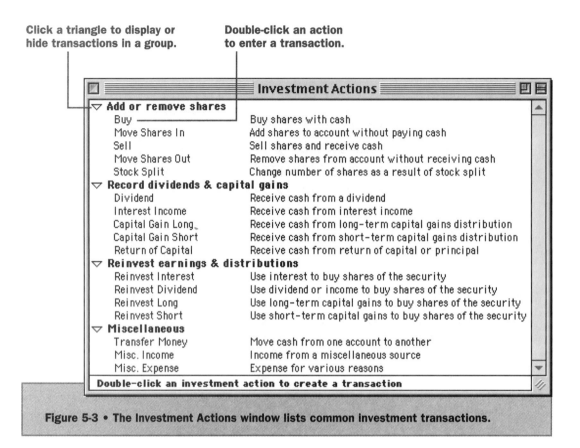

Figure 5-3 • The Investment Actions window lists common investment transactions.

- **Move Shares Out** removes shares from an investment account without an exchange of cash. Use this option for giving shares as gifts or writing off shares of a company that has gone out of business.

- **Stock Split** enables you to record additional shares received as a result of a stock split.

- **Dividend** enables you to record income from dividends paid on shares of a security.

- **Interest Income** enables you to record income from interest paid on cash balances.

- **Capital Gain Long** enables you to record income received from a long-term capital gains distribution.

- **Capital Gain Short** enables you to record income received from a short-term capital gains distribution.

Tip   *Capital Gain Long and Capital Gain Short transactions are relatively common with mutual funds that are not set up to reinvest income.*

- **Return of Capital** enables you to record the return of part of your investment capital.
- **Reinvest Interest** enables you to account for interest income that is reinvested in the security.
- **Reinvest Dividend** enables you to account for dividend income that is reinvested in the security.
- **Reinvest Long** enables you to account for long-term capital gains that are reinvested in the security.
- **Reinvest Short** enables you to account for short-term capital gains that are reinvested in the security.

Tip   *The Reinvest options are common with mutual funds that are set up to reinvest income. The Reinvest Dividend option is common with Dividend Reinvestment Programs (DRIPs).*

- **Transfer Money** enables you to record a transfer of funds from one account to another.
- **Misc Income** enables you to record investment income other than interest or dividends.
- **Misc Expense** enables you to record investment expenses other than commissions.

You can open an Investment Action form window by double-clicking the transaction type in the Investment Actions window. These forms are generally self-explanatory and easy to use. Here are a few common transactions to illustrate how they work.

Purchases

A security purchase normally involves the exchange of cash for security shares. In some cases, you may already own shares of the security or have it listed on your WatchList. In other cases, the security may not already exist in your Quicken data file, so you'll need to set up the security when you make the purchase.

Start by double-clicking the Buy action in the Investment Actions window (see Figure 5-3). A Buy window like the one shown next appears. Enter information into each field and click Record.

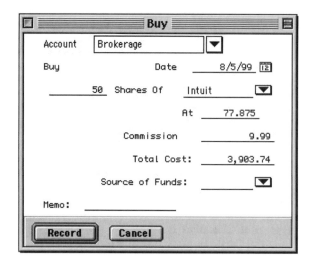

Here's the information you should enter:

- **Account** is the account to which you want to add shares. By default, the current account's name appears in this pop-up menu. Be sure to set the correct account in this field.

- **Date** is the date of the transaction. You can click the calendar icon to display a calendar of dates, if necessary. The date you enter should be the date of the transaction, not the date you entered it.

- **Shares of** has two fields to fill in. On the left line, enter the number of shares you purchased. On the right line, enter the name of the security you purchased. You can use the pop-up menu to pick a security in the Securities list. If you enter the name of a security that is not in the Securities list, Quicken displays a dialog box like the one shown next, enabling you to select or set up a security.

Click Set Up to set up a new security.

Click Select to select a security from the Securities window.

Click Cancel to go back to the form and change your entry.

- **At** is the price you paid per share. You can enter prices as decimal or fractional values. For example, 77.875 could also be entered as 77 7/8. (Be sure to include a space between the whole number and the fraction.)
- **Commission** is the brokerage fee you paid to obtain the shares.
- **Total Cost** is calculated automatically by Quicken based on the number of shares, price per share, and commission. The only way to change this value is to change one of the other values.

> **Tip** *You can use the Commission field to correct slight rounding differences that may occur when recording the purchase of fractional share amounts. This is relatively common when accounting for mutual fund and DRIP reinvestments. Just add a positive or negative number that makes the Total Cost field match the dollar amount of the transaction. Normally, this will only be 1¢ or 2¢, which shouldn't have much of an impact on your investment reports.*

- **Source of Funds** is to record the account that was used to fund the transaction. If the purchase was paid for with cash in the investment account, you can leave this field blank; it will automatically use the same account. If the purchase was paid for with cash in another account—such as your checking account—be sure to choose the correct account for this field.

> **Tip** *To purchase stock on margin—credit offered by a brokerage firm— and later send a check to your brokerage firm to cover the purchase, leave the Source of Funds field blank when entering the purchase transaction. Then, when you send a check to the brokerage firm, record the check in your checking account register, using the investment account as the transfer account in the category field.*

- **Memo** is an optional memo you can include with the transaction.

When you click Record to save the transaction, Quicken adds it to the appropriate account register and updates cash and share balances as necessary.

Moving Shares into an Account

You can use the Move Shares In Investment action to record the beginning share balances for a security if you do not plan to enter all transactions for that security. This action adds shares of a security to an account without affecting the cash balance of any Quicken account.

Double-click the Move Shares In action in the Investment Actions window (see Figure 5-3). A Move Shares In window like the one shown next appears. Enter beginning balance information and click Record.

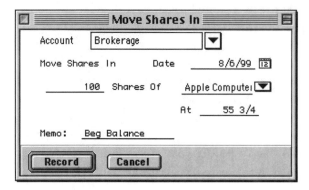

This window has many of the same fields found in the Buy window shown earlier. Here are two tips for entering information:

- The date you enter should be the date you want to begin tracking the security's value.
- The share price you enter should be the price as of the date you entered.

When you click Record to save the transaction, Quicken adds it to the appropriate account register and updates cash and share balances as necessary.

Sales

A security sale also involves the exchange of cash for security shares. Normally, you dispose of shares you already own; but in some instances, you may sell shares you don't own. This is called *selling short*, and it is a risky investment technique sometimes used by experienced investors.

Start by double-clicking the Sell action in the Investment Actions window (see Figure 5-3). A Sell window like the one shown next appears. Enter information into each field and click Record.

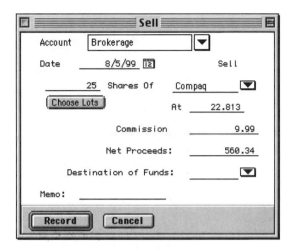

As you can see, this window is very similar to the Buy window shown earlier. The information you enter is basically the same; consult the section titled "Purchases," earlier in this chapter, for details. There are two main differences:

- **Choose Lots** enables you to select the shares you want to sell from individual purchase lots. You can use this option for additional control over capital gains. For example, if you want to take advantage of long-term capital gains tax breaks, you could sell shares that have been in your possession for more than 12 months. If you want to record a loss, you could sell shares that cost more than the selling price. Obviously, your options will vary depending on the lots, their acquisition prices, and your selling price. When you click the Choose Lots button, the Select Specific Shares (Lots) dialog box, which is shown next, appears. Use it to select the lots you are selling and click OK.

SAVE MONEY   By controlling the term and amount of capital gains, you can minimize your tax bill.

Enter the number of shares to sell in the Selected column
for one or more lots, or select an allocation method option
to automatically select lots based on predefined criteria.

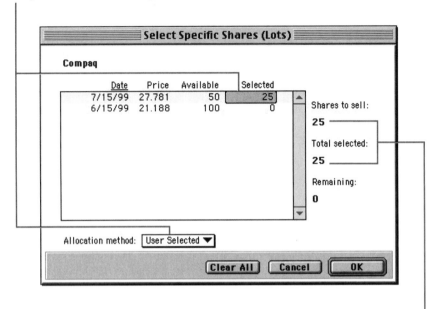

When the Shares to Sell equals
the Total Selected, click OK.

- **Net Proceeds** is the amount of money you will receive as a result of the sale.

When you click Record to save the transaction, Quicken adds it to the
appropriate account register and updates cash and share balances as necessary.

Dividend and Interest Payments

Many investments pay dividends, interest, or other income in cash. (That's why
they're so attractive to an investor!) Recording this activity in the appropriate
account register enables Quicken to accurately calculate performance, while
keeping account balances up-to-date.

Caution *Many mutual funds are set up to reinvest income, rather than
pay it in cash. Do not use the forms in this section to record a reinvestment
of income. Instead, use one of the "Reinvest earnings & distributions"
options in the Investment Actions window (see Figure 5-3) to enter
transaction information.*

Start by double-clicking the Dividend or Interest Income action in the Investment Actions window (see Figure 5-3). Then use the Dividend or Interest Income form that appears (both are illustrated next) to enter transaction information and click Record.

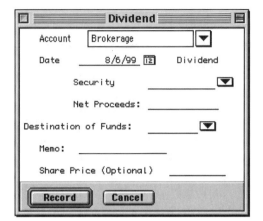 

Again, the information you're prompted for is pretty self-explanatory. Here are two tips:

- If the income arrives as a check that you deposit to a bank account, the Destination of Funds field should be the account to which you deposited the check. If the income is automatically deposited in your brokerage account, you can leave the Destination of Funds field blank to increase the cash balance of that account.
- The Share Price field is optional; you don't have to enter information there unless you want to.

When you click Record to save the transaction, Quicken adds it to the appropriate account register and updates cash balances as necessary.

Other Transactions

Other transactions are just as easy to enter as purchases, sales, and dividends. Simply double-click the appropriate option in the Investment Actions window (see Figure 5-3), and then enter the transaction information in the window that appears. If you have the transaction confirmation or brokerage statement in front of you when you enter the transaction, you have all the information you need to enter it.

Entering Advanced Transactions

Some less common transactions are not included in the Investment Actions window (refer to Figure 5-3). Here are four that you might need to enter, along with instructions for entering them.

Stock Splits and Dividends

You can use the Stock Split action's form (shown next) to record stock received as a result of a stock split or a stock dividend:

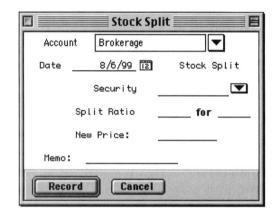

Stock Splits The Stock Split form is designed for stock splits. Simply enter the split ratio in the fields provided. For example, if you got 3 shares of stock for every 2 shares you owned, enter **3 for 2** in the fields.

Stock Dividends A stock dividend is similar to a stock split in that you wind up with more shares than you originally had. In the first Split Ratio box, enter 1 plus the fractional number of shares you received per share of stock you own. In the second Split Ratio box, enter 1. So if you received 0.2 shares for every share you own, you'd enter **1.2 for 1** as the Split Ratio.

Exchange of Shares for IRA Custodial Fees

Some IRAs require annual custodial fees that are paid by deducting shares from your account. You can record this kind of transaction using the Sell action's form shown earlier in this chapter. Enter the number of shares paid and the per share price. Then enter the dollar amount of the fee as the commission to bring the

Net Proceeds field to zero. You can leave the Destination of Funds field empty. When you click Record, the share balance is changed but the account's cash balance remains the same. The fee is recorded as a commission expense.

Accrued Interest for Bond Purchases

When you buy a bond after its original issue date, you normally pay accrued interest—the amount of interest earned but not yet paid—as part of the purchase price. There are two or three steps to properly recording this type of transaction.

1. Record the Bond Purchase as a Buy Transaction.   Record the purchase of the bond, without the accrued interest, using the Buy action form.

2. Record the Accrued Interest as a Misc. Expense Transaction. Record the amount of the accrued interest, as a separate transaction, using the Misc. Expense form. Be sure to enter the correct Account and to select Accrued Int (at the bottom of the category list) as the Category. Here's an example of what it might look like:

Note   *If the bond is not taxable, use Accrued Int NT as the category.*

3. Record the Accrued Interest as a Transfer Money Transaction. If you paid for the accrued interest with cash from another Quicken account, use the Transfer Money form to transfer the funds from the account you used to pay to the accrued interest to the investment account you indicated in step 2. This will properly adjust the cash balance in the investment account. Here's what the form might look like:

Tip *If you wrote a check to pay the accrued interest, you can simply use the investment account's name as the transfer account in the category field for the check transaction. Then you can skip step 3.*

Stock Spin-Off

A stock spin-off occurs when a large company "spins off" one of its subsidiaries as a separate company with its own stock. As the investor, you keep the same number of shares of the parent company, which are now worth less because the company is smaller. But you also get shares in the new company. You need to record the change in value of the parent company while recording the receipt and value of the shares in the new company.

This is a two-step process, and you'll need all the divestiture statements you received from the parent company to complete it accurately.

1. Record the Reduction of the Parent Company's Value as a Return of Capital Transaction. Record the value of the shares you received in the new company as a return of capital on the old company. The date of the transaction should be the date the spin-off occurred. Use the Return of Capital action's form as shown here:

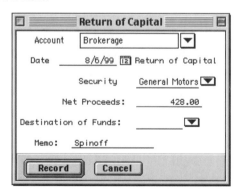

2. Record the Acquisition of the New Company's Shares as a Buy Transaction.   Use a Buy action form to record the purchase of the new company's shares on the spin-off date. To obtain a per-share price, divide the dollar amount entered in step 1 by the total number of shares acquired. When you complete the transaction and click Record, the cash added to the account in step 1 should be removed and the new shares properly recorded.

Editing Transactions and Adjusting Balances

Occasionally, you may need to edit transactions to correct errors or adjust the cash balance in an investment account. Here's how.

Editing Transactions

You can edit a transaction in the account register for the investment account (see Figure 5-2). Simply make changes to the appropriate fields and click Record.

Updating an Account's Cash Balance

You can adjust the cash balance in a brokerage account to account for rounding errors or other inconsistencies. Open the register for the account for which you want to change the balance. Then choose Activities | Adjust Balance to display the Adjust Balance window, shown next. Enter the correct balance and balance date in the top two edit boxes. In the Category box, choose a category to record the gain or loss of cash. Then click OK to record the transaction and change the account balance.

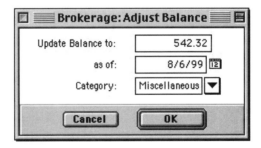

Viewing Your Investments

Quicken includes two different windows you can use to view information about your investments: the Portfolio window and the Security Detail window. Each window also offers options to add transactions or edit securities. Here's a closer look at each of them.

The Portfolio Window

The Portfolio window (see Figure 5-4) displays all of your investments in one place. Information can be viewed in a number of ways to show you what you need to see to understand the performance, value, or components of your portfolio.

Click an account triangle to collapse or expand it.

Use options here to change the view.

Click a column heading to change the sort order.

Use these buttons to open a register or Security Detail window or add a security to your portfolio.

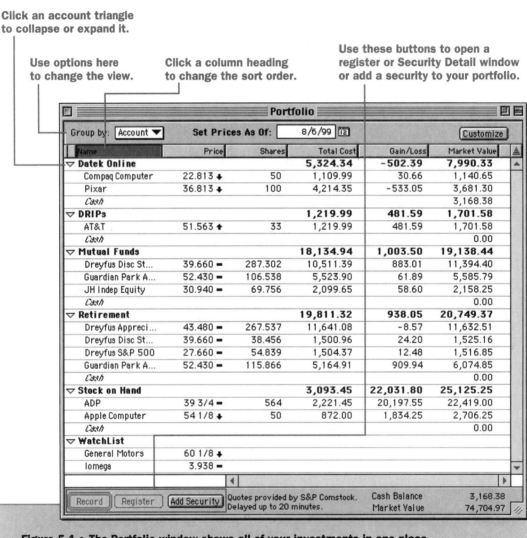

Figure 5-4 • The Portfolio window shows all of your investments in one place.

To open the Portfolio window, use one of these methods:

- Choose Activities | Investment Portfolio or press COMMAND-H.
- Click the Portfolio button near the top of the Investing tab.
- Click the Portfolio button at the bottom of an investment account register window (see Figure 5-2).

The real strength of Portfolio view is its flexibility. It includes many options for working with and viewing your portfolio.

Using Portfolio View Options

You can customize the Portfolio window's appearance by using options at the top of the window. There are many view combinations—far too many to illustrate in this book. Here's a quick look at each option so you can explore them on your own.

Grouping by an Account or Field   The Group By options enable you to select the field by which securities are grouped. Choose an option from the pop-up menu. The options are:

- **Account**, which is the default selection shown in Figure 5-4, shows the securities grouped by account.
- **Security** shows the securities in alphabetical order by security name.
- **Type** shows the securities organized by security type. I tell you about security types earlier in this chapter.
- **Goal** shows the securities organized by investment goal. I tell you about investment goals earlier in this chapter.

Tip   *You can also change the sort order of securities in the Portfolio window by clicking a column heading to sort by that column. To toggle from ascending to descending order, click the button above the top of the vertical scroll bar in the window.*

Setting the Portfolio Date   You can use the "Set Prices as of" text box to set the date for which you want to view the portfolio. For example, suppose you want to see what your portfolio looked like a month ago, before a particularly volatile market period. Enter that date in the text box. Or click the calendar button beside the text box to display a calendar of dates, and then click the date you want to display. The window's view changes to show your portfolio as of the date you specified.

Customizing the Column Display   You can change the columns that are displayed in the Portfolio window. Click the Customize button to display the Portfolio Customization dialog box, shown next. Click to toggle check marks for the columns you want to display, and then click OK to save your settings.

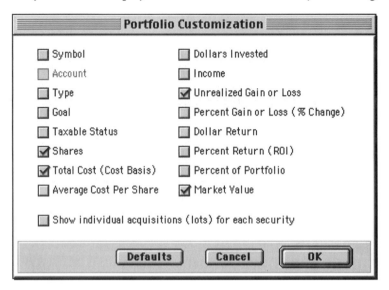

Here's a quick rundown of the available options:

- **Symbol** is the ticker symbol for the security.
- **Account** is the account the security is held in. This option is not available if the Portfolio window is grouped by Account, as shown in Figure 5-4.
- **Type** is the security type. This option is not available if the Portfolio window is grouped by Type.
- **Goal** is the investment goal. This option is not available if the Portfolio window is grouped by Goal.
- **Taxable Status** is the security's tax status.
- **Shares** is the number of shares owned.
- **Total Cost** is the cost basis for the security—what you paid to obtain it.
- **Average Cost per Share** is the total cost of all the shares of a security divided by the number of shares. Quicken can calculate this value on the fly for individual securities and groups of securities.
- **Dollars Invested** is the total amount invested in a security. This includes dividend and capital gain reinvestments.

- **Income** is the amount of income received from the security.
- **Unrealized Gain or Loss** is the dollar amount you would realize as a gain or loss if you sold the security at the most recently entered price for the Portfolio window date. I explain how to enter security prices near the end of this chapter.
- **Percent Gain or Loss** is the percent change in the security's value.
- **Dollar Return** is the dollar amount of your return on investment for the security.
- **Percent Return** is the percent of your return on investment.
- **Percent of Portfolio** is the percentage of your portfolio's value attributable to the security.
- **Market Value** is the total number of shares multiplied by the most recently entered price for the Portfolio window date.
- **Show individual acquisitions (lots) for each security** instructs Quicken to show purchase lots under each security in the Portfolio window.

Tip   *You can change column width by dragging the right border of a column's heading to the right or left. When you release the mouse button, the column's width changes.*

Opening Registers & Security Detail Windows

You can open the register for an investment account or the Security Detail window for a security from within the Portfolio window (see Figure 5-4).

Opening an Investment Register   To open an investment register, use one of these techniques:

- Click the name of an account and then click the Register button at the bottom of the window.
- Double-click the name of an account.

Opening a Security Detail Window   To open a Security Detail window, use one of these techniques:

- Click the name of a security and then click the Detail button at the bottom of the window. (The Register button shown in Figure 5-4 turns into a Detail button when a security is selected.)
- Double-click the name of a security.

Adding Securities to Your Portfolio or WatchList

The Portfolio window offers another way to add securities to your portfolio or to your WatchList, which appears at the bottom of the Portfolio window (see Figure 5-4). Click the Add Security button at the bottom of the window to get the process started. The tiny Security Name dialog box appears. Use it to enter or select a security name.

Tip *If you enter a security name that is not in the Security list window, Quicken offers to let you set up or select the security, as discussed earlier in this chapter.*

When you click OK, the Add Security dialog box, shown next, appears. It offers two options for adding the security:

- **Add shares to account** tells Quicken to add shares to one of your investment accounts. When you select this option and click OK, Quicken displays a dialog box in which you can specify which Investment Action you want to use: Move Shares In or Buy. Select an option there and click OK to display the appropriate action form for adding the shares.
- **Add Security to WatchList** tells Quicken to add the security to the WatchList in the Portfolio window so you can keep track of its prices. Figure 5-4 shows an example with two securities in the WatchList.

The Security Detail Window

The Security Detail window (see Figures 5-5 through 5-8) provides a wealth of information about a specific security, including value and performance information, transactions, and price or market value history. You can also use this window to edit security information and enter or edit prices.

To open the Security Detail window, use one of the following techniques:

- Choose Activities | Security Detail.
- Click the Detail button near the top of the Investing tab.
- Double-click a security name in the Portfolio window.

The Security Detail window has four tabs. Here's a quick overview of each tab and the features it offers.

Tip   *When you open the Security Detail window, it automatically displays the last tab you viewed for the current security. You can switch to a different security by choosing a security from the pop-up menu at the top of the dialog box or clicking the <<Prev Security or Next Security>> button.*

Setup Tab

The Setup tab (see Figure 5-5) provides setup information about the security. You can change any of the information in this tab by clicking the Edit button to display the Edit Security dialog box. I explain how to edit a security earlier in this chapter.

Graph Tab

The Graph tab (see Figure 5-6) displays a graph of security prices that you have entered into your Quicken data file, either manually, as discussed later in this chapter, or automatically via Internet download, as discussed in Chapter 13. If sales volume amounts have been entered, they also appear in the graph.

Tip   *To get the best view of the graph, you may want to enlarge the Security Detail window, as shown in Figure 5-6. This window can be resized like any other Mac OS window.*

You can modify the graph by using options in the bottom of the Security Detail window:

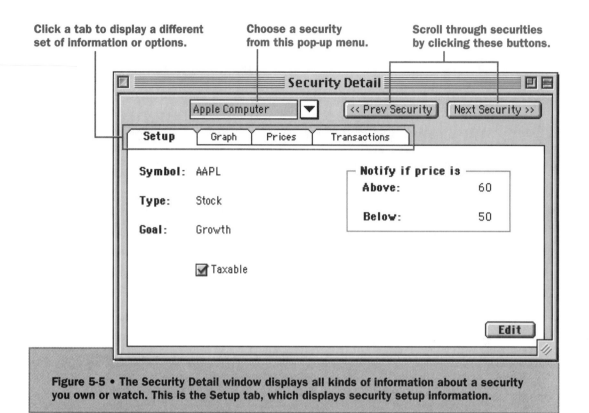

Click a tab to display a different set of information or options.

Choose a security from this pop-up menu.

Scroll through securities by clicking these buttons.

Figure 5-5 • The Security Detail window displays all kinds of information about a security you own or watch. This is the Setup tab, which displays security setup information.

Selecting a Date Range   The Date Range menu enables you to select a period to display in the graph. Your options are One Week, One Month, One Quarter, One Year (the default selection shown in Figure 5-6), Three Years, Five Years, and All.

Charting Multiple Securities   You can chart multiple securities in the same window by clicking the Overlay Securities button. A dialog box like the one shown next appears. Click to turn on check marks beside each security you want

Figure 5-6 • The Graph tab of the Security Detail window shows a chart of security prices.

to display on the graph. When you click OK, the graph is revised to show all securities you selected.

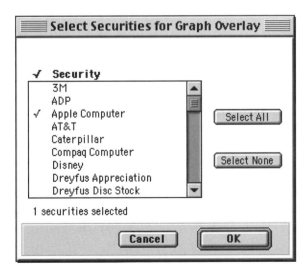

Customizing the Graph Display   When you click the Customize button, the Customize Security Graph dialog box appears. Turn on check marks beside each option you want enabled for the graph.

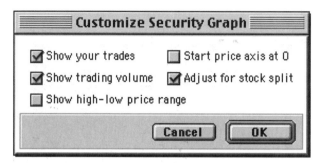

Prices Tab

The Prices tab (see Figure 5-7) displays all the price and volume information entered for the security. This is the same information used to create the graph in the Graph tab (refer to Figure 5-6). You can enter this information manually using the New and Edit buttons at the bottom of this window, as discussed later in this chapter. You can also enter it automatically via Internet download, as discussed in Chapter 13.

Transactions Tab

The Transactions tab (see Figure 5-8) lists all of your transactions for a security. If you make the window wide enough, as shown in Figure 5-8, you can see columns for the Account, Date, Action (or transaction type), Shares, Price, Amount, Commission, and Total Shares (in the account after the transaction). Quicken automatically compiles this information from your account registers when you enter transactions.

Tip   *You can quickly go to a specific transaction in an investment account register by double-clicking the transaction in the Transactions tab.*

Tracking Security Values

As you can see in the Portfolio window (refer to Figure 5-4), Quicken can automatically do all the math to tell you what your investments are worth—if you take the time to enter the per-share prices of each of your securities.

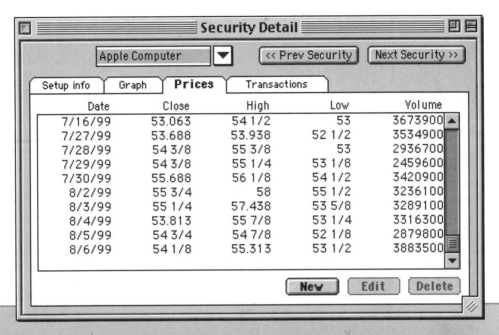

Figure 5-7 • The Prices tab of the Security Detail window lists all available security price and volume information.

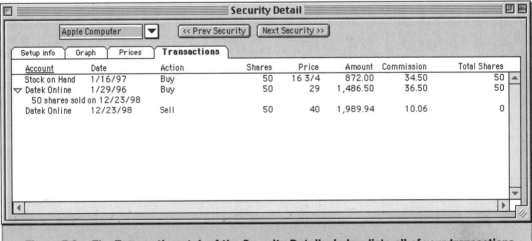

Figure 5-8 • The Transactions tab of the Security Detail window lists all of your transactions for a security.

When you record transactions, Quicken automatically records the security price. It uses the most recently entered price as an estimate to calculate the current value of the investment. Of course, Portfolio view is a lot more valuable with up-to-date security price information and a history of prices.

Note   *If a security price is not for the current date, Quicken displays a gray diamond beside it to indicate that it is an estimate.*

You can enter price information two ways: manually (the hard way) and automatically (the easy way). I show you how to manually enter security prices in this chapter; to learn how to automatically enter prices via Internet download, skip ahead to Chapter 13.

SAVE TIME   If you track more than one or two securities and want to update price information more often than once a week, stop reading now. You don't want to enter security prices manually. Trust me. It's an extremely tedious task. Quicken's ability to download stock prices directly from the Internet—even five-year price histories—can save you tons of time and prevent data entry errors. And best of all, it's free. All you need is an Internet connection. Learn about setting up an Internet connection in Chapter 3 and about downloading quotes in Chapter 13.

Entering Security Prices

Manually entering security prices isn't really hard. It's just time-consuming. And the more securities you track, the more time-consuming it is. But without an Internet connection, this may be the only way you can enter prices into Quicken.

Start by opening the Security Detail window as instructed earlier in this chapter. Click the Prices tab to display its options (see Figure 5-7). Then click the New button at the bottom of the window. The New Price dialog box, which is illustrated next, appears. Use it to enter price and volume information for a specific date. Then click Record to save the information in your Quicken data file.

New Price

Date: 8/6/99 📅
Close:
High:
Low:
Volume: 0

Cancel   Record

Only two pieces of information are required in this dialog box: Date and Close. Date is the date for which you want to enter the price. Close is the closing price on that date. If you're really ambitious, you can also enter the daily high, low, and volume for the date.

You can use two other buttons in the bottom of the Prices tab (see Figure 5-7) to work with prices:

- **Edit** displays the Edit Price dialog box for the currently selected date. This dialog box looks and works the same way as the New Price dialog box.

- **Delete** removes the price information for the selected date.

Caution   *Removing a security price can affect the market value calculations and graph for the security for that date. Quicken will use the previous date's pricing information to estimate prices on the missing date. Quicken cannot plot graph points for dates for which no pricing information exists.*

Viewing Market Values and Performance

Once you've entered price information for your securities, you can view their market value and performance information in the Portfolio window (see Figure 5-4) and Graph tab of the Security Detail window (see Figure 5-6). You can use options within the windows to modify the display of information. I explain how earlier in this chapter.

Monitoring Assets and Loans

In This Chapter:

- *Setting Up Asset and Liability Accounts*

- *Tracking a Loan*

- *Adjusting Asset Values*

- *Using Quicken Home Inventory*

- *Using the Emergency Records Organizer*

Assets and liabilities are what make up your net worth. Bank and investment accounts, which I cover in Chapters 4 and 5, are examples of assets. Credit card accounts, which I cover in Chapter 4, are examples of liabilities. But there are other assets and liabilities you may want to track with Quicken, including a home, car, recreational vehicle, and related loans. By including these items in your Quicken data file, you can quickly and accurately calculate your net worth and financial fitness.

In this chapter, I explain how to set up asset and liability accounts to track your possessions and any outstanding loans you used to purchase them. I also tell you how you can use Quicken Home Inventory and the Emergency Records Organizer to create detailed records of your belongings and other important information.

The Basics

Before you begin, it's a good idea to have a clear understanding of what assets, liabilities, and loans are and how they work together in your Quicken data file.

Assets and Liabilities

An *asset* is something you own. Common examples might be your house, car, camper, computer, television set, and patio furniture. Most assets have value— you can sell them for cash or trade them for another asset.

Although you can use Quicken to track every single asset you own in its own asset account, doing so would be very cumbersome. Instead, you'll normally account for high-value assets in individual accounts and lower-value assets in a Quicken Home Inventory file. For example, you may create separate asset accounts for your home and your car, but group personal possessions such as your computer, television, and patio furniture in a single Quicken Home Inventory file. This makes it easy to track all your assets, so you have accurate records for insurance and other purposes.

A *liability* is something you owe—often to buy one of your assets! For example, if you buy a house, chances are you'll use a mortgage to fund it. The mortgage, which is a loan that is secured by your home, is a liability. You can use Quicken to track all of your liabilities, so you know exactly how much you owe at any given time.

Loans

A *loan* is a promise to pay money. Loans are commonly used to buy assets, although some folks often turn to debt consolidation loans to pay off other liabilities—I tell you more about that in Chapter 17.

Here's how it works: The lender gives the borrower money in exchange for the borrower's promise to pay it back. (The promise is usually in writing, with lots of signatures and initials.) The borrower normally pays back the loan with periodic payments to the lender that include interest on the loan balance or *principal.* In this way, the amount of the loan is reduced after each payment. The borrower also incurs interest expense while the lender earns interest income.

While most people think of a loan as something you owe (a liability), a loan can also be something you own (an asset). For example, say you borrow money from your brother to buy a car. In your Quicken data file, the loan is related to a liability—money that you owe your brother. In your brother's Quicken data file, the loan is related to an asset—money that is due to him from you.

> **Note** | *I tell you more about loans in Chapter 15, including how you can use Quicken.com to help you find the best loan deals.*

Setting Up Asset and Liability Accounts

To track an asset or liability with Quicken, you must set up an appropriate account. Quicken makes it simple by offering two kinds of accounts for tracking assets and liabilities: an Asset account and a Liability account. Chapter 2 explains how to use the Set Up Account window to create new Quicken accounts; refer to that chapter if you need instructions.

All transactions related to the asset or liability will be recorded in the account's register, which looks and works very much like the register for a bank, cash, or credit card account. The first transaction should be the account's opening balance:

- For an asset account, the opening balance should be the asset's fair market value on that date. You can estimate this amount or, if the asset is new, use the purchase price.
- For a liability account, the opening balance should be what you owe on that date. Do not include the amount of any interest you will pay.

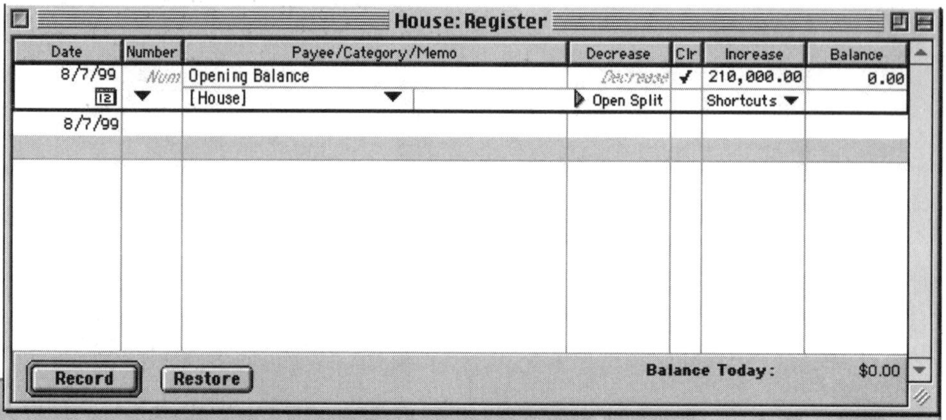

Figure 6-1 • An asset account register window

Open the account's register by double-clicking its name in the Accounts list window or choosing its name from the Rgstrs button menu at the top of the Assets & Debt tab. Figure 6-1 shows an asset account register used to record the value of a house. If necessary, change the date to reflect the balance date. Then enter the opening balance in the Increase field and click Record.

Tracking a Loan

Quicken makes it easy to track the principal, interest, and payments for a loan with regular recurring payments. Once you set up a loan and corresponding liability or asset accounts, you can make payments with Quicken using QuickFill, scheduled transactions, or online payments. The Loan feature keeps track of all the details so you don't have to.

The Loans Window

Quicken lists all of your loans in the Loans window. You can open this window by choosing Lists | Loans or by clicking the Loans button near the top of the Assets & Debt tab. Figure 6-2 shows the Loans window with one loan already created.

**Use buttons to work
with window contents.**

**Click a column heading
to sort by that column.**

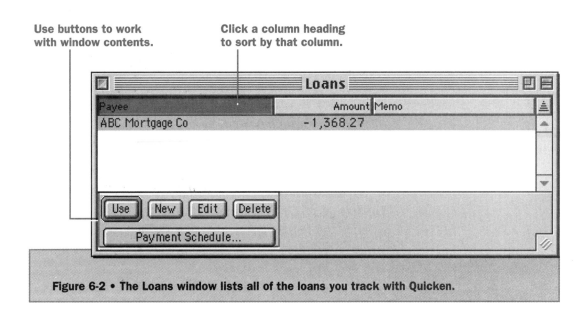

Figure 6-2 • The Loans window lists all of the loans you track with Quicken.

Buttons at the bottom of the window enable you to create new loans or work
with a selected loan in the list:

- **Use** enables you to use the selected loan in a transaction.
- **New** enables you to create a new loan.
- **Edit** enables you to modify the selected loan.
- **Delete** removes the selected loan from the list. This option does not delete
  transactions related to the loan—only the information Quicken uses to
  calculate loan interest and payments.
- **Payment Schedule** displays a list of payment details for each payment on the
  selected loan.

Setting Up a Loan

Setting up a loan is pretty straightforward. A pair of windows prompts you for all
the information Quicken needs to make its loan calculation. To get started, click
the New button in the Loans window.

Providing Basic Loan Information

The first window that appears is the Loan Interview window, shown next. Use it to answer basic questions about the loan:

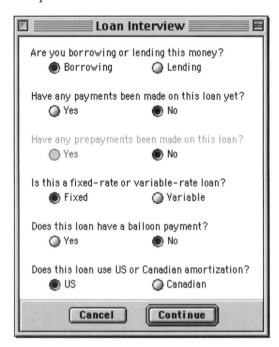

Are you borrowing or lending this money? This question establishes whether the loan should be treated as a liability (borrowing) or asset (lending).

Have any payments been made on this loan yet? If you've had this loan for a while and are just entering it into Quicken now, chances are, the answer to this question will be Yes. Otherwise, if this is a brand new loan and you haven't made any payments yet, click No.

Have any prepayments been made on this loan? This option is only available when you answer Yes to the previous question. It refers to additional payments made on the loan in excess of required payments. If you have made such payments, be sure to click Yes.

> **Tip** *Many people—including me!—contribute additional funds each month to a loan to reduce the loan term and the total amount of interest paid. I tell you more about how you can take advantage of this to save money in Chapter 15.*

Is this a fixed-rate or variable-rate loan?   Fixed loan rates remain the same for the life of the loan. Variable loan rates change periodically over the life of the loan. Choose the appropriate option.

Does this loan have a balloon payment?   A balloon payment is a very large payment at the end of the loan term. This isn't very common; so, if you're not sure whether your loan has a balloon payment, it probably doesn't.

Does this loan use U.S. or Canadian amortization?   *Amortization* refers to the way interest and payments are calculated for a loan. There are different methods in the U.S. and Canada. Choose the country of origin for your loan.

Providing Loan Details

When you click the Continue button in the Loan Interview window, the Set Up Loan window appears. Use it to provide detailed information about your loan. Here's what it looks like when you borrow money:

Loan Info   The Loan Info area is for information about the loan itself. You must provide all requested information:

- **Name of lender** is the name of the individual or organization that loaned you the money.

- **Principal + interest** is the amount of your monthly payment attributable to paying off the loan principal and interest.

- **PMI, property tax, etc.** is the total amount of additional payments for private mortgage insurance (PMI), property taxes, homeowners insurance, and other fees you may have to pay with your mortgage. These fees are usually held in escrow to pay third parties, such as local governments and insurance companies.
- **Total payment** is automatically calculated by Quicken. Check it to make sure it's right.

Caution *If the Total payment does not match the total periodic amount you pay on the loan, you probably made an error in one of the two edit boxes above it. Check the amounts you entered against statements or other documents provided by the lender.*

- **Date of next payment** is the date the next loan payment is due.
- **Frequency** is the frequency of loan payments. Your options are: Weekly, Every two weeks, Twice a month, Every four weeks, Monthly, Every two months, Quarterly, Twice a year, and Annually.
- **Payments remaining** is the number of payments remaining on the loan.
- **Current interest rate** is the current interest rate on the loan. If you indicated that the loan has a fixed interest rate, this field will be labeled *Annual interest rate*.
- **Interest category** is the Quicken category you want to use to record the amount of interest paid. This will normally be something like *Interest Paid* or *Mortgage Int.*
- **Principal account** is the name of the account in which the loan balance is recorded. For a loan in which you borrow money, this will be the liability account you set up for the loan. For a loan in which you lend money, this will be the asset account you set up for the loan.
- **Balance today** is the current balance of the loan. Normally, this will match the balance in the account you indicated as the principal account—in fact, Quicken may fill in the amount for you automatically. If it isn't the same, enter the correct amount and Quicken will update the balance in the loan account.

Note *Other fields may appear in this window depending on options you selected in the Loan Interview window. Field names are self-explanatory, so you shouldn't have any trouble figuring out what to enter. Be sure to enter all requested information.*

Payment Options

Payment Options tell Quicken how you want to record your loan payments:

- **Confirm payment before recording** tells Quicken to display a confirmation dialog box when it's time to record the payment.
- **Schedule payment on Calendar** tells Quicken to create entries on the Calendar for the loan payments. This option ensures that you make payments on time by either automatically entering the payment or reminding you about it. I tell you more about this feature in the section titled "Scheduling Loan Payments," later in this chapter, and in Chapter 7.

Previewing Payments

You can view and edit the loan payment transaction by clicking the Preview Payment button. A window like the one shown next appears. Make changes if necessary and click OK to save the transaction.

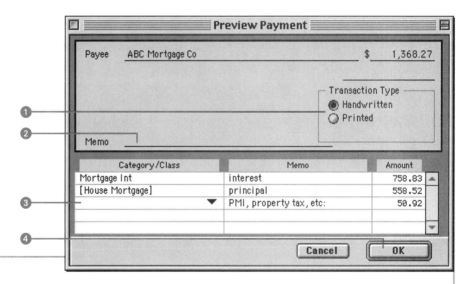

1. Select a transaction type.
2. If desired, enter a note for the transaction.
3. Enter a category for the additional payments included with the loan. If desired, you can split up this amount and allocate it to multiple categories.
4. Click OK.

> **Note** *The amount of the interest and principal paid will change automatically with each loan payment, so you should not change these amounts.*

Scheduling Loan Payments

If you turned on the Schedule Payment on Calendar check box in the Set Up Loan window, Quicken automatically displays the Schedule Future Transaction dialog box, shown next, as well as its Calendar. Enter options in the dialog box to set up the loan payment schedule and click Record.

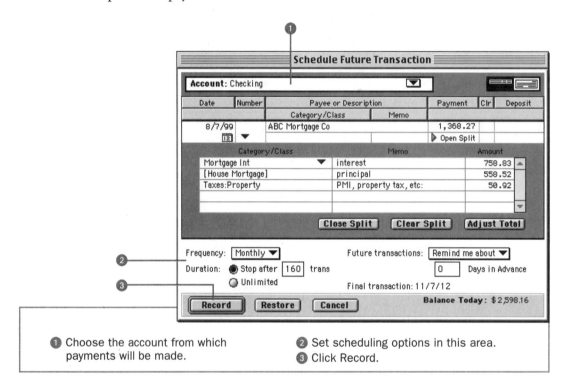

① Choose the account from which payments will be made.

② Set scheduling options in this area.

③ Click Record.

> **Note** *I tell you more about using the Schedule Future Transaction dialog box in Chapter 7; be sure to consult that chapter if you need help setting scheduling options.*

When you click Record, a dialog box like the one shown next may appear. It tells you about the transactions that will be scheduled. Select an option and click OK.

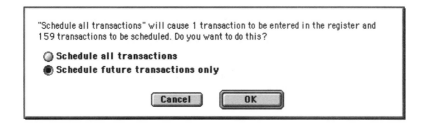

"Schedule all transactions" will cause 1 transaction to be entered in the register and 159 transactions to be scheduled. Do you want to do this?

○ **Schedule all transactions**
● **Schedule future transactions only**

[Cancel]   [**OK**]

Viewing Loan Information

Quicken's Loans window (see Figure 6-2) offers two ways to get information about the loans in your Quicken data file.

Viewing and Editing Loan Details

You can review and, if necessary, edit the information for a loan at any time. This enables you to check values entered for a loan, change interest rate information, change payment amounts, and modify payment transactions.

In the Loans window, click to select the loan you want to view. Then click the Edit button to display the Edit Loan window. This window looks and works very much like the Set Up Loan window shown earlier in this chapter. Make changes as necessary and click the Change button to save them.

Viewing Payment Schedules

You can also view a loan's payment schedule to see what part of each payment is allocated to principal and interest.

In the Loans window, select the loan for which you want to view a payment schedule. Then click the Payment Schedule button. A window like the one shown next appears, providing details for each remaining loan payment. When you have finished reviewing the information in the table, you can click its Close box to dismiss it.

Date	Pmt	Principal	Interest	Balance
			6.875%	132,451.15
8/7/99	1	558.52	758.83	131,892.63
9/7/99	2	561.72	755.63	131,330.91
10/7/99	3	564.93	752.42	130,765.98
11/7/99	4	568.17	749.18	130,197.81
12/7/99	5	571.43	745.92	129,626.38
1/7/00	6	574.70	742.65	129,051.68
2/7/00	7	577.99	739.36	128,473.69
3/7/00	8	581.30	736.05	127,892.39
4/7/00	9	584.63	732.72	127,307.76
5/7/00	10	587.98	729.37	126,719.78
6/7/00	11	591.35	726.00	126,128.43

ABC Mortgage Co Payment Schedule

> **Tip** *A payment schedule like the one Quicken maintains for each loan is also commonly known as a loan amortization table.*

Making a Loan Payment

If you do not take advantage of Quicken's scheduling feature to automatically record future loan payments, you must manually record loan payments. Quicken makes it surprisingly quick and easy to enter these transactions.

When you're ready to make a loan payment, open the account register or Write Checks window for the bank account you want to use to make the payment. When you enter the Lender name in the Payee field, Quicken automatically fills in the rest of the transaction, using amounts from the loan's setup and payment schedule. Quicken may display a Payment dialog box that you can use to confirm the loan information; if so, check and change entries as desired and click OK. Click Record in the account register or Write Checks window and you're done.

What I think is great is that every time you make a payment, Quicken correctly enters the principal and interest paid and updates the information available through the Loans window. So the loan information is always up-to-date and the amount of the principal and interest paid should match statements from the lender.

Recording Other Asset Transactions

Part of tracking assets is keeping track of their current values and modifying account balances when necessary. Like a bank or investment account, which I discuss in Chapters 4 and 5, activity for an asset account appears in its account register.

In this section, I explain how you can record changes in asset values due to acquisitions and disposals, improvements, market values, and depreciation.

Adding and Disposing of Assets

The most obvious change in an asset's value occurs when you add or remove part of the asset. For example, I have a single asset account in which I record the value of my horses and related equipment. If I buy a new saddle, that increases the value of the account. Similarly, if I sell one of my horses, that decreases the value of the account.

In many instances, when you add or dispose of an asset, there is an exchange of money. In that case, recording the transaction is easy: simply use the appropriate bank account register to record the purchase or sale and use the asset account as a transfer account in the category field. Here's what the purchase of a new saddle might look like in my credit card account:

8/7/99	Num	Double C Western World			945.39	Payment	1,357.62
📅	▼	[Horses & Tack] ▼	Saddle	▶ Open Split	Shortcuts ▼		

And here's the same transaction in my Horses and Tack asset account:

8/7/99	Num	Double C Western World			Decrease	945.39	6,545.39
📅	▼	[American Express] ▼	Saddle	▶ Open Split	Shortcuts ▼		

If the asset was acquired without an exchange of cash, you can enter the transaction directly into the asset account, using the Gift Received category (or a similar category of your choice) to categorize the income. Similarly, if the asset was disposed of without an exchange of cash, you can enter the transaction into the asset account register using the Gifts or Charity (or other appropriate category) to categorize the write-off.

Updating Asset Values

A variety of situations can change the value of a single asset. The type of situation will determine how the value is adjusted. Here are three common examples.

Recording Improvements

Certain home-related expenditures can be considered improvements that increase the value of your home. It's important to keep track of improvements, because they raise the property's tax basis, thus reducing the amount of capital gains you have to record (and pay tax on) when you sell the house.

> **Tip**   *Your tax advisor can help you determine which expenditures can be capitalized as home improvements.*

Since most home improvements involve an expenditure, use a banking account register to record the transaction. Be sure to enter the appropriate asset account

(House, Condo, Land, and so on) as a transfer account in the Category field. A home improvement expenditure might look something like this in a banking account register:

8/7/99	*Num*	Mr. Built-It Construction Co		2,500.00	*Deposit*	306.86
🗓 ▼		[House] ▼	New Deck	▶ Open Split	Shortcuts ▼	

And here's what the corresponding entry looks like in an asset account register:

8/7/99	*Num*	Mr. Built-It Construction Co		*Decrease*	2,500.00	212,500.00
🗓 ▼		[Checking] ▼	New Deck	▶ Open Split	Shortcuts ▼	

Adjusting for Market Value

Real estate, vehicles, and other large-ticket item assets are also affected by market values. Generally speaking, real estate values go up, vehicle values go down, and other item values can vary either way depending on what they are.

To adjust for market value, open the account register for the asset account you want to adjust. Then choose Activities | Adjust Balance. The Adjust Balance window, shown next, appears. Enter the new balance and balance date in the first two edit boxes. Then choose a category in which to record the difference between the current balance and the new balance.

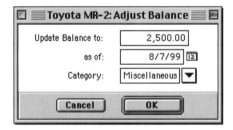

When you click OK, Quicken makes the adjustment. The adjusting entry is added to the account register, as shown here:

8/7/99	*Num*	Balance Adjustment		500.00 ✓	*Increase*	2,500.00
🗓 ▼		Miscellaneous ▼	*Memo*	▶ Open Split	Shortcuts ▼	

Tip *If you don't want the adjustment to affect any category or account other than the asset, choose the same asset account as a transfer account.*

Recording Depreciation

Depreciation is a calculated reduction in the value of an asset. Depreciation expense can be calculated using a variety of acceptable methods, including straight line, sum of the year's digits, and declining balance—consult your accountant or tax advisor for details. Normally, it reduces the asset's value regularly, with monthly, quarterly, or annual adjustments. Depreciation is commonly applied to property used for business purposes since depreciation expense on those assets may be tax deductible.

Tip   *If you think depreciation on an asset you own may be tax deductible, use Quicken to track the depreciation expense. Otherwise, depreciation probably isn't worth the extra effort it requires to track.*

To record depreciation, create an entry in the asset account that reduces the value by the amount of the depreciation. Use a Depreciation Expense category to record the expense. The transaction might look something like this:

7/1/99	*Num*	Depreciation Expense		370.16	*Increase*	21,839.84
🗓	▼	Auto:Depreciation ▼	Monthly Dep Exp	▶ Open Split	Shortcuts ▼	

Shortcut   *You can set up monthly, quarterly, or annual depreciation transactions as scheduled transactions so Quicken will automatically record them when they are due. I tell you about scheduled transactions in Chapter 7.*

Quicken Home Inventory

Quicken Home Inventory is a separate program that comes with Quicken Deluxe. You can open it from within Quicken, enter or edit information about the things in your home, and then manually update your Quicken data file with item valuations.

Quicken Home Inventory is excellent for providing detailed information about your possessions. This information is extremely valuable in the event of a burglary, fire, or other loss when you need to provide details to the police and/or insurance company. Enter this information and print reports to keep in a safe place. Then, once a year or so, update the entries and prepare a fresh report so your printed files are up to date.

Entering and Updating Information

To start, choose Activities | Quicken Home Inventory or click the Home Inv button near the top of the Assets & Debt tab. The Quicken Home Inventory program launches and appears onscreen (see Figure 6-3). You can use this List View window to add or modify summary information about each inventory item.

Note   *The first time you use Quicken Home Inventory, it displays a standard Save As dialog box. Use this dialog box to enter a name and save a new inventory.*

Tip   *Although you can use Quicken Home Inventory to track every possession in every room, from the ceiling lamp to the carpeting, entering that kind of detail isn't really necessary. Instead, enter the most valuable items, the ones that would be most difficult or costly to replace. This will save you time while enabling you to record your most important belongings.*

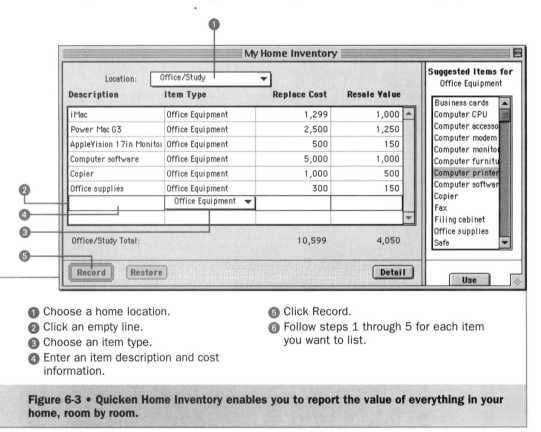

① Choose a home location.
② Click an empty line.
③ Choose an item type.
④ Enter an item description and cost information.
⑤ Click Record.
⑥ Follow steps 1 through 5 for each item you want to list.

Figure 6-3 • Quicken Home Inventory enables you to report the value of everything in your home, room by room.

To add an item to the home inventory, begin by choosing a home location from the pop-up menu near the top of the window. Click in an empty line to start a new entry. Choose an item type from the pop-up menu. Then enter basic information about the item on the line and click Record.

Shortcut   *A quick way to enter a standard item is to choose the item location and type, and then double-click one of the suggested items in the list on the right side of the window. Modify the values as necessary and click Record.*

To add details about an item, select it and click the Detail button. Use the Detail View dialog box, which is illustrated next, to enter more information about the item, such as its make and model, its serial number, and its purchase date. You can also click buttons in this dialog box to enter information about the history of the item's value and receipts you have on hand for the item. When you've finished, click Done.

Customizing Options

You can customize the pop-up menus and lists that appear in Quicken Home Inventory by using commands on the View menu:

- **Item Type List** displays an editable window full of item types, such as Appliances, Bath, Clothing, and Electronics.

- **Location List** displays an editable window full of home locations, such as Attic, Basement, Bedroom, and Bathroom.
- **Policy List** displays an editable list of insurance policies. Not only can you add and remove policies on this list, but you can also specify coverage maximums and quickly determine whether you have enough coverage for all listed items.
- **Claim List** displays an editable list of insurance claims. For each claim, you can provide a description, amount claimed, claim date, amount paid, and payment date. You can use this feature to keep track of progress on claims in the event of a loss.

Printing Home Inventory Reports

The Reports menu in the Quicken Home Inventory program window offers a number of basic reports you can use to print home inventory, insurance policy, and claim information. The inventory reports are extremely useful when applying for homeowner or home office insurance, when the insurance company requires detailed information about certain types of belongings.

Saving Your Entries

When you've finished entering or modifying information in Quicken Home Inventory, choose File | Quit. You may be prompted to back up the Quicken Home Inventory file; click Yes or No as desired. Your information is saved and the Quicken Home Inventory program quits.

Tip *You may want to record the total value of your Quicken Home Inventory file as an asset in your Quicken data file. This enables you to include home inventory items as assets so they appear on net worth and other reports. To do so, simply create an asset account named Home Inventory or Personal Possessions (or a similar name of your choice) and update its balance with the total in your Quicken Home Inventory file. I explain how to update asset balances earlier in this chapter.*

Emergency Records Organizer

The Emergency Records Organizer (ERO) is another program that comes with Quicken Deluxe. It enables you to track personal, financial, and legal information that may come in handy in the event of an emergency. It consists of a number of forms you can fill in with information. You can enter as much or as little information as you like. You can go into great detail on subjects that are important to you and completely ignore others. You can update and print the information at any time. It's this flexibility—and the fact that all information can be stored in one place—that makes the ERO a useful tool.

Entering Information

To open the ERO, choose Activities | Financial Fitness | Emergency Records Organizer. The program launches and its main window, which provides an introduction to its features, appears.

Note *The ERO includes multimedia features. If the Quicken Deluxe CD-ROM is not inserted in your computer when you launch it, you will miss out on these features. Don't worry—you will still be able to use the ERO.*

A dialog box may appear, asking if you want to create a new file or open an existing one. If you've already used this feature, click the Open button to open your existing file. Otherwise, click New and use the standard Save As dialog box that appears to name and save a new ERO file. Read what's in the window or click the Next button to continue.

The ERO steps you through the process of entering a password; personal information; and other data about your emergency contacts, your finances, and your possessions. Follow its instructions—they're very straightforward and easy to understand.

Figure 6-4 shows a typical entry window. Provide information as desired in each edit box. Click buttons to work with information if needed. After completing a window's form, click the Next button to continue.

Tip *You can skip from one topic to another by clicking the topic name in the list on the right side of the window.*

The ERO's information is divided into a number of sections:

- **Who to call** is for providing contact information: emergency contacts, next of kin, lawyers, doctors, business contacts, and other contacts.
- **Legal documents** is for providing information about important legal documents: birth certificates, marriage documents, wills, living wills, living trusts, powers of attorney, Social Security cards, passports, academic documents, professional documents, and other documents.

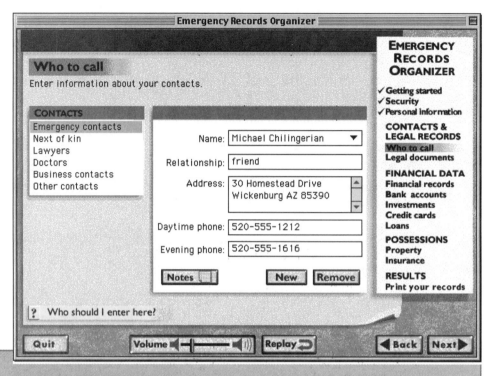

Figure 6-4 • A typical Emergency Records Organizer window gathers information.

- **Financial records** is for providing information about your financial records: tax returns, budgets, financial plans, and other financial records.
- **Bank accounts** is for providing information about your bank accounts.
- **Investments** is for providing information about your investments.
- **Credit cards** is for providing information about your credit card accounts.
- **Loans** is for providing information about outstanding loans.

Tip   *The Bank accounts, Investments, Credit cards, and Loans sections can retrieve account information from your Quicken data file. You just enter the missing information to complete the record.*

- **Property** is for providing information about the things you own: real estate holdings, vehicles, safe deposit boxes, post office boxes, and other property.
- **Insurance** is for providing information about insurance policies.

Printing Reports

When you've finished entering information, you'll get a chance to print reports based on the data you entered. You can give printed reports to people who may need them and lock others up in a secure place for when you need them.

The "Print your records" screen (see Figure 6-5) enables you to view and print three different kinds of reports:

- **Emergency Report** includes information of use in the event of an emergency: contact, medical, and health insurance information.
- **Choose a Section** enables you to select one or more ERO sections. It then prints all the information you entered in each section you selected.
- **Comprehensive Report** includes all the information you entered into the ERO.

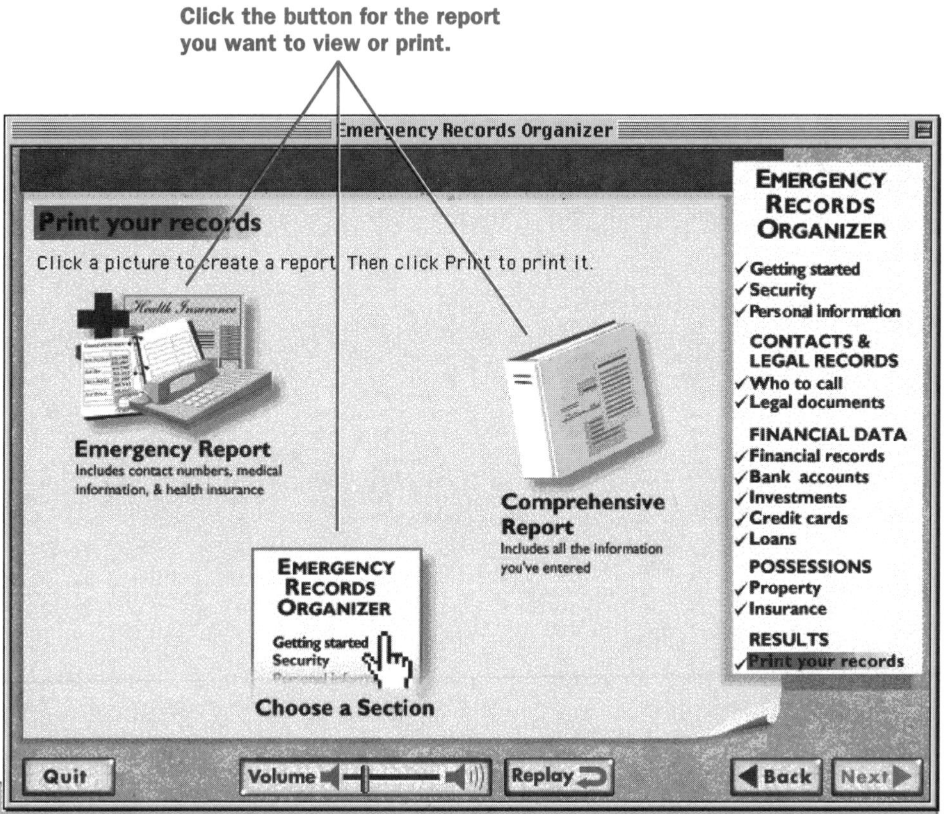

Click the button for the report
you want to view or print.

Figure 6-5 • The "Print your records" screen of the ERO window enables you to select predefined reports to view onscreen or print.

When you select a report, it appears onscreen. You can then click the Print button in its window to print it.

Saving Your Entries

When you've finished entering or modifying information in the ERO, choose File | Quit. Your information is saved and the ERO program quits.

Automating Transactions

In This Chapter:

- *QuickFill*

- *Memorized Transactions*

- *Financial Calendar*

- *Scheduled Transactions*

- *Transaction Groups*

- *Billminder*

Quicken includes a number of features to automate the entry of transactions. You got a glimpse of one of them, QuickFill, in Chapter 4. In this chapter, I tell you about QuickFill and the other features you can use to automate transaction entries or remind yourself when a transaction is due. I'm sure you'll agree that all of these features can make data entry quicker and easier.

Tip   *Before you read this chapter, make sure you have a good understanding of the data entry techniques covered in Chapter 4.*

QuickFill and Memorized Transactions

As you enter transactions, Quicken is quietly working in the background, memorizing information about each one. It creates a database of memorized transactions, organized by payee name. It then uses the memorized transactions for its QuickFill feature.

Note   *By default, Quicken is set up to automatically memorize and use transactions as discussed here. If Quicken does not function as discussed, it's probably because its QuickFill options have been changed. You can set QuickFill options in the Register options in the Preferences window. I tell you how to set preferences in Chapter 1.*

How It Works

QuickFill works in two ways:

- When you enter the first few characters of a payee name in the Write Checks or account register window, Quicken immediately fills in the rest of the name. When you advance to the next text box or field of the entry form, Quicken fills in the rest of the transaction information based on the last transaction for that payee.

- You can select a memorized transaction in the QuickFill Transactions window (see Figure 7-1) and click the Use button to create an account register or Write Checks window entry for that transaction.

QuickFill entries include amounts, categories, and memos. They can also include splits and classes. For example, you might pay the cable or satellite company for television service every month. The bill is usually the same amount each month. The second time you create an entry with the company's name, the rest of the transaction is filled in automatically. You can make adjustments to the amount or other information as desired and save the transaction. It may have taken a minute or so to enter the transaction the first time. But it'll take only seconds to enter it every time after that.

Working with the QuickFill Transactions List

You can view a list of memorized transactions by displaying the QuickFill Transactions window (see Figure 7-1). Choose Lists | QuickFill Transactions, or press COMMAND-T.

You can use buttons at the bottom of the window to use, modify, or delete memorized transactions:

- **Use** creates an entry based on the memorized transaction in the currently open account register or Write Checks window. Modify the entry as desired and click Record to save it.
- **Edit** displays the Edit QuickFill Transaction window for the currently selected transaction. I explain how to use this window later in this chapter.
- **Delete** removes the currently selected transaction. If you delete a memorized transaction, it is removed from the QuickFill Transactions window only—not from any register in the Quicken data file.

A bullet in this column indicates that the transaction is locked.

Click a column heading to sort by that column.

Use buttons to work with window contents.

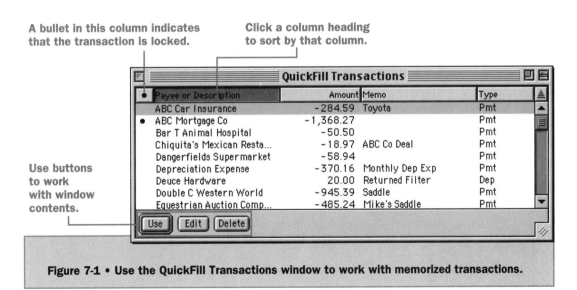

Figure 7-1 • Use the QuickFill Transactions window to work with memorized transactions.

Tip *You may want to periodically delete old QuickFill transactions that you no longer use. This keeps the list manageable and makes it quicker and easier to match memorized transactions when entering a name in an entry's Payee field.*

Editing QuickFill Transactions

Although you can always make minor modifications to the information entered by QuickFill, there are times when you may want to make major changes to an entry and save them as the new memorized transaction. You can do this by editing a QuickFill transaction.

In the QuickFill Transactions window (see Figure 7-1), click to select the entry you want to modify. Then click the Edit button. The Edit QuickFill Transaction window, which is shown next, appears.

Turn on this check box to lock the transaction.

Make changes as desired in window fields.

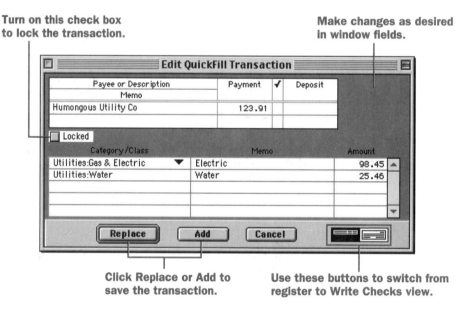

Click Replace or Add to save the transaction.

Use these buttons to switch from register to Write Checks view.

Note *The appearance of the Edit QuickFill Transaction window will vary based on whether the memorized transaction was entered in an account register or the Write Checks window. The window shown here is for a transaction entered in an account register; the window for transactions entered in the Write Checks window looks just like the Write Checks window. You can use the buttons in the bottom-right corner of the window to switch from one view to the other.*

Modifying Transaction Information

To modify the transaction, make changes as desired in the window's fields. You can make any change to the transaction.

Locking Transaction Information

When you lock a transaction, you prevent it from being changed when it is used as a QuickFill transaction in a register entry. For example, if I locked the transaction in the previous illustration, when I used that transaction to make a payment, I would not be able to change the amounts or categories. In this example, that probably wouldn't be a good idea—utility bills vary from month to month. But if the transaction were for something that's the same every month—such as rent—locking the transaction could prevent it from being changed accidentally.

To lock a transaction, turn on the Locked check box in the Edit QuickFill Transaction window. When you save the transaction, a bullet appears before it in the QuickFill Transactions list (refer to Figure 7-1) to indicate that it is locked. You can always edit the transaction again to unlock it if you need to.

Note | *Scheduled payment transactions for loans, which I discuss in Chapter 6, are automatically locked and cannot be either edited or deleted.*

Saving Transaction Changes

The Edit QuickFill Transaction window offers two buttons for saving the transaction:

- **Replace** saves your changes to the transaction, replacing the original transaction.
- **Add** saves your changes to the transaction by adding a new transaction to the QuickFill Transactions list. The original transaction—the one you edited—remains unchanged.

Memorizing Transactions

You can manually memorize a transaction, thus adding it to the QuickFill Transactions list. You might find this useful if, for some reason, you have set Register preferences to disable Quicken's ability to automatically add new transactions to the QuickFill list.

Open the register or Write Checks window in which the transaction you want to memorize has been recorded. Then choose Edit | Memorize transaction or press COMMAND-M. Quicken adds the transaction to the QuickFill Transactions window (see Figure 7-1) as a locked transaction. You can edit this transaction like any other QuickFill transaction if desired.

The Calendar and Scheduled Transactions

Quicken's Calendar feature keeps track of all your transactions by date. It also enables you to schedule one-time or recurring transactions for the future.

Working with the Calendar

To open the Calendar, choose Activities | Calendar. The Calendar window, which is shown in Figure 7-2, appears.

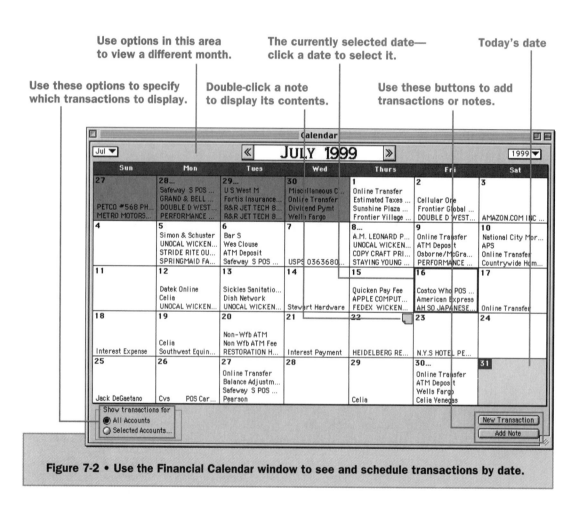

Figure 7-2 • Use the Financial Calendar window to see and schedule transactions by date.

Tip   *You can easily distinguish between scheduled transactions that have not yet been entered in a register and those that have been entered by their color. Blue transactions have not yet been entered; black transactions have been entered.*

Changing the Month Display

You can change which month is displayed by clicking buttons in the Calendar window's heading area:

View the previous month.

View the next month.

Choose a month.

Choose a year.

Changing the Transaction Display

The two "Show transactions for" radio buttons near the bottom of the window enable you to specify which transactions are displayed on the calendar:

- **All Accounts** displays transactions for all Quicken accounts.
- **Selected Accounts** displays the Select Accounts dialog box, shown next. Click to toggle the check marks beside the account names; when a check mark appears, the account will be included in the Calendar. When you've finished, click OK.

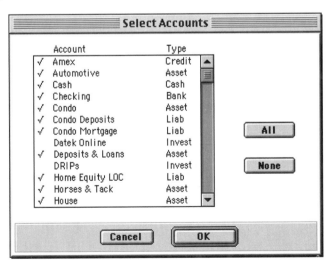

Working with Calendar Notes

You can add a note to any Calendar date. Click the date to select it, and then click the Add Note button at the bottom of the Calendar window. A Note window like the one shown next appears. Enter note text and click the window's Close box to save it.

To view the contents of a note, double-click the note icon in the Calendar window. A Note window like the one previously illustrated appears. You can modify the note's contents if desired. Click its Close box to hide it from view.

To delete a note, click to select the date on which the note's icon appears. Then click the Delete Note button in the bottom of the Calendar window—it appears in place of the Add Note button. The note is removed.

Viewing Transactions

When you double-click a calendar date, a window listing all the transactions for that date appears, as shown next. You can use buttons at the bottom of the window to work with transactions:

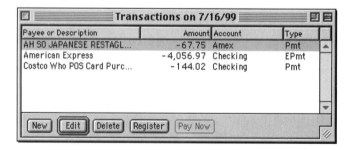

- **New** displays the Enter Transaction window so you can create a new transaction. I explain how to use this window a little later in this chapter.

- **Edit** displays the Edit Transaction window so you can modify the currently selected transaction. The Edit Transaction window looks and works very much like the Enter Transaction window, which I discuss later in this chapter.
- **Delete** removes the selected transaction.
- **Register** opens the account register for the selected transaction.
- **Pay Now** processes or records the selected transaction immediately. This option is only available for transactions that have not yet been processed.

Scheduling a Transaction

You can create a scheduled transaction from within the Calendar window (see Figure 7-2). Here are three different ways to get started:

- Click the New Transaction button in the bottom of the Calendar window.
- Choose Edit | New Transaction or press COMMAND-N.
- Double-click a date to open its Transactions window. Then click the New button.

The Enter Transaction window appears, as shown next. It looks a lot like a register entry area, but it also has additional options for scheduling transactions. Use it to enter information about the transaction.

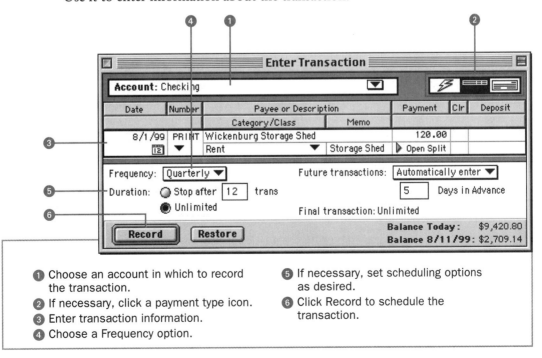

① Choose an account in which to record the transaction.
② If necessary, click a payment type icon.
③ Enter transaction information.
④ Choose a Frequency option.
⑤ If necessary, set scheduling options as desired.
⑥ Click Record to schedule the transaction.

> **Tip** | *The payment type icons at the top-right corner of the window enable you to specify whether the transaction should be an online payment, register entry, or Write Checks window entry. The button you click will determine the appearance of the Enter Transaction window. The online payment button is only available if you have online payments enabled for the selected account.*

If you want to schedule the transaction as a recurring transaction, choose an option from the Frequency pop-up menu. Your options are Only once, Weekly, Every two weeks, Twice a month, Every four weeks, Monthly, Last day of month, Every two months, Quarterly, Twice a year, and Annually. When you select a Frequency option other than Only once, the scheduling options in the bottom half of the window can be set:

Duration   Duration is the number of payments you want to schedule. For example, if you are scheduling a transaction for monthly payments on a four-year car loan and four payments have already been made, you'd choose Monthly from the Frequency pop-up menu and enter 44 in the "Stop after" edit box. Selecting Unlimited in this area tells Quicken to continue making payments indefinitely.

Future Transactions   Future transactions options enable you to specify how you want future transactions recorded.

- **Remind me about** tells Quicken to remind you to record the transaction. It does this by displaying a dialog box when you first launch Quicken on the date the reminder is due.
- **Automatically enter** tells Quicken to automatically enter the transaction without bothering you about it.

Days in Advance   Days In Advance enables you to specify how many days before the transaction date the transaction should be entered (or you should be reminded about it). For example, you might want transactions for checks and other payments to be entered a week in advance so your account balance reflects these items before they're actually paid. This can prevent you from spending money that will be needed for future transactions.

> **Caution** | *Scheduling future transactions is not the same as recording them. You must record a transaction in order to have it appear in the appropriate register or print a check for it. Choosing the "Automatically enter" option from the Future transactions pop-up menu is a good way to ensure that a scheduled transaction is properly recorded.*

Working with the Scheduled Transactions List

The Scheduled Transactions window, which is shown next, displays a list of all scheduled transactions. To view and work with the list, choose Lists | Scheduled Transactions.

Click a column heading to sort by that column.

Payee	Next Due Date	Account	Frequency	Amount
Countrywide Home L...	8/10/99	Checking	Monthly	-414.16
Frontier Village Con...	9/1/99	Checking	Monthly	-70.00
National City Mortgage	8/10/99	Checking	Monthly	-1,368.27
Paycheck	8/7/99	Checking	Weekly	712.84
Wickenburg Storage ...	11/1/99	Checking	Quarterly	-120.00

Scheduled Transactions

New   Edit   Delete

Use buttons to work with window contents.

You can use buttons at the bottom of the window to create, modify, or delete scheduled transactions:

- **New** displays the Enter Transaction window, which you can use to create a new scheduled transaction. I explain how to use this window earlier in this chapter.
- **Edit** displays the Edit Transaction window, which looks and works very much like the Enter Transaction window, so you can modify the selected transaction.
- **Delete** removes the scheduled transaction. It does not remove any transactions that have already been entered in a register.

Using Transaction Groups

Quicken's transaction group feature enables you to group together multiple transactions for entry on the same date. For example, say you make payments on all your credit card bills each month on the same date. You can group together all of these payments and schedule the group for payment at once.

Working with the Transaction Groups Window

Start by choosing Lists | Transaction Groups to display the Transaction Groups window. The following illustration shows this window with one group already created:

Click a column heading to sort by that column.

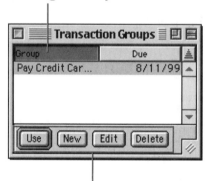

Use buttons to work with window contents.

You can use buttons at the bottom of the Transaction Groups window to work with window contents:

- **Use** displays the Recall Transaction Group dialog box, shown next. Use this dialog box to record entries in the selected transaction group.

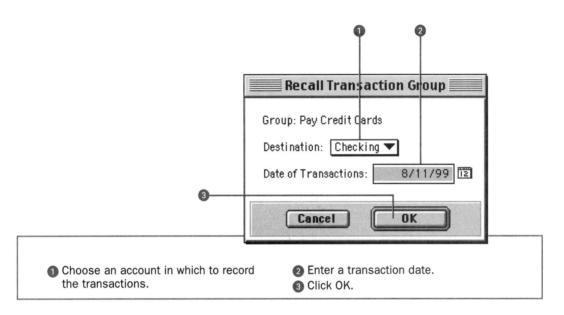

1. Choose an account in which to record the transactions.
2. Enter a transaction date.
3. Click OK.

- **New** displays the Set Up Group window, which you can use to create a new transaction group. I tell you more about creating groups with this window later in this section.
- **Edit** displays the Edit Group window, which looks and works very much like the Set Up Group window, so you can modify the information for the selected group.
- **Delete** removes the selected transaction group. When you delete a group, you remove it from the Transaction Groups window—you do not remove any entries in your Quicken data file.

Creating and Scheduling a Transaction Group

To create and schedule a new Transaction Group, click the New button at the bottom of the Transaction Groups window. The Set Up Group window, which is illustrated in Figure 7-3, appears. Use it to enter options for the group and click Create to save it.

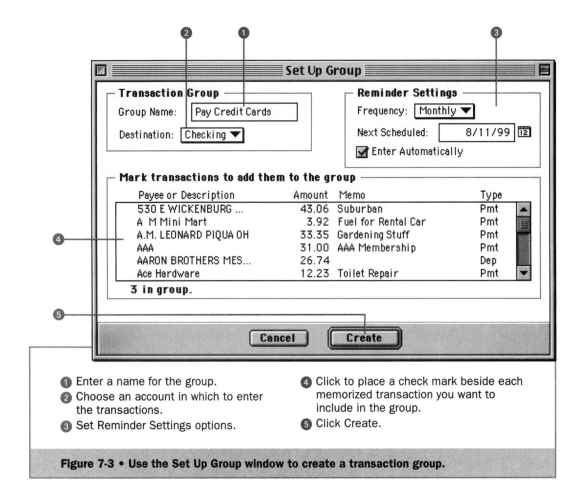

Figure 7-3 • Use the Set Up Group window to create a transaction group.

Here's a quick overview of the information you need to provide for each group you create.

Transaction Group Options   The transaction group options are for basic information about the group:

- **Group Name** is a name for the group. You can name it just about anything you like.
- **Destination** is the account in which you want to record the group's transactions. All transactions in the group must be recorded in the same account.

Reminder Settings   Reminder settings enable you to set how Quicken should remind you to record the transaction. They also enable you to set scheduling options:

- **Frequency** is how often the group's transactions should be entered.
- **Next Scheduled** is the next date the group's transactions should be entered.
- **Enter Automatically** tells Quicken to enter the transactions automatically on the date you specified. This option is only available if you choose a Frequency option other than "Only once."

Transactions to Include   The middle of the window displays a list of memorized transactions. Click to turn on check marks beside each transaction you want to include in the group.

Tip | *To edit a transaction, double-click it and use the Edit Transaction window that appears to make changes as desired.*

Using Billminder

Quicken's Billminder feature tells Quicken to remind you about postdated checks and scheduled transaction groups, so you don't forget to record them. It can remind you at one or two different times:

- When you start your computer.
- When you start Quicken.

Note | *Transactions scheduled in Quicken's Calendar have their own reminder feature so they are not included in Billminder's reminders.*

Setting Up Billminder

By default, Billminder is disabled. You can turn it on and configure it in the Billminder options of the Preferences window, which is shown next. To open this window, choose Edit | Preferences. Then click the Billminder icon in the left side of the window (you may have to scroll down to see it).

Turn on this check box to be reminded
when you turn on your computer.

Enter the number of days in advance of
transactions that you want to be reminded.

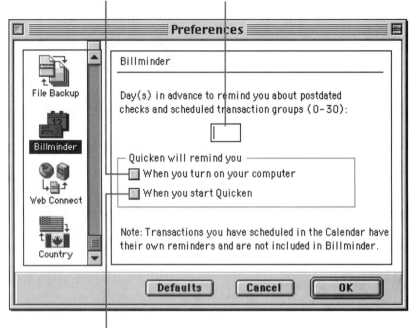

Turn on this check box to be
reminded when you start Quicken.

Set options as desired and click OK. Your settings take effect the next time
you start Quicken or your computer.

Tip *The more often you use Quicken, the lower you can set the number
of days in advance to be reminded about transactions.*

Billminder Reminder Windows

Billminder displays two different, yet very similar windows when it needs to
remind you about checks to print or transactions to enter:

The window Billminder displays at system startup

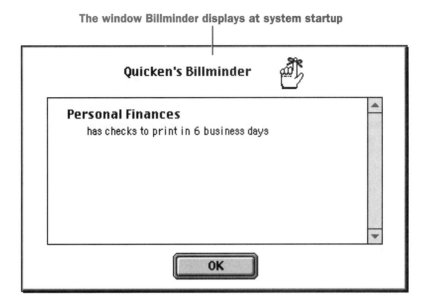

The window Billminder displays at Quicken startup.

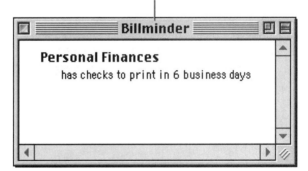

To dismiss a Billminder window, click OK or its Close box.

Managing Your Financial Records

This part of the book explains how to manage the information you enter in your Quicken data file. It explains how to reconcile your bank and credit card accounts; use the Quicken Insights window; view your data in reports and graphs; and create budgets and forecasts. These tasks can ensure that your data is accurate and provide you with useful tools for managing your finances. This part has three chapters:

Chapter 8:   *Reconciling Accounts*

Chapter 9:   *Centers, Reports, and Graphs*

Chapter 10: *Budgeting and Forecasting*

Part Three

Reconciling Accounts

In This Chapter:

- *The Importance of Reconciling Accounts*

- *Starting a Reconciliation*

- *Comparing Transactions*

- *Making Adjustments*

- *Recording a Credit Card Payment*

One of the least pleasant tasks of manually maintaining a bank account is balancing or reconciling it monthly. If you're good about it, you faithfully turn over your bank statement each month and use the form your bank provides to balance the account. There's a lot of adding when it comes to totaling the outstanding checks and deposits; and, the longer you wait to do the job, the more adding there is. And for some reason, it hardly ever comes out right the first time you try. Maybe you've even failed so many times that you've given up. I know someone who opens a new checking account once a year just so she can start fresh after 12 months of not being able to balance her account. That's *not* something I recommend.

In this chapter, I explain why you should reconcile your bank statements and how you can do it quickly and easily with Quicken.

The Importance of Reconciling Accounts

Reconciling your checking account is very important. It enables you to locate differences between what you think you have in the account and what the bank says you have. It can help you track down bank errors (which do happen once in a while) or personal errors (which, unfortunately, seem to happen more frequently). Completely balancing your checking account and making adjustments as necessary can prevent you from accidentally bouncing checks when you think you have more money than you really do. That can save you the cost of bank fees and a lot of embarrassment.

If you keep track of all bank account activity with Quicken, reconciling your bank accounts is easy. You don't need to use the form on the back of the bank statement. You don't even need a calculator. Just use Quicken's reconciliation feature to enter beginning and ending bank balances, check off cleared transactions, and enter the transactions you missed. You'll find you're successful a lot more often with Quicken helping you out.

Tip   *You can use Quicken's reconciliation feature to balance any Quicken banking account, including credit card accounts. Although this chapter concentrates on checking accounts, I provide additional information for reconciling credit card accounts, too.*

Reconciliation Basics

Reconciling an account refers to the process of comparing transactions in your account register to transactions on the account statement sent to you by your bank. Transactions that match are simply checked off. Transactions that appear only in one place—your account register or the bank's account statement—need to be accounted for.

In this section, I cover the basics of reconciling an account with Quicken: comparing transactions, making adjustments, and finishing up.

Getting Started

To reconcile a bank account, you must have the statement for the account. Bank statements usually come monthly, so you won't have to wait long.

With statement in hand, open the account register for the account you want to reconcile. Then click the Reconcile button at the top of the Banking tab or choose Activities | Reconcile. The Reconcile Startup window, which gathers basic statement information prior to reconciling the account, appears:

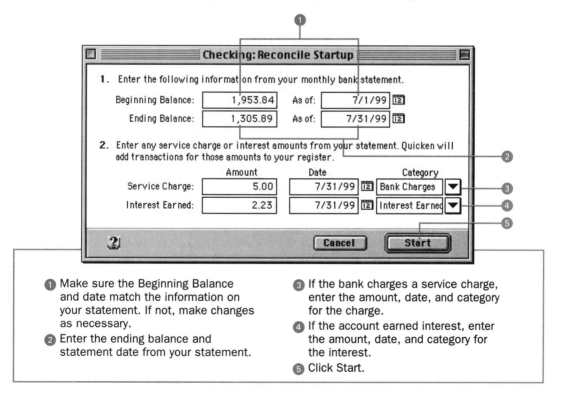

① Make sure the Beginning Balance and date match the information on your statement. If not, make changes as necessary.

② Enter the ending balance and statement date from your statement.

③ If the bank charges a service charge, enter the amount, date, and category for the charge.

④ If the account earned interest, enter the amount, date, and category for the interest.

⑤ Click Start.

Enter balance, service charge, and interest earned information in the appropriate edit boxes and click Start to continue.

Comparing Transactions

The next step to reconciling the account is to compare transactions that have cleared on the statement with transactions in your account register. For this, Quicken displays the Reconcile window (shown in Figure 8-1), which displays all payments, checks, and deposits.

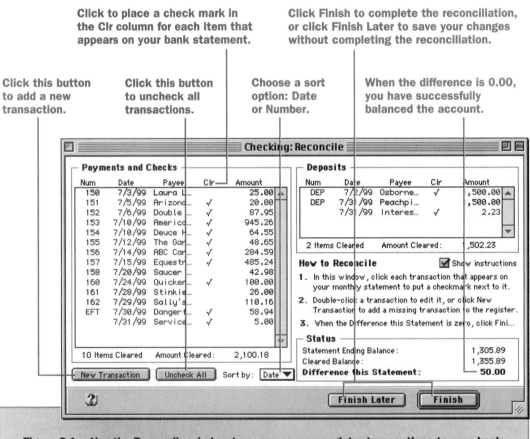

Figure 8-1 • Use the Reconcile window to compare your register transactions to your bank statement transactions.

Your job is to check off the items in the window that also appear on your bank statement. While you're checking off items, be sure to check off the same items with a pen or pencil on your bank statement. Here are some of the differences you might encounter:

- An item that appears on the bank statement but not in your account register is an item that you did not enter. There are a number of reasons why you may have omitted the transaction. Perhaps it was a bank adjustment you were not informed about. Or maybe you simply forgot. In Figure 8-1, the $50 difference between the Cleared Balance and the Statement Ending Balance is due to the failure to enter an ATM transaction—something many of us forget to do! To enter an omitted transaction, click the New Transaction button to switch to the register window. Enter the transaction in the register and click the Record button. Then switch back to the Reconcile window and click to place a check mark in the Clr column beside the item to mark it cleared.

- An item that appears on both your account register and bank statement but has a different amount or date could be due to an error—yours or the bank's. If the error is yours, you can edit the transaction by double-clicking it in the Reconcile window. This displays the account register window with the transaction selected. Edit the transaction and click Record. Then switch back to the Reconcile window to continue the reconciliation.

- Items that appear in your account register but not on the bank statement are items that have not cleared the bank yet. These are usually transactions prepared just before the bank's closing date, but they can be older. Do not check them off. Chances are, you'll check them off the next time you complete a reconciliation.

Tip *If, during a bank reconciliation, you discover any uncleared items that are older than two or three months, you should investigate why they have not cleared the bank. You may discover that a check (or worse yet, a deposit) was lost in transit.*

Finishing Up

When you reconcile a bank account with Quicken, your goal is to make the difference between the Cleared Balance and the Statement Ending Balance zero. You can monitor this progress at the bottom of the Reconcile window, as shown in Figure 8-1.

When the Difference Is Zero

If you correctly checked off all bank statement items and the difference is zero, you've successfully reconciled the account. Congratulations! Click the Finish button.

If You Can't Get the Difference to Zero

Sometimes, try as you might, you just can't get the difference to zero. Here are a few last things to check before you give up:

- Make sure all the amounts you checked off in your account register are the same as the amounts on the bank statement.
- Make sure you included any bank charges or earned interest.
- Make sure the beginning and ending balances you entered are the same as those on the bank statement.

If you checked and rechecked all these things and still can't get the difference to zero, click Finish. Quicken displays a dialog box like the one below that indicates the amount of the difference and offers to make an adjustment to your account register for the amount. Click Adjust Register to enter the adjustment.

> **Checking: Adjust Ending Balance**
>
> The total of the items you have marked is $50.00 more than the total of the items shown on your statement.
>
> You may have Quicken enter a balance adjustment transaction in your register for this amount, dated 7/31/99, or click Return to Reconcile to go back to reconciling.
>
> [**Adjust Register**]   [**Return to Reconcile**]

But next month, don't give up!

Other Reconciliation Tasks and Features

Quicken offers a number of other reconciliation features that you might find useful. Here's a quick look at them.

Reconciling Credit Card Accounts

You can reconcile a credit card account the same way you reconcile a bank account. If you try to enter all credit card transactions as you make them throughout the month, it's a good idea to use the reconciliation feature to compare your entries to the credit card statement, just to make sure you didn't miss any. If you simply enter all credit card transactions when you get your statement, reconciling to the statement really isn't necessary.

The Reconcile Startup window that appears at the beginning of the reconciliation process is shown next. As you can see, it's similar to the Reconcile Startup window that appears when you begin reconciling a bank account. Enter information in the appropriate text boxes and click Start to move on to the Reconcile window for a credit card account, which looks and works almost exactly like the Reconcile window shown in Figure 8-1.

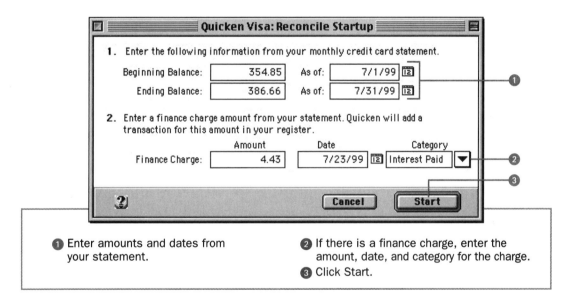

① Enter amounts and dates from your statement.

② If there is a finance charge, enter the amount, date, and category for the charge.

③ Click Start.

At the conclusion of a credit card reconciliation, Quicken displays a dialog box that asks whether you want to pay your credit card bill now. This is a particularly handy offer if you like to pay your credit card bill after reconciling your statement to your entries. If you click Yes, the Pay Credit Card Bill dialog box, shown next, appears. Select an account and payment method and click Pay. Quicken prepares the transaction for you in the Write Checks or account register window. Edit the transaction as necessary and click Record to save it.

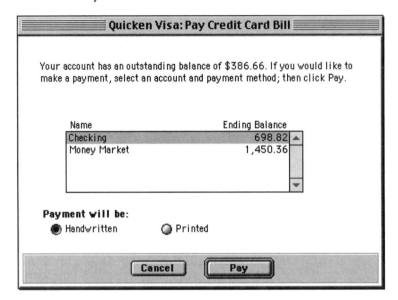

Identifying Reconciled Items

Quicken uses the Clr column in an account register to identify items that have either cleared the bank or have been reconciled:

- A plain check mark indicates that the item has cleared the bank. You'll see a plain check mark in the Clr column beside items that you have checked off during a reconciliation if you have not completed the reconciliation. You'll also see a plain check mark beside items downloaded and accepted using Quicken's online banking feature, which I discuss in Chapter 12.
- A bold check mark indicates that the item has been reconciled. The following illustration shows some examples.

Date	Number	Payee/Category/Memo		Payment	Clr	Deposit	Balance
7/14/99	156	ABC Car Insurance		284.59	✓		1,977.84
		Insurance:Auto	Toyota				
7/15/99	157	Equestrian Auction Company		485.24	✓		1,492.60
		Gifts	Mike's Saddle				
7/20/99	158	Saucer Network		42.98			1,449.62
		Utilities:Cable TV					
7/24/99	160	Quicken Visa		100.00	✓		1,349.62
		[Quicken Visa]	Payment on Acct.				

Caution   *To prevent errors in your account registers, do not edit transactions that have been reconciled.*

Centers, Reports, and Graphs

In This Chapter:

- *Quicken Insights*

- *Customizing the Insights Window*

- *Creating Reports and Graphs*

- *Customizing Reports and Graphs*

- *Printing Reports, Graphs, and Quicken Windows*

At this point, you'll probably agree that entering financial information into Quicken is a great way to organize it. But sometimes organizing information isn't enough. Sometimes you need to see concise summaries of the information you entered, in the form of balances, activity reports, and graphs.

Quicken's Insights window, reports, and graphs are three highly customizable features you can use to view and analyze your financial information. As you'll see in this chapter, they quickly and easily provide the information you need about your accounts and categories.

Quicken Insights

Quicken's new Insights feature provides "snapshots" of your financial information, complete with balances and graphs. It also provides useful links for accessing Quicken features and, if you have Internet access, Web pages on Quicken.com and other Internet destinations.

To open the Insights window, click the Insights button near the top of any tab. You'll see a window similar to the one in Figure 9-1.

Overview of the Insights Window

The Insights window combines three elements—snapshots, observations, and actions—to provide you with a centralized place for getting financial information and working with it. Here's an overview of each of these elements.

Snapshots

A *snapshot* is an up-to-the-minute view of information in your Quicken data file. Some snapshots are text-based lists while others are charts or graphs. By default, the Insights window offers five different snapshots, each of which is illustrated in Figure 9-1.

- **Accounts** displays a list of your accounts and their balances. You can click an account's name to open its register.
- **Scheduled Transactions** lists upcoming scheduled transactions.
- **WatchList** displays the securities on your WatchList, along with their most recently entered or downloaded prices. You can click a security name to open its Security Detail window.

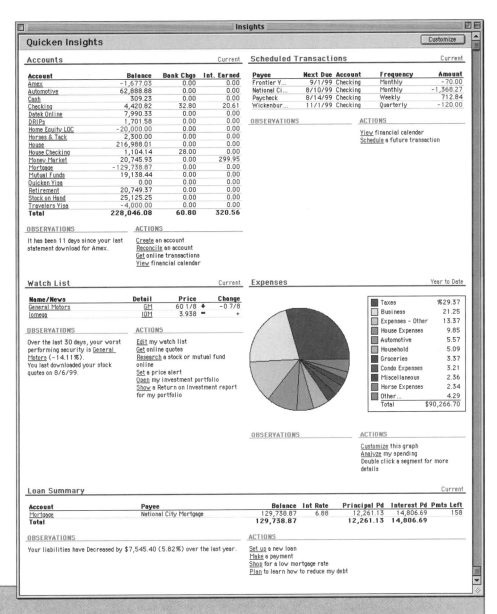

Figure 9-1 • The Insights window provides information about your finances.

- **Expenses** displays a pie chart of your largest expense items year-to-date. A legend beside the chart identifies the colored slices and provides percentage information.

- **Loan Summary** lists all of your loans and provides information about the balance, rate, principal and interest paid, and number of remaining payments. You can click the name of a loan account to open its register.

A number of other snapshots are available and can be added to the Insights window:

- **Budgets** provides information about items you have budgeted within Quicken, including the category name, budgeted and actual amounts, and the difference for the current month.
- **Credit Card Analysis** lists your credit card accounts, their balances, and your credit limits. It also displays the total amount charged on each card for the current year-to-date.
- **Income** lists your income categories, along with the year-to-date amounts earned.
- **Income vs. Expenses** shows a column chart of income and expenses for the year, with a pair of columns for each month.
- **Investment Accounts** displays a list of all of your investment accounts, along with their balances. You can click an account name to open its register.
- **Investment Returns** displays a column chart of your year-to-date returns, organized by investment.
- **Net Worth Graph** displays a column chart showing your assets and liabilities, on a month-by-month basis, for the current year. An overlaid line graph shows the change in your net worth.

Observations

Observations are notable pieces of information about the data in a snapshot. For example, the Observations area in the Credit Card Analysis snapshot may inform you about the total amount of interest paid to credit card companies or that one of your credit cards is getting close to its limit. These tidbits can provide valuable analysis of your financial records.

Actions

Actions are clickable links to other Quicken tasks or features related to a snapshot. For example, the Investment Accounts snapshot includes actions to add an investment, get online quotes, or view your full portfolio. Most Actions areas also include links to customize a snapshot; I tell you more about that a little later in this chapter.

Customizing the Insights Window

There are two ways to customize the Insights window: add, remove, or rearrange snapshots or customize individual snapshots.

Tip | *By customizing the Insights window to show the information that interests you most—in the way you want to see it—you can make it into a useful analysis tool.*

Selecting Snapshots

In the Insights window, click the Customize button. The Customize Insights dialog box appears:

To add an item to the window, select it in the Available Items list and click Add.

To remove an item from the window, select it in the Selected Items list and click Remove.

To change the order in which items appear in the window, select an item in the Selected Items list and click Move Up or Move Down.

To add an item, select it in the Available Items list and click Add. Its name appears in the Selected Items list. You can include any combination of items in the Insights window. You can rearrange the order of items in the Selected Items list by selecting an item and clicking the Move Up or Move Down button. To remove an item from the Insights window, select it in the Selected Items list and click Remove. When you've finished making changes, click Done. The Insights window is redrawn to reflect your changes.

Customizing a Snapshot

Many snapshots can be customized to change the content or display. Customization options, when available, vary from one snapshot to another.

For example, you can customize the Expenses snapshot's Pie Chart by clicking the "Customize this graph" link in the Actions area beneath it. A dialog box like the one shown next appears, enabling you to set options for the chart. Make changes as desired and click OK. Your changes take effect immediately. If you don't like what you see, don't worry. You can always customize it again.

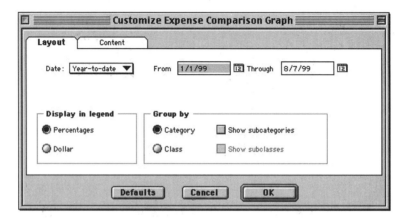

Note   *I tell you more about customizing reports and graphs in the second half of this chapter.*

Reports and Graphs

Quicken offers a variety of reports and graphs, each of which can be customized to meet your needs. I like to think of reports and graphs as the "fruits of my labor"—I spend time entering data into Quicken so Quicken can crunch the numbers and create reports and graphs that I can use to analyze my spending habits, find ways to save money, and submit to financial institutions when I apply for loans.

Here's a real-life example. In late May, I applied by phone for a home equity line of credit. The bank representative asked a lot of questions about my finances, including balances on my accounts and the market value of my investments. Because I track all my finances in Quicken, all the information I needed was right in front of me, in Quicken windows and reports that I could generate within seconds. The application process took less than 15 minutes and I got a preliminary approval right away.

In this section, I tell you about the types of reports and graphs Quicken offers. I also explain how you can create, customize, and print a report or graph based on the financial information in your Quicken data file.

Types of Reports and Graphs

Within Quicken are essentially four kinds of reports and graphs: EasyAnswer, predefined, customized, and memorized. Here's an overview of each one.

EasyAnswer

EasyAnswer reports and graphs answer specific, predefined questions such as:

- How much did I spend during the period…?
- Where did I spend my money during the period…?
- How much did I spend during the period … compared to the period…?
- Did I meet my budget during the period…?
- What am I worth as of…?

You select a question, and then provide information such as a date range, category, or account. Quicken gathers the information and generates the report or graph.

Predefined

Quicken includes a number of predefined reports and graphs. The reports are organized by topic:

- **Standard** reports include reports for your budget, categories, net worth, and taxes. Standard graphs include all categories of graphs: personal, business, and investment.
- **Business** includes reports of use to a small business owner, including accounts payable, accounts receivable, balance sheet, and income statement.
- **Investment** includes reports for capital gains, investment income, investment transactions, and investment performance.

Custom

You can create custom reports and graphs by customizing the predefined reports and graphs. This multiplies your reporting capabilities, enabling you to create reports or graphs that show exactly what you need to show.

Memorized

Memorized reports are reports you have created and customized, and then memorized to use again and again. This makes it possible to prepare frequently needed, custom reports or graphs quickly with just a few clicks of your mouse.

Creating Reports and Graphs

With Quicken, creating a report or graph is as simple as clicking a few buttons. There are several techniques: using the Reports and Graphs windows, using Shortcut commands in an account register, and clicking links in the Insights window. In this section, I explain how to use all of these techniques.

Using the Reports and Graphs Windows

The most obvious way to create a report or graph is with the Reports or Graphs window. Start by clicking the Reports or Graphs button near the top of the Reporting tab to display the Reports window (see Figure 9-2) or Graphs window (see Figure 9-3). Then click one of the tabs along the top of the window to display a list of the available reports or graphs.

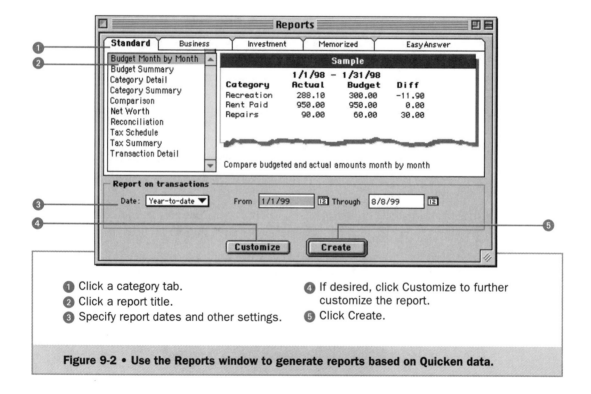

Figure 9-2 • Use the Reports window to generate reports based on Quicken data.

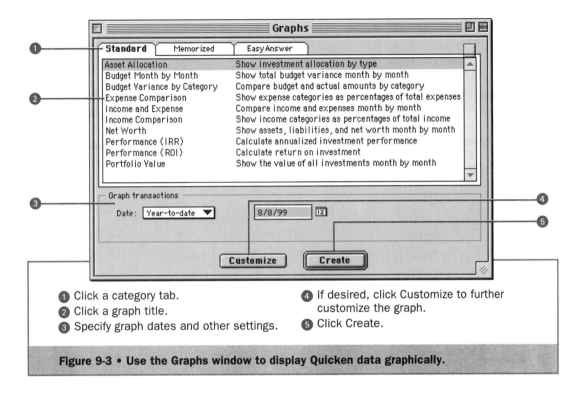

① Click a category tab.
② Click a graph title.
③ Specify graph dates and other settings.
④ If desired, click Customize to further customize the graph.
⑤ Click Create.

Figure 9-3 • Use the Graphs window to display Quicken data graphically.

Note   *The Memorized tab in the Reports window is gray until you have memorized at least one report. This also applies to the Graphs window.*

To create a report or graph, click its name and enter options in the settings area at the bottom of the window. Then click Create to display the report or graph. Figures 9-4 and 9-5 show examples.

Tip   *In many instances, you can double-click on part of a graph to get a new, detailed view of that part of the graph.*

Using Shortcuts Commands in Register Windows

The active entry in an account register includes a Shortcuts pop-up menu like the one shown next. Often, you can use this menu to generate Transaction Detail

Click buttons to print, preview, or customize the report.

Double-click a value to create a detailed report or
view a transaction's register entry.

Drag a diamond to change column width.

Set options to make quick changes to the report.

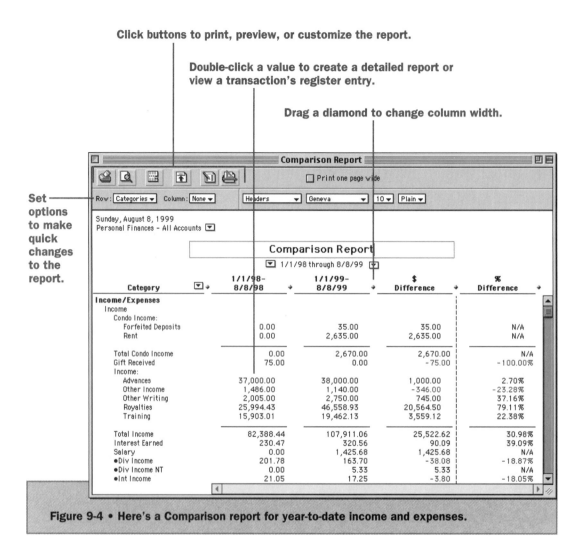

Figure 9-4 • Here's a Comparison report for year-to-date income and expenses.

Shortcut Reports for the payee or category of the current entry. Simply choose
the report option you want:

• **Report on *Payee Name*** generates a listing of year-to-date transactions for the
payee or description in the entry.

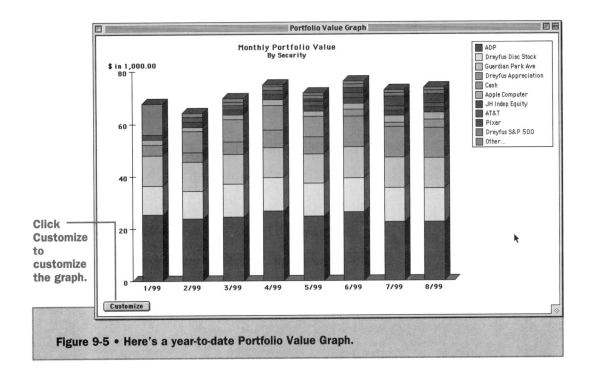

Click Customize to customize the graph.

Figure 9-5 • Here's a year-to-date Portfolio Value Graph.

- **Report on** *Category Name* generates a listing of year-to-date transactions for the category in the entry.

Clicking Links in the Insights Window

The Actions areas within the Insights window (refer to Figure 9-1) often includes clickable links for creating reports. For example, you can generate a Return on Investment report for your portfolio by clicking a link in the Actions area of the WatchList snapshot.

Customizing Reports and Graphs

You can customize just about any report or graph you create so it shows only the information you want to display. When you can customize it, however, depends on how you create it:

- When you create a report or graph using the Reports or Graphs window, you can customize it before or after you create it.
- When you create a report using Shortcuts menu options or links in the Insights window, you can only customize it after you create it.

Customization options vary from one type of report or graph to another. It's impossible to cover all variables in this chapter. I will, however, tell you about the most common options so you know what to expect. I'm sure you'll agree that Quicken's reporting feature is very flexible when you go beyond the basics.

Using the Customize Report Window

To customize a report, click the Customize button at the bottom of the Reports window (see Figure 9-2) or the Customize button at the top of the report window (see Figure 9-6, later in this chapter). The Customize Report window appears. Here's what it looks like for a Comparison Report:

Click a tab to view its options.   Set customization options in the window.

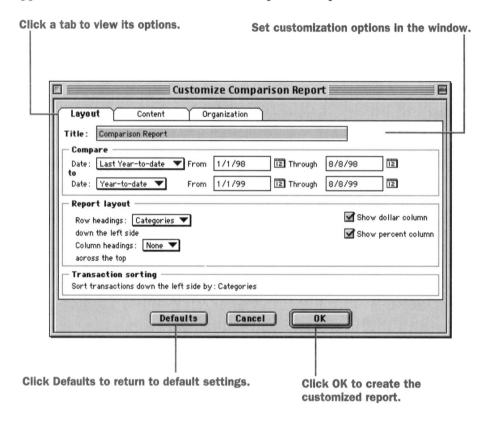

Click Defaults to return to default settings.   Click OK to create the
                                                        customized report.

The Customize Report window normally includes three tabs of options that you can set to customize the report:

- **Layout** (shown in the previous illustration) enables you to set display options for the report, such as the title, report dates, and row and column headings.

- **Content** enables you to select the transactions that should appear in the report based on entry fields such as accounts, categories, classes, payees and descriptions, memos, check numbers, and amounts. You can also specify whether Quicken should include uncleared items, cleared items, reconciled items, payments, deposits, and unprinted checks. This is a powerful feature for creating reports because of the amount of flexibility it offers; you can specify virtually any combination of options to report exactly what you need to see.

- **Organization** enables you to specify how transactions should be organized and whether account transfers should be included.

Once you have set options as desired, click the OK button. Quicken creates the report to your specifications. If it isn't exactly what you want, that's okay. Just click the Customize button in the report window and change settings in the Customize Report window to fine-tune the report. You can repeat this process until the report is exactly the way you want it.

Using the Customize Graph Window

To customize a graph, click the Customize button in the Graphs window or, when available, in the graph window itself. The Customize Graph window appears. Here's what it looks like for a Portfolio Value Graph:

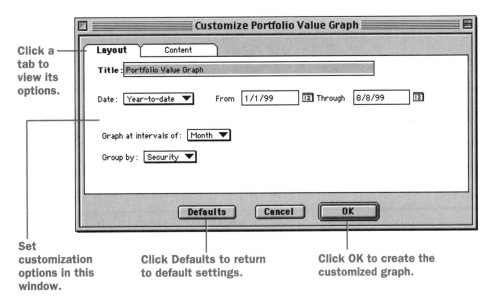

Click a tab to view its options.

Set customization options in this window.

Click Defaults to return to default settings.

Click OK to create the customized graph.

The window has two tabs for setting options:

- **Layout** (shown in the previous illustration) enables you to specify a graph title, dates, and organization.
- **Content** enables you to select the transactions that should appear in the graph based on entry fields such as accounts, categories, classes, and securities.

When you've finished setting options, click the OK button. Quicken creates the graph to your specifications. If it isn't exactly what you want, repeat the process to fine-tune the graph until it is the way you want it.

Using Customization Options in the Report Window

The top of the report window offers a number of buttons and options for working with the report. All of these options are identified in Figure 9-6.

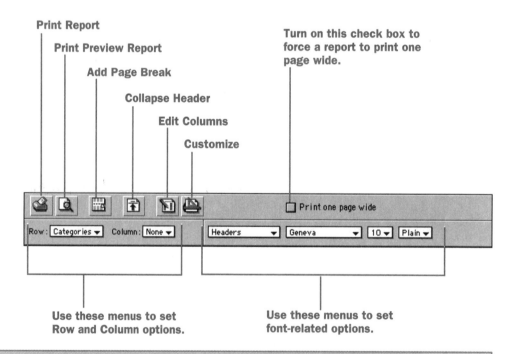

Print Report

Print Preview Report

Add Page Break

Collapse Header

Edit Columns

Customize

Turn on this check box to force a report to print one page wide.

☐ Print one page wide

Row: Categories ▾   Column: None ▾   Headers ▾   Geneva ▾   10 ▾   Plain ▾

Use these menus to set Row and Column options.

Use these menus to set font-related options.

Figure 9-6 • The top of a report window offers customization options.

Note *The options that appear at the top of the report window can vary based on the report displayed, so don't expect every report to offer the same options shown in Figure 9-6.*

The buttons along the top of the window offer a number of options:

- **Print Report** displays the Print dialog box so you can print the report. I tell you more about printing reports later in this chapter.
- **Print Preview Report** displays a preview of the report, the way it will appear when printed.
- **Add Page Break** inserts a page break above the currently selected report line. A page break appears as a dashed line across the report. Once a page break has been inserted, you can remove it by selecting the line immediately below it and clicking this button again.
- **Collapse Header** hides all report lines above the column headings. Once hidden, you can display them by clicking this button again.
- **Edit Columns** displays a dialog box like the one shown next, which lists the report columns. Click to toggle check marks beside columns to show or hide them. When you've finished, click OK. The report changes immediately.

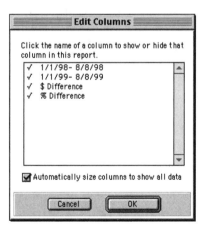

- **Customize** displays the Customize Report window, which you can use to set a variety of options for the report. I show and discuss the Customize Report window earlier in this chapter.

Tip *If you point to a button, a tiny box with the button's name appears to identify it.*

You can also use pop-up menus near the top of the report window to change the rows and columns and font formatting of a report. Simply choose options from the menus; the report changes a moment later.

Tip *Pop-up menus within the report itself enable you to change more report options, such as report dates, accounts, and categories. The options that are offered vary from one report type to another. Don't be afraid to experiment. You can always re-create the report if you need to.*

Dragging Column Borders

You can change the width of columns on some reports by dragging the column markers. Column markers, when available, look like three-dimensional diamonds between column headings in the report window (see Figure 9-4). Move the mouse pointer onto a column marker and a pair of vertical lines with two arrows appears. Press the mouse button down and drag to the right or left. When you release the mouse button, the column's width changes.

Setting Report and Graph Preferences

You can use the Preferences window to change the default settings for Reports and Graphs. Choose Edit | Preferences to display the Preferences window. Then click the Reports or Graphs icon on the left side of the window to display appropriate preference options. I discuss these options in detail in Chapter 1; consult that chapter if you need more information.

Memorizing Reports and Graphs

Often, you'll create a predefined report and customize it to create a report you want to be able to see again and again. Rather than creating and customizing the report from scratch each time you want to see it, you can memorize its settings. Then, when you want to view the report again, just select it from a list and it appears. You can do the same for graphs.

Memorizing a Report or Graph

To memorize a report or graph, start by creating and customizing one. When it looks just the way you want it, choose Edit | Memorize or press COMMAND-M. The Memorize Report Template dialog box (shown next) or Memorize Graph Template dialog box (which looks the same) appears.

Enter a name and description for the report or graph in the appropriate edit boxes. Then toggle the "Use current date" check box on or off as desired. With the check box turned on, the report or graph always shows the date it is created. With the check box turned off, Quicken uses the currently selected date option (today's date) each time it displays the report or graph. When you've finished setting options, click the Memorize button to memorize the report or graph.

Tip *If you make changes to a report or graph and then close it without memorizing it, Quicken may ask if you want to memorize it. If you click the Yes button, Quicken displays the Memorize Report Template so you can memorize it.*

Viewing a Memorized Report or Graph

When you memorize a report or graph, it appears in the Memorized tab of the Reports window (see Figure 9-2) or Graphs window (see Figure 9-3). The next illustration shows what the tab might look like with a few memorized reports. Select the report or graph you want and click Create to display it.

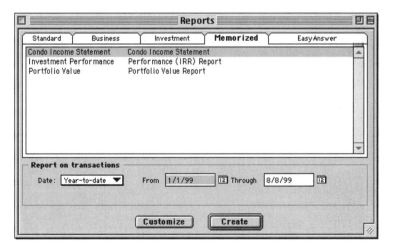

Printing Reports, Graphs, and Quicken Windows

You can print reports and graphs. This enables you to create hard copies for your paper files or for use when applying for loans or completing your tax returns. You can also print the contents of many Quicken windows to create simple reports of lists and register entries.

Note *Before previewing or printing a report, you may want to use Apple's Chooser to select a printer and use the Page Setup dialog box to set general printing options for your printer. Consult the documentation that came with Mac OS or your printer for assistance if necessary.*

SAVE TIME When I applied for my mortgage, I was able to create and print all kinds of useful reports to include with my mortgage application forms. I don't know if it helped me get the mortgage, but it saved the time I would have spent manually duplicating needed information.

Previewing a Report

Before you print a report, you may want to preview it to make sure it looks the way you want it to. This can save time and paper if the report isn't just right the first time you're ready to print it.

To preview a report, click the Print Preview Report button at the top of the report window (see Figure 9-6) or choose File | Print Preview Report. A preview window like the one in Figure 9-7 appears. Use it to see what the report will look like when you print it.

Printing a Report or Graph

To print a report or graph, choose File | Print Report or File | Print Graph, click the Print Report button at the top of the report window (see Figure 9-6), or click

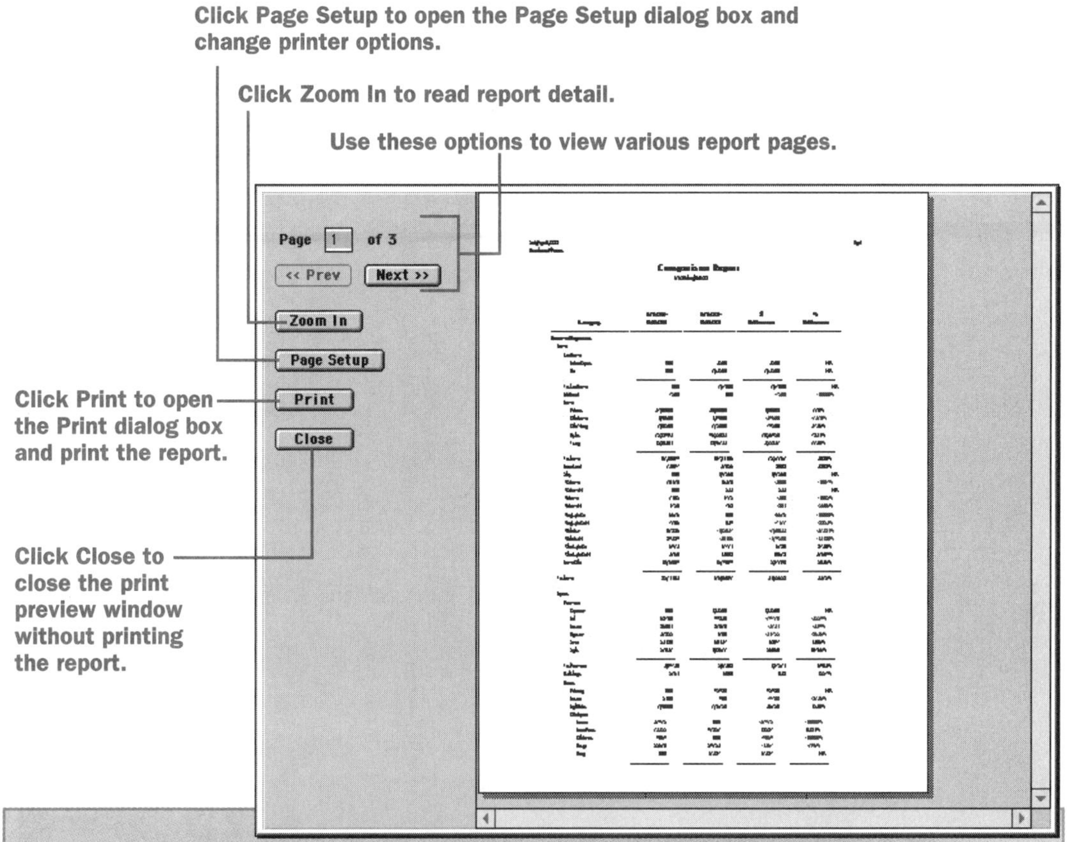

Click Page Setup to open the Page Setup dialog box and change printer options.

Click Zoom In to read report detail.

Use these options to view various report pages.

Click Print to open the Print dialog box and print the report.

Click Close to close the print preview window without printing the report.

Page [1] of 3

<< Prev   Next >>

Zoom In

Page Setup

Print

Close

Figure 9-7 • Use a report preview window to see what a report will look like when printed.

the Print button in the print preview window (see Figure 9-7). The Print dialog box appears. Here's what it looks like for a LaserWriter printer; it may look different for your printer.

Set print options as desired.

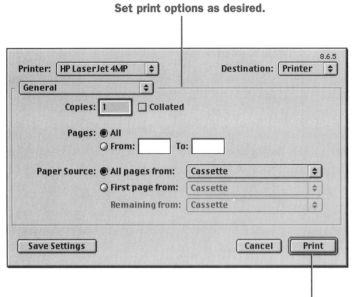

Click Print to print the report or graph.

The printing options that appear in the Print dialog box within Quicken are the same as the options available in any other program, so they should be familiar to you. Set options as desired and click Print to print the report or graph.

Printing a Quicken Window

You can print the contents of many Quicken windows. Simply open the window you want to print and choose the appropriate Print command from the File menu. For example, if a register window is open, you'd choose File | Print Register to print it. If the Categories & Transfers window is open, you'd choose File | Print Categories & Transfers. The same Print dialog box discussed previously appears. Set options as desired and click Print to print the window's contents.

Budgeting and Forecasting

In This Chapter:

- *Budgeting and Forecasting Basics*

- *Creating a Budget*

- *Fine-Tuning a Budget*

- *Managing Multiple Budgets*

- *Monitoring Budgets*

- *Creating a Forecast*

- *Modifying a Forecast*

Chapter 10

When money is tight or you're interested in meeting financial goals, it's time to create a budget and monitor your spending. But if you're serious about managing your money, you might want to create a budget before you need one. While Quicken's categories give you a clear understanding of where money comes from and where it goes, budgets enable you to set up predefined amounts for each category, thus helping you control spending.

Budgets also make it easier to create forecasts of your future financial position. This makes it possible to see how much cash will be available at a future date—before the holidays, for summer vacation, or for the day you plan to put down a deposit on a new car.

In this chapter, I tell you how to create a budget and use it to monitor your spending habits. I also explain how to create a forecast so you can glimpse your financial future.

Budgeting

The idea behind a budget is to determine expected income amounts and specify maximum amounts for expenditures. This helps prevent you from spending more than you earn. It also enables you to control your spending in certain categories. For example, say you realize that you go out for dinner a lot more often than you should. You can set a budget for the Dining category and track your spending to make sure you don't exceed the budget. You'll eat at home more often and save money.

In this section, I explain how to set up a budget and use it to keep track of your spending. I think you'll agree that budgeting is a great way to keep spending under control.

Creating a Budget

Quicken's budgeting feature enables you to create budgets for any combination of categories. You can enter budget amounts manually or tell Quicken to automatically generate a budget for you based on past transactions.

Choose Activities | Budgeting | Budget Setup to display the Create Budget window, shown next. Enter a name for the budget; then set options as desired and click Create.

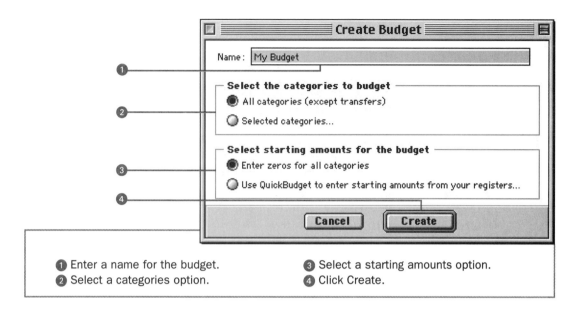

① Enter a name for the budget.
② Select a categories option.
③ Select a starting amounts option.
④ Click Create.

> **Note**   *If you have already created a budget, the Budget Setup window will appear (see Figure 10-1, later in the chapter) instead of the Create Budget window. To display the Create Budget window, choose New Budget from the pop-up menu in the top-left corner of the Budget Setup window.*

Selecting Budget Categories

The first pair of radio buttons in the Create Budget window enables you to specify which categories should be included in the budget:

All Categories   The "All categories (except transfers)" option includes all categories in the budget. Transfer accounts are not included. Selecting this option makes it easy to create a budget that includes all of your income and expenditures.

Selected Categories   The "Selected categories" option enables you to select which categories to include. This makes it possible to create a budget for a specific purpose—for example, a budget to monitor just those expenditures that you can control, like dining, clothing, and entertainment. When you select this option, the Select Categories dialog box, shown next, appears. Click to toggle check marks beside category names or click the buttons on the right side of the dialog box to include or exclude specific types of categories. When you click OK, the categories that are checked will be included in the budget.

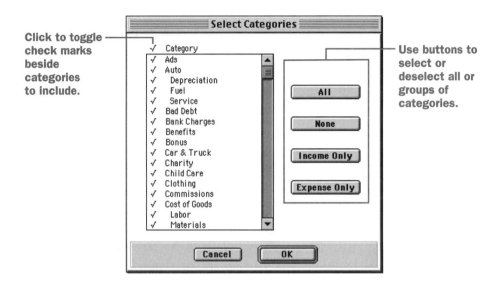

Click to toggle check marks beside categories to include.

Use buttons to select or deselect all or groups of categories.

Selecting Starting Amounts

The second pair of radio buttons in the Create Budget window enables you to specify how you want to enter starting amounts for the budget:

Enter Zeros   The "Enter zeros for all categories" option enters 0.00 for each category in the budget. You can then modify the budgeted amounts to create your budget from scratch.

Use QuickBudget   The "Use QuickBudget to enter starting amounts from your registers" option enables you to create a budget based on amounts already entered in your account registers. When you select this option, the QuickBudget window, shown next, appears. Set the following options and click OK:

- **Date** is the period for which register transactions should be used for the budget. You can choose an option from the Date pop-up menu or enter beginning and ending dates in the From and Through edit boxes. For best results, choose a recent 12-month period—this ensures that you'll include both regular and seasonal income and expenses.

- **Calculate amounts as** options specify how Quicken should fill in monthly amounts. "The monthly average amount" calculates an average for each month based on all the transactions in the date period. It then enters that average for each month. This is a good option if you selected a date period less than a full year or your income and expenses don't have seasonal peaks.

"The actual amount for each month" enters actual amounts from the registers for each month. Be sure to use this option if you do have a lot of seasonal income or expenses.

- **Round amounts to the nearest** enables you to choose a rounding amount from a pop-up menu: $1, $10, or $100. The amount you choose will be used to round budget entries.

- **Inflate amounts by** enables you to enter an inflation percentage. The amount you enter is applied to each budgeted category.

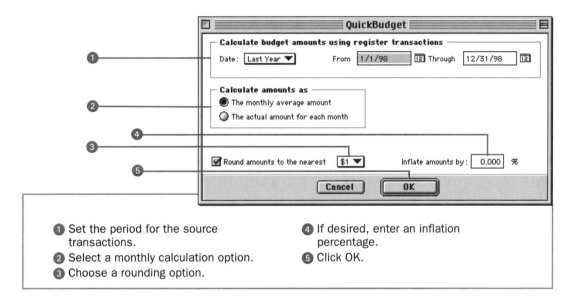

① Set the period for the source transactions.
② Select a monthly calculation option.
③ Choose a rounding option.
④ If desired, enter an inflation percentage.
⑤ Click OK.

Fine-Tuning a Budget

You can view and fine-tune a budget in the Budget Setup window (see Figure 10-1). You can open this window in a number of ways:

- Use the Create Budget window, which is discussed in the previous section, to set budget options. When you click Create, the Budget Setup window appears.

- Once a budget has been created, choose Activities | Budgeting | Budget Setup, or click the Budget button near the top of the Planning tab.

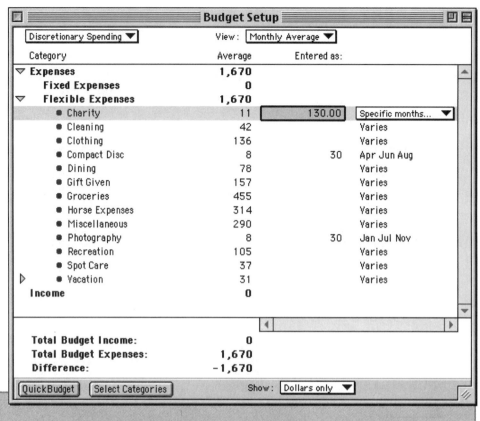

Figure 10-1 • Use the Budget Setup window to fine-tune a budget.

Changing the Budget View

There are a number of ways to change the way information appears in the
Budget view window.

Setting the View   By default, the Budget Setup window displays your budget
in Monthly Average view. You can change the view by choosing a different
option from the View menu in the top of the window:

- **Monthly Average** (see Figure 10-1) displays the average amount for
  each month.
- **Quarterly Average** displays the average amount for each quarter.
- **Yearly Total** displays the total amount for the entire year.

- **All Months** displays the amount entered for each month (see Figure 10-2). When you choose All Months, another pop-up menu appears at the top of the window. Use it to select the first month you want to display.

Tip   *All Months view is particularly handy for modifying budgeted amounts, especially when your income or expenses vary throughout the year.*

Setting Value Options   You can also change the way values appear in the Budget Setup window. Choose an option from the Show pop-up menu at the bottom of the window. The options are self-explanatory: Dollars only or Dollars & cents.

Changing the Category Display   You can add or remove categories from a budget at any time. Click the Select Categories button at the bottom of the Budget Setup window. This displays the Select Categories dialog box illustrated earlier in this chapter. Click to toggle check marks on or off to specify which categories should appear. When you click OK, your changes are applied to the Budget Setup window.

Rearranging Categories   Expense categories are separated into Fixed Expenses and Flexible Expenses. You can move any expense category from one

Category	Total	January	February	March	April	May
▽ **Expenses**	20,040	2,680	360	1,430	1,360	2,130
Fixed Expenses	0	0	0	0	0	0
▽ **Flexible Expenses**	20,040	2,680	360	1,430	1,360	2,130
• Charity	130	0.00	0	0	0	0
• Cleaning	500	0	0	140	120	120
• Clothing	1,630	580	0	0	100	190
• Compact Disc	90	0	0	0	30	0
• Dining	940	160	0	40	120	160
• Gift Given	1,880	160	50	0	0	330
• Groceries	5,460	560	50	870	310	370
• Horse Expenses	3,770	0	0	380	400	370
• Miscellaneous	3,480	280	200	0	160	430
• Photography	90	30	0	0	0	0
• Recreation	1,260	910	60	0	60	0
• Spot Care	440	0	0	0	60	70
▷ • Vacation	370	0	0	0	0	90
Income	0	0	0	0	0	0
Total Budget Income:	0	0	0	0	0	0
Total Budget Expenses:	20,040	2,680	360	1,430	1,360	2,130
Difference:	-20,040	-2,680	-360	-1,430	-1,360	-2,130

Figure 10-2 • You also can display individual months in the Budget Setup window.

area to the other. Simply drag its category line to the new position. When you release the mouse button, the category moves.

Changing Budgeted Amounts in Average or Total View

In Monthly Average, Quarterly Average, or Annual Total view, you can modify the amounts that appear in the "Entered in" column of the Budget Setup window (see Figure 10-1). This, in turn, will recalculate the monthly or quarterly average or annual total, thus changing your budget.

To change a budgeted amount, begin by choosing an option from the frequency pop-up menu to the right of the amount in the "Entered in" column. Your options are Per week, Every two weeks, Twice a month, Every four weeks, Per month, Every two months, Per quarter, Twice a Year, Per year, or Specific months. ("Varies" may appear as an option for some categories when QuickBudget enters values for you as discussed earlier in this chapter.) Choose the option that corresponds to the frequency of the budgeted amount. If you choose Specific months, a dialog box appears, enabling you to select the months to budget.

Next, enter a value in the edit box beside the pop-up menu. The value should correspond to the amount you expect to receive or want to spend for the category for the frequency you chose.

For example, say you get paid every two weeks and want to enter your budgeted take-home pay. You'd select the "Every two weeks" option, and then enter the amount of your take-home pay in the edit box beside it. Quicken automatically calculates the Average and total for the year. Here's what it might look like in the Budget Setup window:

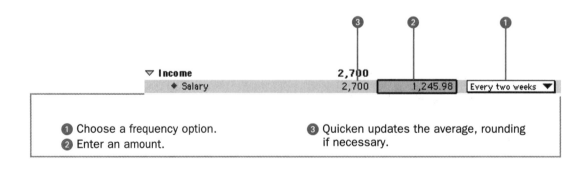

Changing Budgeted Amounts in All Months View

Changing budgeted amounts in All Months view (see Figure 10-2) is a little more straightforward. Simply click to select the value you want to change and enter a new value. The total is automatically updated.

Tip   *To copy a selected value to all months after the selected month, click the Fill Row button at the bottom of the Budget Setup window (see Figure 10-2). The value appears in all month columns to the right of the selected value for that category.*

Using QuickBudget

You also can use QuickBudget to change all the budgeted amounts for your budget. Click the QuickBudget button at the bottom of the Budget Setup window. A QuickBudget window like the one shown next appears. It offers the same basic options as the QuickBudget window discussed earlier in this chapter, along with two others:

- **Replace already budgeted amounts in Budget Setup with QuickBudget amounts** clears out the current budgeted amounts and replaces them with the result of QuickBudget calculations, as determined by the other settings in the window.
- **For which categories** enables you to specify whether you want All categories or Selected categories. If you select the Selected option, the Select Categories dialog box appears so you can specify which categories you want to include.

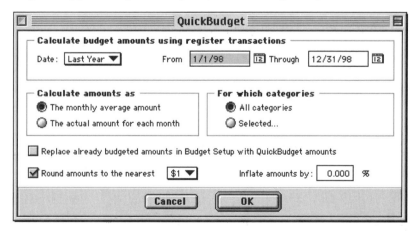

When you've finished setting QuickBudget options, click OK to apply your settings to the current budget.

Managing Multiple Budgets

Quicken enables you to have more than one budget. The pop-up menu at the top-left corner of the Budget Setup window (see Figures 10-1 and 10-2) offers options for creating and managing multiple budgets.

Creating a New Budget

To create additional budgets, choose New Budget from the pop-up menu at the top left of the Budget Setup window. This displays the Create Budget window, which I discuss earlier in this chapter. Use it to name, set options for, and create a new budget.

Switching from One Budget to Another

The name of each budget you create automatically appears on the pop-up menu at the top left of the Budget Setup window. To switch from one budget to another, simply choose a budget name from the menu. The window's contents change to reflect the information for the budget you selected.

Renaming a Budget

You can also change the name of a budget. Switch to the budget that you want to rename. Then choose Rename from the pop-up menu at the top left of the Budget Setup window. The Rename Budget window, shown next, appears. Enter a new name for the budget and click Rename.

Deleting a Budget

If you have a budget that you no longer use, you can delete it. Switch to the budget you want to delete and choose Delete from the pop-up menu at the top left of the Budget Setup window. A confirmation dialog box appears, asking if you really do want to delete the budget. Click Yes. The budget's information is removed from your Quicken data file.

Monitoring Budget Status

Once you have created a budget you can live with, it's a good idea to periodically compare your actual income and expenditures to budgeted amounts. Quicken lets you do this a number of different ways.

Tip *Make sure you compare budgeted amounts to actual results for the period for which you have recorded data. For example, don't view a year-to-date Budget Report if you began entering data into Quicken in March. Instead, customize the report to show actual transactions beginning in March.*

Budget Reports

The Reports window offers two different reports for comparing budgeted amounts to actual results:

- **Budget Month by Month** displays the actual and budgeted transactions by month.
- **Budget Summary** (see Figure 10-3) displays the total actual and budgeted transactions for the period you specify.

I tell you about creating reports, including how to customize them, in Chapter 9.

Budget Graphs

The Graphs window offers two options that graphically represent a comparison of budgeted and actual results:

- **Budget Month by Month** shows the favorable and unfavorable differences between actual and budgeted income amounts.
- **Budget Variance by Category** shows the budgeted and actual values for each category.

I explain how to create graphs, including how to customize them, in Chapter 9.

Budget Snapshot

Quicken's Insights window includes a "snapshot" you can view to keep track of your budgets. Follow the instructions in Chapter 9 to add the snapshot to your Insights window. You can then customize the snapshot by clicking the

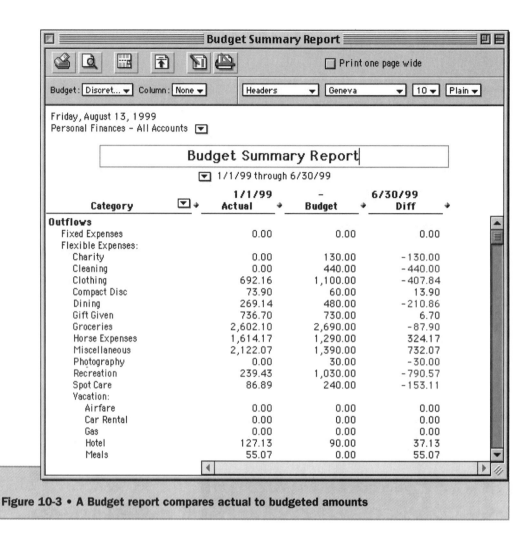

Figure 10-3 • A Budget report compares actual to budgeted amounts

"Customize this report" link in the actions area beneath it. I tell you more about customizing the Insights window's contents in Chapter 9.

Budget Monitoring Window

Quicken's Budget Monitoring window graphically compares budgeted to actual amounts. You select the budget you want to monitor, and then set up the Budget Monitoring window so it displays the categories you want to monitor. The window uses color to tell you, at a glance, how you're doing.

Choose Activities | Budgeting | Budget Monitoring to display the Budget Monitoring window, shown next. Choose a budget and a period from the pop-up menus at the top of the window. Here's what it might look like for the budgeted expense items in Figures 10-1 and 10-2:

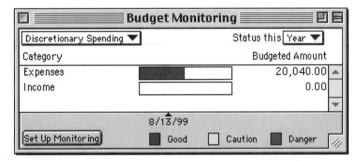

To monitor individual categories, click the Set Up Monitoring button. A dialog box like the one shown next appears. It lists all the categories included in the currently selected budget. Click to toggle check marks beside each category you want to monitor and click OK.

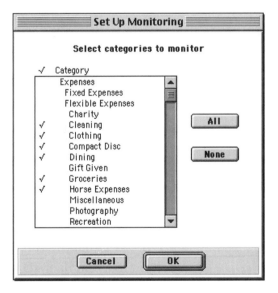

When you click OK, the Budget Monitoring window changes to display each category you want to monitor. You can enlarge the Budget Monitoring window to show all selected categories, like this:

Budget Monitoring		
Discretionary Spending ▼		Status this Year ▼
Category		Budgeted Amount
Cleaning		500.00
Clothing		1,630.00
Compact Disc		90.00
Dining		940.00
Groceries		5,460.00
Horse Expenses		3,770.00
Spot Care		440.00

8/13/99

Set Up Monitoring ■ Good □ Caution ■ Danger

> **Tip** *You can click a category bar in the Budget Monitoring window to learn the actual amount for the category.*

Forecasting

Forecasting uses known and estimated transactions to provide a general overview of your future financial situation. This "crystal ball" can help you spot potential cash flow problems (or surpluses) so you can prepare for them.

Working with the Forecast Window

Your financial forecast appears in the Forecast window (see Figure 10-4), which also offers commands and options to modify the forecast. To open this window, choose Activities | Forecast or click the Forecast button near the top of the Planning tab. Quicken automatically creates a forecast for you based on the upcoming transactions in the Calendar. You can use options at the bottom of the Forecast window to change the window's view.

> **Note** *I explain how to use the Calendar to schedule transactions in Chapter 7.*

Choosing the Accounts to Forecast

The Show Forecast For area of the Forecast window offers two options for specifying which accounts should appear in the forecast:

- **All Accounts** displays all accounts in the forecast.

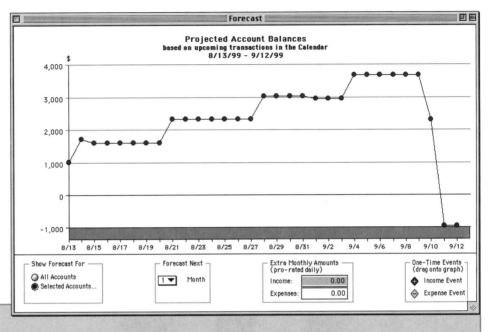

Figure 10-4 • The Forecast window graphically displays your financial position over time.

- **Selected Accounts** displays the accounts you select in the forecast. When you choose this option, the Select Accounts dialog box, shown next, appears. Click to toggle check marks beside the accounts you want to include. Then click OK.

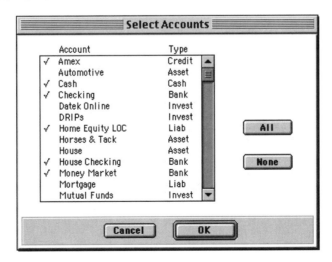

> **Tip**   *You may find it more meaningful to include only your most liquid accounts in a forecast. Normally, that will be bank and credit card accounts.*

Choosing the Period to Forecast

The Forecast Next area offers a pop-up menu you can use to specify how many months should be included in the forecast. The options are 1, 3, 6, or 12. When you change this option, the contents of the Forecast window change accordingly.

Modifying Forecast Data

There are two ways to modify a forecast:

- Add or remove scheduled transactions in the Calendar window.
- Add monthly amounts in the Forecast window.
- Add one-time amounts in the Forecast window.

> **Tip**   *You can quickly open the Calendar window for a specific date by double-clicking the graph point at that date.*

I explain how to use the Calendar in Chapter 7. In this section, I'll explain how to add amounts in the Forecast window.

Adding Extra Monthly Amounts

If you don't use Quicken's Calendar feature to schedule all transactions, you may find it helpful to add monthly amounts not included in the Calendar right in the Forecast window. For example, suppose you don't include your biweekly paycheck on the Calendar. You can add the monthly amount of your take-home pay as an extra monthly income amount.

To add an extra monthly amount, enter the amount you want to add in the Income or Expense edit box at the bottom of the Forecast window (see Figure 10-4) and press RETURN or ENTER. The forecast is adjusted accordingly.

Adding One-Time Events

In some instances, you may know about specific one-time income or expense events that you have not scheduled on Quicken's Calendar. You can add these events to the Forecast so Quicken includes them in its forecast calculations.

To add a one-time Income event, drag the blue diamond on the bottom-right corner of the Forecast window (see Figure 10-4) onto the Forecast graph at the appropriate date. When you release the mouse button, the Set Up Income Event dialog box, which is shown next, appears. Enter the date, amount, and event name in the edit boxes and click OK. The Forecast graph is updated for your entry and a blue diamond appears on the graph's x-axis (bottom line), at the date you specified.

As you probably guessed, you can add one-time expense items the same way. Just drag the yellow diamond onto the graph, enter information in the dialog box that appears, and click OK.

Tip   *You can edit a one-time income or expense item by double-clicking its diamond on the graph's x-axis.*

Saving Time with Online Features

This part of the book explains how you can save time by taking advantage of Quicken's online features for banking, tracking credit card transactions, and monitoring your investments. It also gives you a formal introduction to Quicken.com and other Quicken features accessible via the Internet.

This part of the book has three chapters:

Introducing Quicken.com

In This Chapter:

- *An Introduction to Web Surfing*

- *Accessing Quicken on the Web*

- *Quicken.com Features*

- *Quicken Financial Partners*

- *Applying for Online Financial Services*

Chapter 11

The World Wide Web has had a greater impact on the distribution of information than any innovation since the invention of moveable type hundreds of years ago. The Web makes it possible to publish information almost instantly, as it becomes available. Accessible by anyone with a computer, an Internet connection, and Web browsing software, it gives individuals and organizations the power to reach millions of people worldwide without the delays and costs of traditional print and broadcast media.

While this power to publish has flooded the Internet with plenty of useless and trivial information, it has also given birth to exceptional Web sites, full of useful, timely, and accurate information that can make a difference in your life. Quicken.com, Intuit's site, is one of the best financial information sites around.

In this chapter, I'll lead you on a short tour of Quicken.com and other Quicken features on the Web. My goal is to introduce you to what's out there so you can explore the areas that interest you most.

Tip *Chapter 3 explains what an Internet connection is and what it requires. It also shows you how to set up and test Quicken for accessing its online features, including the Web. If you haven't already read that chapter and completed Quicken's brief online setup process, go back and do that now.*

Keep one thing in mind as you read through this chapter: Quicken.com is an incredibly dynamic Web site that changes frequently. The screen illustrations and features I tell you about will probably appear differently when you connect. In addition, brand-new features might be added after the publication of this book. That's why I won't go into too much detail in this chapter. The best way to learn about all the features of Quicken.com when you're ready for them is to check them out for yourself.

An Introduction to Web Surfing

Before I start my overview of Quicken on the Web, let me take a moment to explain exactly what you're doing when you connect to Quicken.com and the other Quicken features on the Web. If you're brand-new to Web surfing—that is, exploring Web sites—be sure to read this section. But if you're a seasoned surfer, you probably already know all this stuff and can skip it.

One more thing: This section is not designed to explain everything you'll ever need to know about browsing the World Wide Web. It provides the basic information you need to use the Web to get the information you need.

Going Online

When you access Quicken's online features, you do so by connecting to the Internet through your ISP. It doesn't matter whether you connect via a modem or a network, or whether your ISP is America Online or Joe's Dial-up Internet Service. The main thing is having a connection or a conduit for information.

Think of an Internet connection as some PVC piping running from your computer to your ISP's, with a valve to control the flow of information. Once the valve is open (you're connected), any information can flow through the pipe in either direction. You can even exchange information through that pipe in both directions at the same time. This makes it possible to download (or retrieve) a Web page with your Web browser while you upload (or send) e-mail with your e-mail program.

Quicken's online features use the pipe (or connection) in two ways:

- Your Web browser—normally Netscape Navigator (or Communicator) or Microsoft Internet Explorer—sends your requests for information and displays the information in its browser window (see Figure 11-1). It's live and interactive—click a link and a moment later your information starts to appear.
- The Online Account Access and Online Payment features work in the background to communicate with financial institutions with which you have accounts. Quicken sends information you prepared in advance and retrieves the information the financial institution has waiting for you.

There's one important thing to remember when using Quicken's online features to browse the Web: You browse Web pages with your Web browser, not with Quicken software. Although selecting certain options within Quicken will display Web pages, those Web pages appear in your Web browser window. To go back to Quicken when you've finished browsing the Web, select Quicken Deluxe 2000 (or the Quicken icon) from the Application menu at the top-right corner of your screen, as shown here:

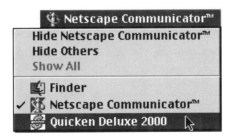

A hypertext link

The address or URL for
the link being pointed to

A form

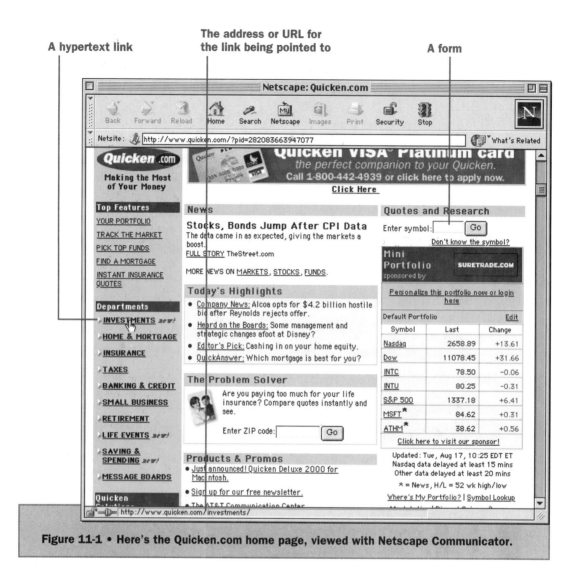

Figure 11-1 • Here's the Quicken.com home page, viewed with Netscape Communicator.

This chapter concentrates on Web browsing—the interactive features of Quicken.com. But it also provides some information to help you find financial institutions that work with Quicken for the Online Account Access and Online Payment features.

Navigating

The main thing to remember about the Web is that it's interactive. Every time a Web page appears on your screen, it'll offer a number of options for viewing other information. This is known as "navigating the Web."

Hyperlinks and Forms

You can move from page to page on the Web in two ways, both of which are illustrated in Figure 11-1:

- **Hyperlinks** (or **links**) are text or graphics that, when clicked, display another page. Hypertext links are usually underlined, colored text. Graphic links sometimes have a colored border around them. You can always identify a link by pointing to it—your mouse pointer will turn into a hand with a pointing finger.
- **Forms** offer options for going to another page or searching for information. Options can appear in pop-up menus, text boxes that you fill in, check boxes that you turn on, or radio buttons that you select. Often there are multiple options. You enter or select the options you want and click a button to send your request to the Web site. The information you requested appears a moment later.

Other Navigation Techniques

The toolbar at the top of your Web browser window (refer to Figure 11-1) includes a number of buttons you might find handy for navigating the Web and working with Web pages. Here are the ones I think you'll use most with Quicken.

- **Back** displays the previously viewed page.
- **Forward** displays the page you viewed after the current page. This button is only available after you have used the Back button.
- **Reload** (in Netscape Navigator or Communicator) or **Refresh** (in Microsoft Internet Explorer) refreshes the information on the page by loading a new copy from the Web site's server. This button is handy for updating stock quotes or news that appears on a page.
- **Print** prints the currently displayed Web page.

- **Stop** stops the loading of the current page. This may result in incomplete pages or error messages on the page. You might use this button if you click a link and then realize that you don't really want to view the information you requested.

Working Offline

When you've finished working with online features, if you have a dial-up connection, you may want to disconnect. This frees up your telephone line for incoming calls. You can continue working offline with Quicken features that don't require Internet access.

To work offline, choose Apple menu | Remote Access Status to display the Remote Access window, shown next. Click the Disconnect button to sever your Internet connection.

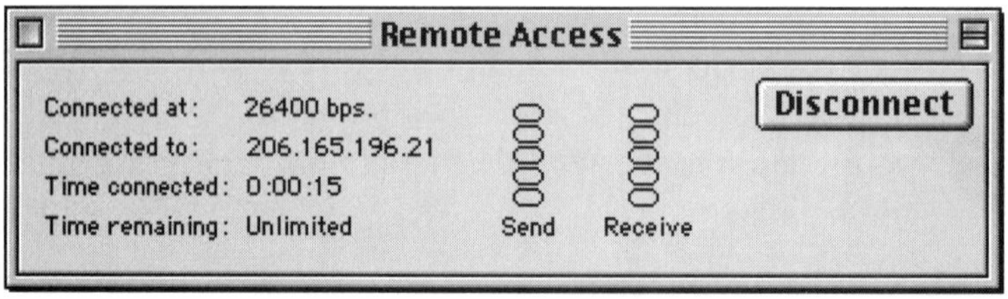

Tip   *If you're connected via a direct network connection, there's no reason to disconnect.*

Accessing Quicken on the Web

You can access Quicken's online features using commands on its Online menu. One of these commands, To the Web, is really a submenu full of options for Quicken Web features, as shown next:

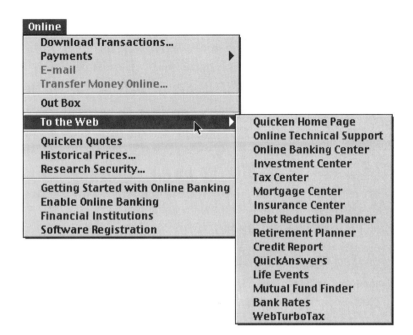

Here's a quick overview of some of these options.

Quicken Home Page   The Quicken Home Page command takes you to the home page for Quicken.com, Intuit's financial Web site. Although designed to be of most use to Quicken users, most of its features are accessible to anyone. (Tell your friends about it!)

Note *Quicken.com is divided into different departments. You can go to a department by clicking its link on the navigation bar on the left side of the Quicken.com home page (refer to Figure 11-1). Most Quicken.com departments are also accessible directly from the To the Web submenu shown previously.*

Online Technical Support   The Online Technical Support command takes you to the Quicken Support Network page. This is where you can find answers to frequently asked questions, information about solving problems with Quicken, and program updates. Use this command when you can't find the information you need in this book or with Quicken's Online Help feature.

 Tip *The Technical Support page covers all Intuit products, not just Quicken.*

Online Banking Center   The Online Banking Center command displays the Online Banking page. This is where you can learn all about online banking and find banks that offer online features. It's also a great place to start searching for a credit card, loan, or bank account online.

Investment Center   The Investment Center command is a shortcut to Quicken.com's Investments Department, where you can find information of interest to investors—including news, quotes, and research tools. There's specific information about stocks, mutual funds, and bonds, as well as a retirement link. If you're new to investing, be sure to check out the Investing Basics section for the concepts and terms you'll need to know to get started as an investor. I tell you more about Investments Department options in Chapters 13 and 16.

Tax Center   The Tax Center command is a shortcut to Quicken.com's Taxes Department, which provides information you can use to prepare and file your tax returns, including federal tax forms, IRS publications, and state tax forms. News, articles, and advice offer additional insight into the world of taxation, to help you understand and minimize your tax burden. I tell you more about the Taxes Department options in Chapter 14.

Mortgage Center   The Mortgage Center command is a shortcut to Quicken.com's Home & Mortgage Department. This department should be your first stop if you're looking for a home or shopping for the right mortgage. In addition to current information about national mortgage rates, you'll find interactive tools to help you find out what kinds of loans you qualify for and how much you can afford. Even if you're not shopping for a home, this department might help you decide whether now is the right time to refinance your current home. You learn more about Home & Mortgage Department options in Chapter 15.

Insurance Center   The Insurance Center command takes you to the home page for Quicken InsureMarket, which provides a wide range of tools for evaluating your insurance needs. A number of links offer information about insurance basics so you know what your agent is talking about when he or she throws around words like "annuity" and "rider." You can even shop for insurance online. I cover some of the Quicken InsureMarket and Quicken.com Insurance Department options in Chapter 15.

Debt Reduction Planner   The Debt Reduction Planner command displays the first page of Quicken.com's Debt Reduction Planner, an interactive tool you can use to create a debt reduction plan. I cover this excellent money-saving resource in detail in Chapter 17.

Retirement Planner   The Retirement Planner command takes you to the first page of Quicken.com's Retirement Planner, an interactive tool you can use to plan for your retirement. I discuss the Retirement Planner in Chapter 17.

Credit Report   The Credit Report command takes you to a page where you can order a credit report and sign up for a credit monitoring service. You might find these features useful if you're not sure about your credit history and want to make sure all your credit records are correct. I tell you more about credit reports in Chapter 15.

QuickAnswers   The QuickAnswers command takes you to the QuickAnswer Calculator page on Quicken.com. This page offers links with interactive calculators you can use to answer specific questions. For example, clicking the "What will your investment be worth in the future?" link brings up a page that can calculate an investment's future value based on its current value, expected annual return, and expected holding period.

Life Events   The Life Events command is a shortcut to Quicken.com's Life Events Department. This department is full of features that can help you plan for major events in your life, such as college, weddings, parenthood, and retirement. Interactive tools and timely information make this a great destination when you need to plan for the future. I discuss the Life Events Department's options in Chapter 17.

Mutual Fund Finder   The Mutual Fund Finder command takes you to the Mutual Fund Finder page in the Investments Department of Quicken.com. Use this page to search for mutual funds based on specific criteria. I tell you more about using the Mutual Fund Finder in Chapter 16.

Bank Rates   The Bank Rates command is a shortcut to the Quicken.com Banking & Credit Department. This department offers a wealth of up-to-date information about current interest rates on savings and loans, as well as banking-related news stories. This is where you can follow links to find a bank account, get your credit report, and shop for a credit card. If you don't know much about banking or credit, this is the place to come to learn. I cover Banking & Credit Department options in Chapters 15 and 17.

WebTurboTax   The WebTurboTax command takes you to the WebTurboTax main page. WebTurboTax is a Quicken.com feature that enables you to prepare your federal income tax returns online, without any special software. I tell you a little more about WebTurboTax in Chapter 14.

Quicken Financial Partners

If you're interested in keeping track of your finances with the least amount of data entry, you should be considering Quicken's online features for bank account access and payment, credit card account access, and investment tracking. Back in Chapter 3, I tell you about the benefits of these features. The next two chapters tell you how to use them. But you can't use them until you've set up an account with a Quicken financial partner and have applied for the online financial services you want to use.

Finding a Quicken Partner

Finding a Quicken financial partner is easy. Choose Online | Financial Institutions. The Financial Institutions window, shown next, appears. This window, which can be updated to add new partners that come on board, provides the name and contact information for each financial institution that directly supports Quicken 2000 software.

Working with the Financial Institutions List

Buttons along the bottom of the Financial Institutions window enable you to work with items in the list:

- **Use** copies the financial institution's name into the Enable Online Banking window, which you use to set up Online Account Access and Online Payment. (I explain how to use this window in Chapter 12.)
- **Update Item** connects to the Internet to update the information about the selected financial institution.

Tip   *It's a good idea to use the Update button to update the information for your financial institution before you set up for Online Account Access or Online Payment.*

- **Apply** displays a Web page with information about how you can apply for Online Account Access or Online Payment with the selected financial institution. (You may have to click the Update Item button to update information about the financial institution before you can click the Apply button.)
- **Update List** connects to the Internet to update the list of Quicken partner institutions.

Tip   *Click the Update List button if your financial institution does not appear on the list and you want to see if it has been added since the last time the list was updated.*

- **Hotline** displays the phone number for the currently selected financial institution. You can use the number to call and ask questions about the online features it offers.

Types of Services

Quicken partner institutions offer three types of services:

- **Banking account access** enables you to download bank account transactions directly into your Quicken data file.
- **Credit/charge card account access** enables you to download credit or charge card transactions directly into your Quicken data file.
- **Payment** enables you to send payment instructions from within Quicken. This makes it possible to pay bills and send payments to anyone without writing a check.

If Your Financial Institution Is Not on the List

If your bank or credit card company is not on the list, you have four options:

- **Change financial institutions.** I know it sounds harsh, but if your bank or credit card company doesn't support Online Account Access with Quicken and you really want to use this feature, you can find a financial institution that does support it and open an account there.

- **Wait until your financial institution appears on the list.** The list of partner institutions is updated quite often. If your bank or credit card company doesn't appear there today, it may appear next month. Or next year. You can hurry things along by asking your financial institution to become a Quicken partner institution. If enough customers ask for it, they might add this feature.

- **Check to see if your financial institution supports Quicken Web Connect.** This feature enables you to download transactions from your financial institution in a specially formatted, Quicken-compatible .QFX file. You can then import the transactions into your Quicken data file. This method limits your online activities to Online Account Access; Online Payment is not supported. Contact your financial institution for details and step-by-step instructions for using this feature.

- **Use Intuit Online Payment or CheckFree.** If all you're interested in is the Online Payment feature, you can use Intuit Online Payment. This enables you to process online payments via CheckFree Corporation, which can prepare checks from your existing bank accounts. There's no need to change banks or wait until your bank signs on as a Quicken partner. Intuit Online Payment is listed as one of the Quicken partners in the Financial Institutions window.

Applying for Online Financial Services

To apply for online financial services, click to select the financial institution's name in the Financial Institutions window. Then click the Apply button. Follow the instructions on the Web page that appears to apply by phone or online. This gets the wheels turning to put you online. It may take a few days to get the necessary access information, so apply as soon as you're sure you want to take advantage of the online financial services features.

Using Online
Account Access
and Payment

In This Chapter:

- *Benefits and Costs of Online Financial Services*

- *Setting Up Online Financial Services*

- *Downloading Transactions*

- *Comparing Downloaded Transactions to Register Transactions*

- *Setting Up Payees*

- *Entering Online Payments*

- *Exchanging E-Mail with Your Financial Institution*

- *Transferring Money Online*

Quicken's Online Account Access and Online Payment features enable you to do most (if not all) of your banking from the comfort of your own home. These two individual features can be used separately or together:

- **Online Account Access** enables you to download bank and credit card account activity and transfer money online between accounts.
- **Online Payment** enables you to pay bills online, without manually writing or mailing a single check.

In this chapter, I explain how these two features work and how you can use them to save time and money.

Note *The instructions in this chapter assume that you have already configured your computer for an Internet connection. If you have not done so, do it now. Chapter 3 provides the instructions you need to set up and test an Internet connection. This chapter also assumes that you understand the topics and procedures discussed in Chapters 2, 4, and 7. This chapter builds on many of the basic concepts discussed in those chapters.*

Why Do Your Banking Online?

Consider the following scenario: Every week (or two), you go to the bank to deposit your paycheck. (If you're lucky, you can use an ATM or drive-up window where you don't have to wait in line.) Throughout the month, you stop at ATMs and withdraw cash. You use your debit card at the pharmacy. You write checks for groceries, dentist visits, and car repairs. Periodically, you sit down to pay your bills. You write checks, insert them with statement stubs in window envelopes, put your return address on the envelopes, and stick on stamps. (Forgot the stamps? Remember to wait in line at the post office to get them!) Once in a while, you call your bank to transfer money from one account to another. At month's end, you get a bank statement full of surprises: ATM withdrawals, debit card transactions, and checks you neglected to enter. Your bank balance may be dangerously close to zero because of these omissions. Or maybe you even bounced a few checks. And what about late payments (and fees) for the bills that sat on a table by the door, waiting for days to be mailed?

Sound familiar? At least some of it should. Life can be pretty hectic sometimes—too hectic to keep track of your bank accounts, pay bills before they're overdue, and buy stamps. But with Online Account Access and Online Payment, banking can be a lot less of a chore.

Benefits

The benefits of online financial services vary depending on the services you use. I've been doing my banking online for years. Here are some of the benefits I've seen.

Online Account Access

Online Account Access performs three primary tasks:

Download Transactions That Have Cleared Your Account   Bank account transaction downloads include all deposits, checks, interest payments, bank fees, transfers, ATM transactions, and debit card transactions. Credit card transaction downloads include all charges, credits (for returns), payments, fees, and finance charges. Quicken displays all the transactions, including the ones you have not yet entered in your account register, as well as the current balance of the account. A few clicks and keystrokes is all it takes to enter the transactions you missed. This feature makes it virtually impossible to omit entries, while telling you exactly how much money is available in a bank account or how much money you owe on your credit card account. No more surprises in that monthly statement.

Transfer Money Between Accounts   If you have more than one bank account at the same financial institution, you can use Online Account Access to transfer money between accounts. Although many banks offer this feature by phone, it usually requires dialing a phone number and entering an account number and PIN while navigating through voice prompts. Even if you get a real person on the phone, you still have to provide the same information every time you call. With Online Account Access, you merely enter a transfer transaction and let Quicken do the rest.

Send E-Mail Messages to Your Financial Institution   Ever call the customer service center at your bank or credit card company to ask a question? If you're lucky, real people are waiting to answer the phone. But if you're like most people, your financial institution uses a call routing system that requires you to listen to voice prompts and press telephone keypad keys to communicate with a machine. Either way, when a real person gets on the line, you have to provide all kinds of information about yourself just to prove that you are who you say you are. Then you can ask your question. But the e-mail feature that's part of Online Account Access makes communicating with your bank or credit card company's customer service department easy. You normally get a response within one business day.

Online Payment

Online Payment enables you to send a check to anyone without physically writing, printing, or mailing a check. You enter and store information about the payee within Quicken. You then create a transaction for the payee that includes the payment date and amount. You can enter the transaction weeks or months in advance if desired—the payee receives payment on the date you specify.

Online Payment is one of the least understood Quicken features. Many folks think it can only be used to pay big companies like the phone company or credit card companies. That just isn't true. You can use Online Payment to pay any bill, fund your IRA, donate money to a charity, or send your niece a graduation gift.

How It Works   Suppose you use Quicken to send Online Payment instructions to pay your monthly bill at Joe's Hardware Store. You've already set up Joe as a payee by entering the name, address, and phone number of his store, as well as your account number there. Quicken sends your payment instructions to your bank, which stores it in its computer with a bunch of other Online Payment instructions. When the payment date nears, the bank's computer looks through its big database of payees that it can pay by wire transfer. It sees phone companies and credit card companies and other banks. But because Joe's store is small, it's probably not one of the wire transfer payees. So the bank's computer prepares a check using all the information you provided. It mails the check along with thousands of others due to be paid that day.

Joe's wife, who does the accounting for the store, gets the check a few days later. It looks a little weird, but when she deposits it with the other checks she gets that day, it clears just like any other check. The amount of the check is deducted from your bank account and your account balance at Joe's. If you use Online Account Access, the check appears as a transaction. It also appears on your bank statement. If your bank returns canceled checks to you, you'll get the check along with all your others.

> **Tip**   *If your bank doesn't return canceled checks, you can see for yourself what an Online Payment check looks like. Just use the Online Payment feature to write a check to yourself. It'll arrive in the mail on or before the date you specified. Although the check looks different, it works like any other check.*

When the Money Leaves Your Account   The date the money is actually withdrawn from your account to cover the payment varies depending on your bank. There are four possibilities:

- One to four days before the payment is processed for delivery

- The day the payment is processed for delivery
- The day the payment is delivered
- The day the paper check or electronic funds transfer clears your bank

You can find out when funds are withdrawn from your account for online payments by contacting your bank.

The Benefits of Online Payment   Online Payment can benefit you in several ways. You can pay your bills as they arrive, without paying them early—the payee never receives payment before the payment date you specify. You don't have to buy stamps and the bank never forgets to mail the checks.

Costs

The cost of Online Account Access and Online Payment varies from bank to bank. Check with your bank to see what the exact fees are. Here's what you can expect:

- Online Account Access is often free to all customers or to customers who maintain a certain minimum account balance. Otherwise, you could pay up to $5 for this service. My bank claims it charges $3, but I haven't been billed once. (Don't tell anyone.)
- Online Payment is sometimes free; but, more often, it costs from $5 to $10 per month for 20 to 25 payments per month. Each additional payment usually costs 40¢ to 60¢. Again, some banks waive this fee if you maintain a certain minimum balance. My bank, for example, requires a $5,000 minimum account balance to waive the fee.

If you think this sounds expensive, do the math for your bank's deal. Here's an example: I get 25 payments per month for $5. If I had to mail 25 checks, it would cost me $8.25. So I'd actually save $3.25 per month if I made 25 online payments. Although I don't make 25 payments a month—it's more like 15 to 20 for me—I also don't have to stuff envelopes, apply return address labels, or stick on stamps. Or wait in line at the post office. My bills get paid right on time, I earn more interest income, and I haven't bounced a check in over four years.

Does it sound like I'm sold on this feature? You bet I am!

Security

If you're worried about security, you must have skipped over the security information in Chapter 3. Go back and read that now. It explains how Quicken and financial institution security works to make Online Account Access and Online Payment safe.

Setting Up Online Financial Services

To use either Online Account Access or Online Payment, you must configure the appropriate Quicken accounts. This requires that you enter information about your financial institution and the account with which you want to use these online financial services features.

Applying for Online Account Access and Online Payment

Before you can use Online Account Access or Online Payment, you must apply for it. I tell you how at the end of Chapter 11. Normally, all it takes is a phone call, although some banks and credit card companies do allow you to apply online. The process usually takes a week, but may take less. You'll know that you're ready to go online when you get a letter with setup information.

The setup information your financial institution sends usually consists of the following information:

- **A PIN (or Personal Identification Number).** You'll have to enter this code into Quicken when you access your account online. This is a security feature, so don't write down your PIN on a sticky note and attach it to your computer screen. There is a chance that your bank may send this information separately for additional security.
- **A customer ID number.** This is often your social security number or taxpayer identification number.
- **The bank routing number.** This information tells Quicken which bank your account is with. You may not get this information for a credit card account.
- **Account number for each online-access-enabled account.** This tells your financial institution which account you want to work with.

Setting Up

With a PIN, a routing number, and account numbers in hand, you're ready to set up your account(s) for online financial services features. There are a number of ways to set up for online banking. Rather than cover them all, I'll cover the most straightforward method.

Choose Lists | Accounts, or press COMMAND-A to display the Accounts window. How you proceed depends on whether you want to set up online banking for an existing account or for a new account.

Setting Up a New Account

To set up online banking for a new Quicken account, click the New button at the bottom of the Accounts window. Use the Set Up Account dialog box that appears to enter options for a Bank or Credit Card account. (I explain the options for setting up an account in Chapter 2.) Then click the Enable Online Banking button. If a dialog box appears, telling you that it will save changes to the account, click Save.

The Select Account to Enable dialog box, which is shown next, may appear. Use it to select the account you just created. Then click OK.

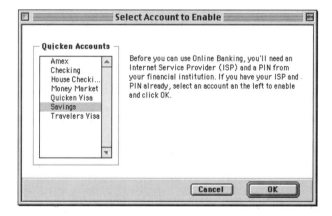

The Enable Online Banking window should appear next. Skip ahead to the section titled "Enabling Online Banking" to continue.

Setting Up an Existing Account

To set up online banking for an existing Quicken account, select the account in the Accounts window and click the Edit button at the bottom of the window. In the Edit Account window that appears, click the Enable Online Banking button. This should display the Enable Online Banking window, which I discuss next.

Enabling Online Banking

You set online banking options with the Enable Online Banking window, which is shown next.

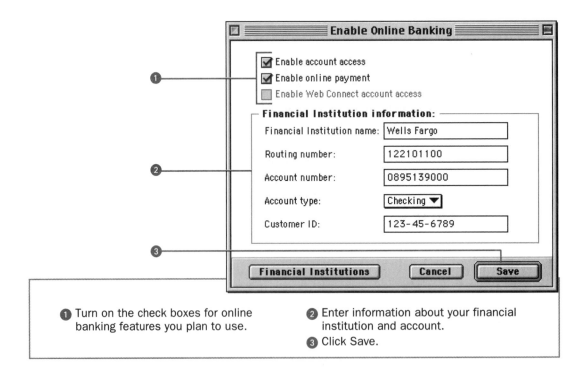

❶ Turn on the check boxes for online banking features you plan to use.

❷ Enter information about your financial institution and account.

❸ Click Save.

Selecting Online Banking Features   Start by turning on the check box for each online banking feature you plan to use:

- **Enable account access** allows you to download transactions and balances and transfer funds between accounts.
- **Enable online payment** allows you to send payment instructions for paying bills and making other payments online.
- **Enable Web Connect account access** allows you to download transactions and balances from a financial institution that doesn't directly support Quicken's Online Account Access feature but does support the Web Connect feature. This option is only available when the other two options are not selected; likewise, if this option is selected, the other two options are not available.

Note   *Procedures for using the Web Connect feature vary from one financial institution to another. For detailed instructions about using Web Connect, contact your financial institution.*

Financial Institution Information   Next, you need to enter information about your financial institution and account:

- **Financial Institution** is the name of your bank or credit card company. You can enter this information by typing it into the edit box. As you type, Quicken attempts to match the name with the names in its database. If you prefer, you can click the Financial Institutions button to display the Financial Institutions list window, shown next. Then select the name of your bank or credit card company and click the Use button to enter it into the Financial Institution edit box. This prevents you from entering an invalid financial institution name.

- **Routing number** is the routing number provided by your financial institution. This number may not be required when entering information for a credit card account.

- **Account number** is your account number. Enter the entire number, without spaces or dashes.

- **Account type** is the type of account. For a bank account, your options are None, Checking, Savings, Money Market, and Line of Credit. (If you're setting up a credit card account, Credit Card is also offered as an option.) Be sure to choose the correct account type from the pop-up menu.

Caution   *If you enter the incorrect account type, the online banking feature will not work. If your financial institution tells you what kind of account to enter, use that account type, even if it seems incorrect. For example, my bank instructed me to classify my money market account as a savings account. If I don't follow my bank's instructions, online banking for that account just won't work.*

- **Customer ID** is usually your social security number, but it may be another number provided by the bank. Be sure to enter the correct number.

Note   *When setting up a Quicken credit card account for online banking, you'll also have to provide a PIN. Enter it in the appropriate edit box. The PIN is stored in your Quicken data file and is automatically used when you connect.*

Completing the Setup Process

When you've finished entering information in the Enable Online Banking window, click the Save button. A Service Agreement Information dialog box may appear next. It tells you that online financial services are provided by your financial institution and not Intuit. (I think the lawyers at Intuit whipped this one up.) Read the contents of the dialog box and click OK.

Back in the Accounts window, a tiny lightning bolt appears beside the name of the account:

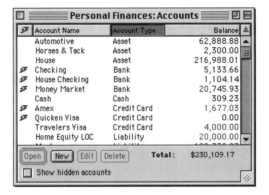

You're now ready to use online features for that account.

Downloading Transactions

When you enable online account access, you can use the Download Transactions window to download transactions from your financial institution and compare them to transactions in your account register. You can check off the transactions that appear in your register and add the transactions that don't. This enables you to see which transactions have cleared and prevents you from failing to enter transactions.

In this section, I explain how to download, compare, and accept transactions in the Download Transactions window.

Opening the Download Transactions Window

Choose Online | Download Transactions or click the Download button near the top of the Banking tab. Figure 12-1 shows what this window looks like for my setup.

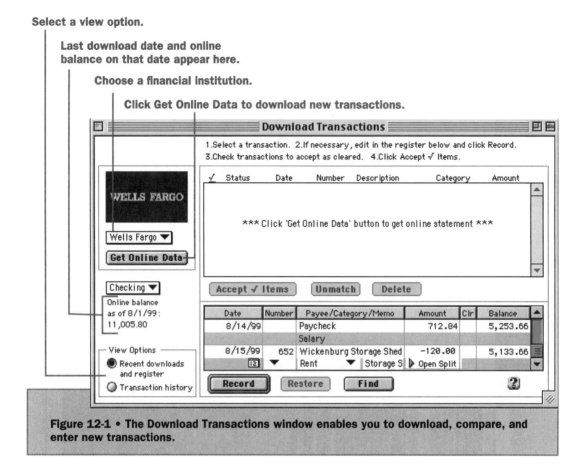

Select a view option.

Last download date and online
balance on that date appear here.

Choose a financial institution.

Click Get Online Data to download new transactions.

Figure 12-1 • The Download Transactions window enables you to download, compare, and
enter new transactions.

Getting Online Data

To download transactions from your financial institution, begin by selecting the
bank or credit card company name from the first pop-up menu in the Download
Transactions window (see Figure 12-1). Then click the Get Online Data button.
In most cases, a PIN dialog box like the one shown next should appear. Enter
your PIN in the edit box and click OK.

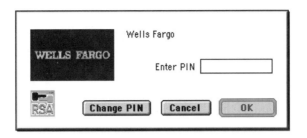

Tip　 *You can change your PIN by clicking the Change PIN button in the PIN dialog box. The dialog box that appears prompts you to enter your current PIN once and your new PIN twice. When you click OK, your PIN is changed. Be sure to use the new PIN from then on.*

If you have a dial-up connection to the Internet, your computer connects. Then Quicken displays a dialog box like the one shown next. It indicates the connection status.

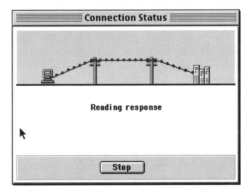

When the connection is finished, Quicken displays the Online Transmission Summary dialog box (see Figure 12-2). It summarizes the transactions that were downloaded. You can click the Print button to print the summary for reference if desired.

Note　 *The first time you connect, the bank sends all transactions from the past 60 days. After that, only new transactions will be downloaded.*

When you've finished reviewing the summary, click OK to return to the Download Transactions window.

Figure 12-2 • The Online Transmission Summary window lists downloaded transactions and other transmission information.

Comparing Downloaded Transactions to Register Transactions

Once the information has been downloaded, you can compare the transactions to the transactions already entered in your account register. This enables you to identify transactions that you neglected to enter or that you entered incorrectly.

In the Download Transactions window, select the account for which you want to compare transactions. As shown in Figure 12-3, the downloaded transactions appear in the top half of the Download Transactions window.

The Status column in the top half of the window identifies two types of transactions:

- **Match** identifies downloaded transactions that match those in the register.
- **New** identifies transactions that do not appear to be in the register.

Choose an account to view and compare downloaded transactions for.

Choose a financial institution.

A transaction that has been reviewed and checked off

A matched transaction

A new transaction

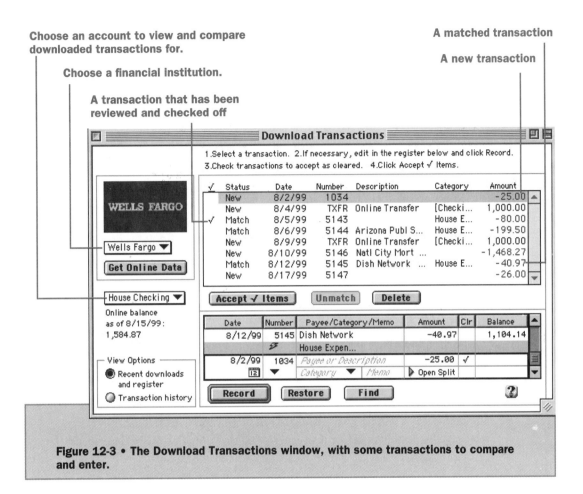

Figure 12-3 • The Download Transactions window, with some transactions to compare and enter.

Checking Off a Matched Transaction   If a transaction matches one in the register, you can check it off by clicking in the √ column beside it to place a check mark there.

Tip   *You can view a matched transaction by clicking it in the top half of the window to select it in the bottom half of the window.*

Entering and Checking Off a New Transaction   To enter a new transaction into the register, select the new transaction in the top half of the window. Quicken begins preparing a register transaction entry for it in the bottom half of the window, as you can see in Figure 12-3. Fill in the missing details, including the payee, category, and memo. Then click Record. Quicken records the transaction and changes its status in the top half of the window to "Match." You can then click in the √ column beside the transaction to place a check mark there.

SAVE TIME Because Quicken will automatically enter a date, transaction number, and amount—and, in the case of a debit card transaction, the payee and category (based on previous memorized transactions)—using this method to enter a transaction can be much faster than entering it manually in the account register window.

Matching a New Transaction If a downloaded transaction identified as New should match one in the register, you can modify the information in the register to match the information in the downloaded transaction. When you click the Record button for the register transaction, the word "Match" should appear beside the downloaded transaction. You can then click in the √ column beside the transaction to place a check mark there.

Unmatching a Matched Transaction If a matched transaction really shouldn't be matched, select it in the top half of the window and click the Unmatch button. You can then treat it as a new transaction.

Deleting a New Transaction To delete a new transaction, select the transaction in the top half of the window and click the Delete button. The transaction is removed from the downloaded Transaction List.

Tip *This option is especially useful the first time you download transactions. You may download transactions that have already been reconciled. Use the Unmatch button to unmatch them as necessary, and then use the Delete button to delete them from the downloaded Transaction List.*

Accepting All Checked Transactions   To accept all transactions that you have checked off in the top half of the window, click the Accept √ Items button. This removes the items from the top half of the window and places a plain check mark beside them in the Clr column of the register window. (I explain how the Clr column works in Chapter 7.)

Finishing Up   When you've finished comparing downloaded transactions to register transactions and have accepted the checked transactions, you can close the Download Transactions window. If transactions still appear in the top half of the window, they'll remain there. You can work with them the next time you open the Download Transactions window.

Caution   *Transactions with a New status in the top half of the Download Transactions window may not be entered in your account register. Thus, your register balance may be misstated until you accept all downloaded transactions.*

Paying Your Credit Card Bill

If payment on your credit card bill is due, you're notified in the Online Transmission Summary window when you successfully download transactions. When you've finished reviewing, comparing, and accepting downloaded transactions, you can use Quicken to review your bill and enter a payment transaction.

The Pay Credit/Charge Card dialog box, shown next, may appear automatically when you click the Accept √ Items button in the Download Transactions window. To pay your bill, set payment options and click Pay. To dismiss the dialog box without paying your bill, click Cancel.

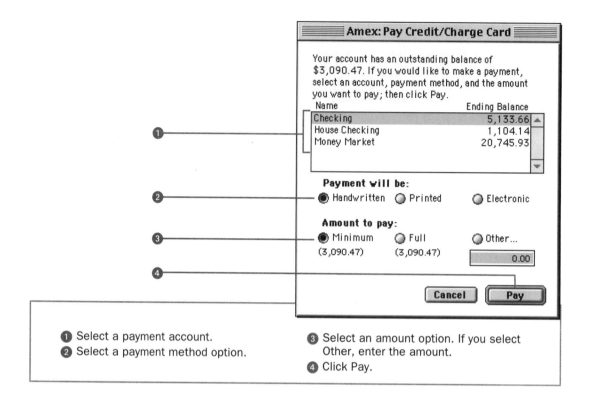

1 Select a payment account.
2 Select a payment method option.
3 Select an amount option. If you select Other, enter the amount.
4 Click Pay.

Tip *If the Pay Credit/Charge Card dialog box does not appear automatically, you can display it manually. Click the Payment Info button in the bottom of the Download Transactions window for the credit card account. Then click the Pay button in the Payment Info dialog box that appears.*

The option you select in the "Payment will be" area determines what happens when you click Pay:

- **Handwritten** displays the account register window, with the payment transaction already filled in. Edit the transaction as necessary and click the Record button to complete it. You must then write the check by hand.

- **Printed** displays the Write Checks window, with the payment transaction already filled in. Edit the transaction as necessary and click the Record Check button to complete it. The check can be printed the next time you use the Print Checks command.

- **Electronic** displays the Enter Online Payment window with the payment transaction already filled in. Edit the transaction as necessary and click the Put in Out Box button to complete it. The payment instruction will be sent to your bank the next time you send the items in your Out Box to the bank. I tell you more about using the Enter Online Payment window and the Out Box later in this chapter.

Tip   *To use the Electronic option, one of your bank accounts must be set up for Online Payment through your bank or Intuit Online Payment. In addition, the credit card company must be set up as an online payee.*

Making Payments

You can make online payments from any account for which the Online Payment feature is enabled. Use the Set Up Payee window to enter information for each organization or individual you want to pay with online payments. Then, when you're ready to make a payment, use the Enter Online Payment window to enter payment information. Use the Out Box to send your payment instructions to the bank and you've finished.

In this section, I provide the details for these steps.

Entering Online Payee Information

To send payments from your account, your bank must know who and where each payee is. To ensure that your account with the payee is properly credited, you must also provide account information. You do this by setting up online payees.

Opening the Payees Window

Choose Online | Payments | Online Payees to display the Payees list window. This window, which is shown next, lists all the payees for which you have provided payment information.

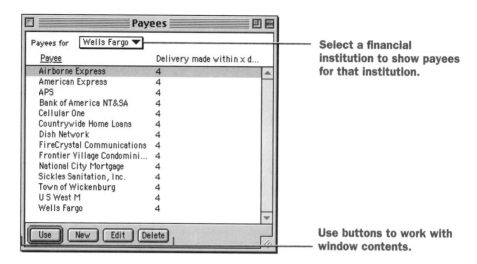

Buttons at the bottom of the window enable you to work with window contents:

- **Use** copies the selected payee's name into the Payee field of the Enter Online Payment window.
- **New** enables you to enter information about a new payee.
- **Edit** enables you to modify information about the selected payee.
- **Delete** removes the selected payee's information from the Payees list.

Note *Deleting a payee simply deletes the payee's information from the Payees list. It does not change any transactions for a payee. You cannot delete a payee for which unsent payment instructions exist in the Out Box window.*

Creating a New Payee

To create a new online payee, click the New button. Then fill in the edit boxes in the Set Up Payee dialog box, shown here, and click Create:

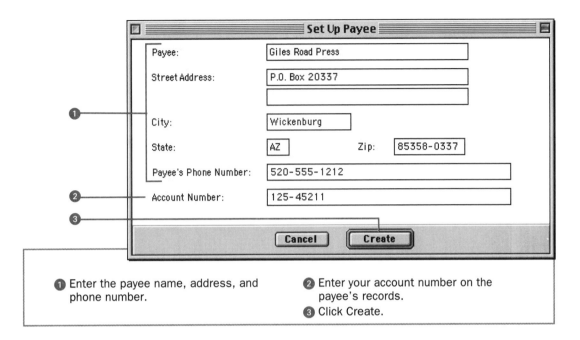

① Enter the payee name, address, and phone number.

② Enter your account number on the payee's records.

③ Click Create.

When you click Create, a dialog box containing the information you just entered appears. Check the information in this box and click Yes. The payee is added to the list with the delivery lead time "to be determined." I explain what delivery lead time is all about later in this chapter.

Caution *Check the payee information carefully! If there is an error, your payment might not reach the payee or it might not be properly credited to your account. Remember, your bank will not be sending a billing stub with the payment—just the check.*

Modifying a Payee

If necessary, you can change information for a payee. (I did this recently when one of my payees moved to a new location.) Select the payee name in the Payees window and click the Edit button. Then use the Edit Payee window, which looks and works just like the Set Up Payee window shown earlier, to change the payee's information. Click Change to complete the change.

Entering Payment Instructions

To send a payment to a payee, you must enter payment instructions. The easiest way to do this is with the Enter Online Payment window, shown next. To open this window, begin by opening the register for the account from which the payment will be made. Then choose Online | Payments | Enter Payment or choose Enter Payment from the EPay button's menu near the top of the Banking tab.

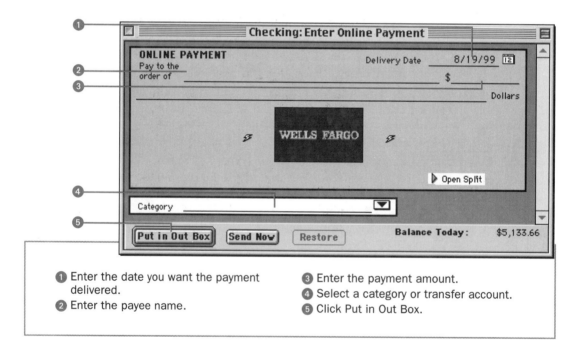

1. Enter the date you want the payment delivered.
2. Enter the payee name.
3. Enter the payment amount.
4. Select a category or transfer account.
5. Click Put in Out Box.

As you can see, this window looks and works a lot like the Write Checks window, which I cover in Chapter 4. Here are the details about the information you have to enter:

- **Delivery Date** is the date you want the payee to receive payment. This is the date the bank will either write on the check or make the electronic funds transfer. The check may be received before that date, depending on the mail. The date you enter, however, must be at least the same number of business days in advance as the delivery lead time for the payee—usually four days. That means if you want to pay a bill on Wednesday, October 30, you must enter and send its instructions to your bank on or before Friday, October 25. Quicken will adjust the date for you if necessary.

Tip   *Whenever possible, I give the bank an extra two days. So, in the previous example, if the bill is due on October 30, I'd instruct the bank to pay on October 28. This isn't because I don't have confidence in Quicken or my bank. It's because I have less confidence in the postal service.*

- **Payee** is the online payee to receive payment. Quicken's QuickFill feature fills in the payee's name as you type it. If you enter a payee that is not in the Payees list, Quicken offers to set up a new payee for you. This enables you to create online payees as you enter payment instructions.
- **$** is the amount of the payment.
- **Category** is the category in which the payment should be recorded. You can either enter a category, choose one from the pop-up menu, or click the Open Split triangle to enter multiple categories.

When you've finished entering information for the transaction, click Put in Out Box. The transaction is added to the Out Box window, which I discuss a little later. You can repeat this process for as many payments as you want to make.

Tip   *You can also enter online payment instructions in the account's register window. Be sure to select Send in the Number field. When you click Record, Quicken adds the instruction to its Out Box window.*

Scheduling Repeating Online Payments

Some payments, such as your rent or your monthly cable television bill, are exactly the same every month. You can set these payments up as repeating online payments.

Here's how it works. You use the Schedule Transaction or Schedule Future Transaction window, which I discuss in Chapter 7, to enter payment information for an online payee. Be sure to click the Online Payment button (which looks like a lightning bolt) in the window. Enter the frequency, duration, and reminder information as desired in the bottom of the window. Here's an example of a transaction entered in Quicken's Calendar:

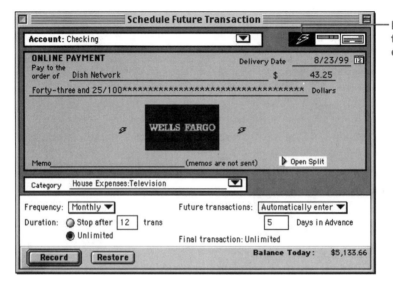

When you click Record, the payment is scheduled just like any other scheduled transaction. But each time the transaction needs to be recorded, Quicken puts the payment instruction in its Out Box for delivery to the bank with your other payment instructions.

Setting Up Online Loan Payments

You can also set up loan payments as repeating online payments. Just follow the instructions in Chapter 6 to set up a loan. In the Preview Payment window, which is shown next, select the Online Payment radio button. This enables you to schedule the payment as a repeating online payment.

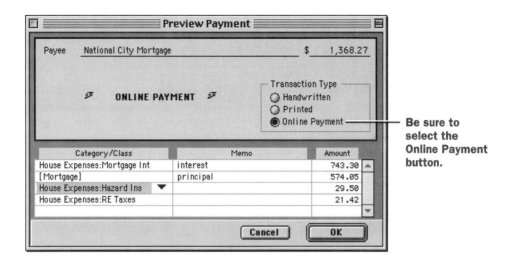

Sending Payment Instructions

Remember the bills I told you about? The ones waiting on a table by the door to be mailed? Payment instructions that have not yet been sent to the bank are just like those stamped envelopes. They're ready to go, but they won't get where they're going without your help.

Once your payment instructions have been completed, you must connect to your bank to send the instructions. Choose Online | Out Box or click the Out Box button near the top of the Banking tab. The Out Box window (see Figure 12-4) appears. It lists all of the transactions waiting to be sent, as well as other instructions to your bank.

Tip   *As you can see in Figure 12-4, Quicken's Out Box also includes instructions to update account statement data—in other words, download transactions. But although you can use this window to download transactions, you must switch to the Download Transactions window to review and accept them, as discussed earlier in this chapter.*

Make sure check marks appear beside each instruction you want to send. Then click the Send Now button. In most cases, a PIN dialog box like the one shown earlier in this chapter should appear. Enter your PIN in the edit box and click OK.

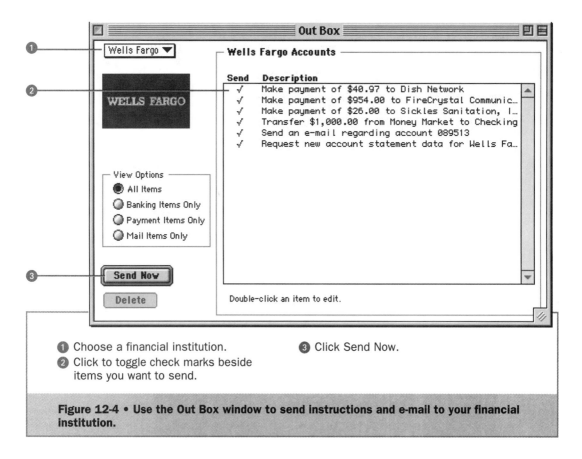

① Choose a financial institution.
② Click to toggle check marks beside items you want to send.
③ Click Send Now.

Figure 12-4 • Use the Out Box window to send instructions and e-mail to your financial institution.

If you have a dial-up connection to the Internet, your computer connects. Then Quicken displays a connection status dialog box like the one shown earlier in this chapter. When the connection is finished, Quicken displays the Online Transmission Summary window (refer to Figure 12-2). It summarizes the online session and provides details about payment instructions that were sent. You can click the Print button to print the summary for reference if desired.

Canceling a Payment

Occasionally, you may change your mind about making a payment. Perhaps you found out that your spouse already sent a check. Or that you set up the payment for the wrong amount. For whatever reason, you can cancel an online payment that you have sent to your bank—as long as there's enough time to cancel it.

Here's how it works. When you send a payment instruction to your bank, it waits in the bank's computer. When the processing date (determined by the number of days in the payee's delivery lead time and the payment date) arrives, the bank makes the payment. Before the processing date, however, the payment instructions can be canceled. If you send a cancel payment instruction to the bank before the processing date, the bank removes the instruction from its computer without sending payment to the payee. Quicken won't let you cancel a payment if the processing date has already passed. If you wait too long, the only way to cancel the payment is to call the bank directly and stop the check.

Tip   *Canceling a payment instruction isn't the same as stopping a check. If you send the cancel payment instruction in time, there should be no bank fee for stopping the payment.*

Canceling an Online Payment

In the account register window, select the payment you want to cancel. Then choose Online | Payments | Cancel Payment. If it isn't too late to cancel the payment, a dialog box like the one shown next will appear. Click the Put in Out Box button to add the cancellation instruction to the Out Box window or Send Now to send the cancellation instruction immediately.

Caution   *You must send the cancel payment instruction to your bank to cancel a payment. If you don't send the instruction immediately by clicking the Send Now button, be sure to use the Out Box to send the instruction before quitting Quicken. If you fail to do this, the cancel payment instruction may not reach your bank in time to cancel the payment.*

Stopping All Future Payments for a Repeating Online Payment

In the Scheduled Transactions window, select the payment you want to stop and click Delete. Click Yes in the confirmation dialog box that appears. The transaction is removed from the list and no further payment instructions will be created or sent to your bank.

Exchanging E-Mail with Your Financial Institution

You can use Quicken to exchange e-mail messages for any financial institution for which you have the Online Account Access feature enabled. This is an easy way to communicate with your bank or credit card company about issues that are not time-sensitive.

Caution *If you need to communicate about a time-sensitive issue— such as a lost or stolen checkbook or credit card—do not use Quicken's e-mail feature. Instead, drop everything and call your bank or credit card company immediately.*

Opening the E-mail Window

Quicken's E-mail window enables you to create new e-mail messages, read incoming e-mail messages, and review e-mail messages waiting to be sent. To open this window, choose Online | E-mail. The window might look something like this with the Create New Mail view option selected:

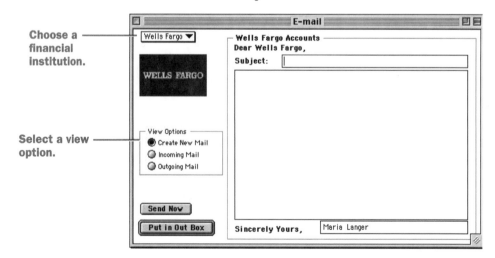

Creating an E-Mail Message

In the E-mail window, select the Create New Mail view option. Then fill out the e-mail form (consult the previous illustration) by entering a subject and message. When you have finished, click the Put in Out Box button to add the message to your Out Box or the Send Now button to send the message immediately.

> **Tip**   *You can also send an e-mail message about a specific transaction. Open the account register in which the transaction appears, select the transaction, and choose Online I Payments I Payment Query. Quicken creates an e-mail message that already includes a subject and all information about the transaction. Just add your message text and click Put in Out Box or Send Now to save it.*

Exchanging E-Mail Messages

Using e-mail is a lot like having a box at the post office. When you write a letter, you have to get it to the post office to send it to the recipient. When you receive a letter, you have to go to the post office and check your box to retrieve it. E-mail works the same way. Connecting is a lot like going to the post office to send and retrieve messages. If you don't use the Send Now button to send an e-mail message right after you compose it, you'll have to use the Out Box to send the message with your other instructions.

   In the Out Box window (see Figure 12-4), select the financial institution for which outgoing messages are waiting to be sent and click the Send Now button. Quicken displays the PIN dialog box; enter your PIN and click OK. Then wait while Quicken establishes an Internet connection with your financial institution and exchanges e-mail.

   When Quicken is finished, it displays the Online Transmission Summary dialog box. Review the information in this dialog box and click OK.

Reading an E-Mail Message

When your financial institution sends you an e-mail message, it appears in the E-mail window. To read the message, open the E-mail window and select the Incoming Mail view option. Then select the message you want to read. Its contents appear in the bottom half of the window. If desired, you can click the Delete Mail button to delete the message when you've finished with it or the Reply button to compose a reply.

Transferring Money Between Accounts

If you have more than one account enabled for Online Account Access at the same financial institution, you can transfer money from one account to another.

SAVE MONEY You can take advantage of this feature to maximize the interest earned on your money. Keep excess funds in an interest-bearing savings or money market account. Then, the day before a transaction will be made, transfer the funds to cover the transaction from the interest-bearing account to your checking account. Your money stays where it earns interest as long as possible, but is transferred just in time to make the payment.

Preparing an online transfer is very much like preparing any other account transfer in Quicken. Choose Online | Transfer Money Online to open the Transfer Money Online window, which is shown next. (This window looks and works very much like the Transfer Money window I discuss in Chapter 4.) Fill in the amount and account information and click Put in Out Box.

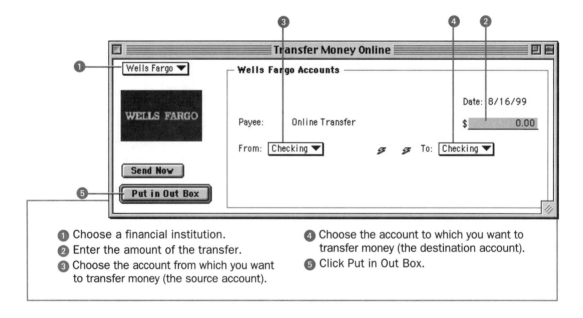

1. Choose a financial institution.
2. Enter the amount of the transfer.
3. Choose the account from which you want to transfer money (the source account).
4. Choose the account to which you want to transfer money (the destination account).
5. Click Put in Out Box.

Like payment instructions, you must send transfer instructions to your bank in order for the transaction to take place. If you don't use the Send Now button to send the instruction immediately, make sure you use the Out Box to send the instruction with all of your other instructions.

In the Out Box window (see Figure 12-4), select the financial institution for which transfer instructions are waiting to be sent and click the Send Now button. Quicken displays the PIN dialog box; enter your PIN and click OK. Then wait while Quicken establishes an Internet connection with your financial institution and sends the instructions.

When Quicken is finished, it displays the Online Transmission Summary dialog box. Review the information in this window and click OK.

Updating Your Portfolio's Value with Quicken Quotes

Chapter 13

In This Chapter:

- *Benefits and Costs of Quicken Quotes*

- *Downloading Current Quotes*

- *Downloading Historical Prices*

The Quicken Quotes feature enables you to obtain current and historical quotes for individual stocks, mutual funds, and other investments. This automates the tracking of market values to keep your portfolio balance up-to-date. Quicken can also notify you, with a dialog box, when a security you track reaches a high or low price you specify.

In this chapter, I tell you about this feature and explain how it can help you save time and stay informed about your investments.

Tip   *The instructions in this chapter assume that you have already configured your computer for an Internet connection. If you have not done so, do it now. Chapter 3 provides the instructions you need to set up and test an Internet connection. This chapter also assumes that you understand the topics and procedures discussed in Chapters 2 and 5, and builds on some of the basic concepts discussed in those chapters.*

Benefits and Costs of Quicken Quotes

Consider the following scenario: You wake up one morning and realize that your future financial security is very important to you. (This happened to me about five years ago.) You make a conscious effort to save and invest money. After a few years, you own shares of a few stocks and mutual funds, which you track in your Quicken data file. With your growing portfolio, you find that half the time you spend with Quicken is spent entering up-to-date stock quotes. You like keeping the market value information current, but you'd like to spend more of your time researching new investments and following news stories about the investments you already have.

With Quicken Quotes, you can download quotes throughout the day or at the day's end. If you miss a few days, don't worry. You can get up to five years of stock quotes for any company with the click of a mouse.

The cost? It's free to Quicken Deluxe users, courtesy of Intuit. All you need is an Internet connection.

Getting Quotes Online

Getting quotes online is easy—provided that you have properly set up your Quicken data file with required security information. In this section, I explain how to set up, download, and review online quotes.

Setting Quotes Preferences

Quicken's Preferences window offers one option you can set to fine-tune the way Quicken Quotes works. To set this option, choose Edit | Preferences to display the Preferences window. Then click the Quotes icon on the left side of the window to display Quicken Quotes preferences, which is shown next. Change the value in the edit box as desired and click OK.

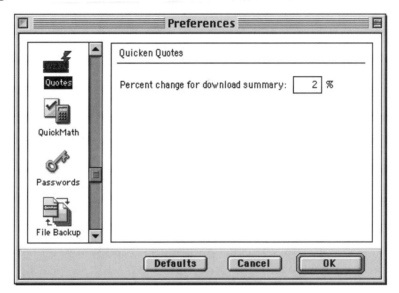

The value you enter in the edit box determines the minimum percentage change in an investment account's balance for Quicken to notify you about the change. For example, with this option set to 2% (the default value), if an account's balance changes by 2.56% due to an increase (or decrease) in security market values, Quicken will notify you. If the account's balance changes by only 1.87%, Quicken will not notify you.

Setting Up Securities for Downloading Quotes

To download a security's price, you must enter the ticker symbol for the security in the Set Up Security or Edit Security window. You may also want to set up the price notification feature to notify you of high or low prices. If you did all this when you first set up the security, you can skip this section. If not, read on.

Looking Up a Ticker Symbol

You can't download quotes for a security if its correct ticker symbol is not entered in Quicken. If you don't know a security's ticker symbol, you'll have to look it up.

Choose Online | To the Web | Investment Center or click the InvCntr button near the top of the Investing tab. This launches your Web browser and displays the Quicken Investments Department main page. Click the "Don't know the symbol?" link in the Quotes and Research area near the top of the page. In the Symbol Lookup area of the Ticker Search page that appears, select a security type and enter all or part of the security name. Here's an example:

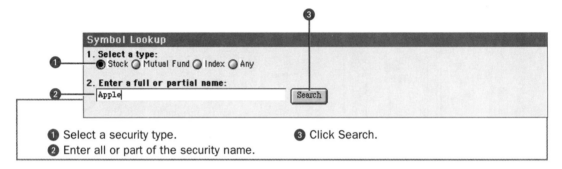

❶ Select a security type.   ❸ Click Search.
❷ Enter all or part of the security name.

When you click Search, Quicken displays a list of possible matches, along with their ticker symbols:

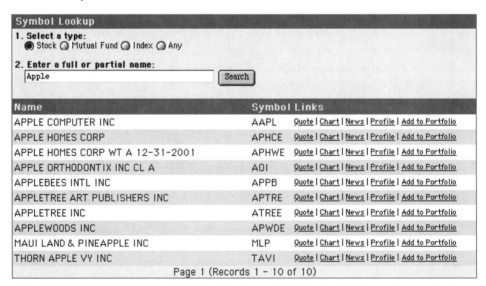

Entering the Ticker Symbol and Notification Prices

If necessary, switch back to Quicken. Then choose Lists | Securities to display the Securities window. Select the security for which you want to download quotes and click the Edit button. The Edit Security window, which is shown next, appears. Be sure the correct ticker symbol appears in the Security edit box. You can also set options to have Quicken notify you when the security reaches either a high or low price that you specify. When you've finished, click Change.

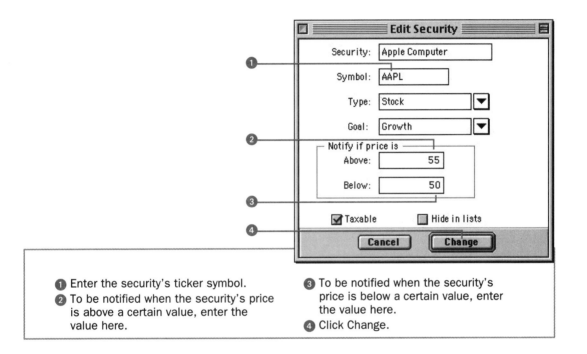

① Enter the security's ticker symbol.
② To be notified when the security's price is above a certain value, enter the value here.
③ To be notified when the security's price is below a certain value, enter the value here.
④ Click Change.

Repeat this process for each security for which you want to download quotes.

Downloading Current Quotes

You can update quotes any time you like. Choose Online | Quicken Quotes or click the Quotes button near the top of the Investing tab. If you are not connected to the Internet, Quicken connects. A Quicken Quotes Progress dialog box appears while Quicken requests and receives the security price information. When it's finished, a Download Summary window like the one shown next should appear. It tells you what Quicken did while you were waiting. It also displays any price notifications or account value notifications.

Note *The prices downloaded by the Quicken Quotes feature during trading hours are delayed by 15 minutes or more. Mutual fund closing prices for the day are not updated until approximately 6:00 P.M. ET. Quicken does not download quotes for hidden securities.*

In Quicken 2000, market values of your securities are automatically updated when you download quotes. You can see recent prices for the securities you track by clicking the View Latest Prices button in the Download Summary window. Here's what it might look like:

Symbol	Volume	High	Low	Current	Change	Time/Date
AUD	490800	40.063	39.563	39.625	unchanged	8/20/99
AUD	899300	40.313	39.250	39.625	-.875	8/19/99
AUD	958500	40.688	39.813	40.500	-.125	8/18/99
AUD	1142800	40.688	39.750	40.625	.125	8/17/99
AUD	930800	40.875	40.313	40.500	unchanged	8/16/99
AAPL	2076100	59.375	58.188	58.563	-.187	8/20/99
AAPL	4910900	60.500	58.563	58.750	-1.375	8/19/99
AAPL	2865500	60.375	58.938	60.313	-.187	8/17/99
AAPL	2472600	60.688	59.500	60.500	.437	8/16/99
T	8407300	48.063	46.375	46.875	-1.313	8/20/99
T	6919900	48.438	47.750	48.188	-.437	8/19/99
T	7841800	49.875	48.938	49.750	.687	8/17/99
T	6826100	49.875	48.250	49.063	-.187	8/16/99
CPQ	6793000	24.563	24.125	24.500	.500	8/20/99
CPQ	8876900	24.188	23.125	24.000	.500	8/19/99
CPQ	10130800	24.813	23.125	23.500	-.625	8/18/99
CPQ	8994100	24.750	23.875	24.125	.250	8/17/99
CPQ	7190000	23.875	22.813	23.875	.812	8/16/99
DIS	7035500	30.000	28.750	29.938	.563	8/20/99
DIS	9888800	29.375	28.813	29.375	.187	8/19/99
DIS	11459600	29.313	28.500	29.188	.688	8/18/99
DIS	10824000	28.500	27.500	28.500	.562	8/17/99
DIS	6047600	28.000	27.563	27.938	.750	8/16/99
DGAGX	0	.000	.000	44.420	.460	8/17/99
DDSTX	0	.000	.000	40.570	.340	8/17/99

All quotes are at least 15 minutes delayed

Viewing Portfolio Values

After downloading quotes, the Price and Market Value columns in the Portfolio window (see Figure 13-1) reflect the most recently downloaded prices for both the securities you own and WatchList items—even if you download quotes several times in the same day.

Portfolio					
Group by: Account ▼ Set Prices As Of: 8/20/99 🗓 Customize					
Name	**Price**	**Shares**	**Total Cost**	**Gain/Loss**	**Market Value**
▽ **Datek Online**			5,324.34	–355.59	8,137.13
Compaq Computer	24 3/8 ↑	50	1,109.99	108.76	1,218.75
Pixar	37 1/2 ↑	100	4,214.35	–464.35	3,750.00
Cash					3,168.38
▽ **DRIPs**			1,219.99	333.09	1,553.08
AT&T	47.063 ↓	33	1,219.99	333.09	1,553.08
Cash					0.00
▽ **Mutual Funds**			18,134.94	1,154.03	19,288.97
Dreyfus Disc St...	39.940 —	287.302	10,511.39	963.45	11,474.84
Guardian Park A...	52.970 —	106.538	5,523.90	119.42	5,643.32
JH Indep Equity	31.120 —	69.756	2,099.65	71.16	2,170.81
Cash					0.00
▽ **Retirement**			19,811.32	1,101.03	20,912.35
Dreyfus Appreci...	43.770 —	267.537	11,641.08	69.01	11,710.09
Dreyfus Disc St...	39.940 —	38.456	1,500.96	34.97	1,535.93
Dreyfus S&P 500	27.880 —	54.839	1,504.37	24.54	1,528.91
Guardian Park A...	52.970 —	115.866	5,164.91	972.51	6,137.42
Cash					0.00
▽ **Stock on Hand**			3,093.45	22,256.80	25,350.25
ADP	39 3/4 ↑	564	2,221.45	20,197.55	22,419.00
Apple Computer	58 5/8 ↓	50	872.00	2,059.25	2,931.25
Cash					0.00
▽ **WatchList**					
General Motors	63.188 ↑				
Iomega	3 7/8 ↓				

Record	Register	Add Security	Quotes provided by S&P Comstock. Delayed up to 20 minutes.	Cash Balance	3,168.38
				Market Value	75,241.78

Figure 13-1 •The Portfolio window reflects most recently downloaded prices for the day.

Symbols to the right of the security price indicate the price change:

- **Up arrow** indicates that the security's price has risen since the last closing price.
- **Down arrow** indicates that the security's price has fallen since the last closing price.
- **Dash** indicates that the security's price has not changed since the last closing price.
- **Gray diamond** (not shown) indicates that the security's price has not been downloaded since the start of the trading day.

Note | *I tell you more about using the Portfolio window in Chapter 5.*

Getting Historical Prices

You can also download historical price information for the securities you track with the Quicken Quotes feature. Choose Online | Historical Prices or click the HistPrice button near the top of the Investing tab. Quicken displays the Download Historical Prices dialog box, which is shown next. Choose a time period from the drop-down list at the top of the dialog box. Make sure check marks appear beside all securities for which you want to get historical prices. Then click the Download button.

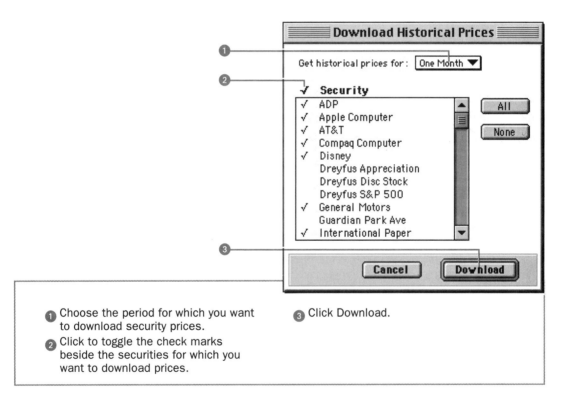

1 Choose the period for which you want to download security prices.

2 Click to toggle the check marks beside the securities for which you want to download prices.

3 Click Download.

Quicken connects to the Internet and retrieves the information you requested. When it has finished, it updates the price information for each security.

You can review the quotes that were downloaded in the Security Detail window. Here's what the Graph tab looks like for one of my investments:

Saving Money and Achieving Your Goals

Part V

This part of the book tells you about the Quicken and Quicken.com features you can use to save money on big-ticket items such as income tax, insurance, a home, and a vehicle. It shows you how using Quicken to help you make big financial decisions can save you money. It also highlights how you can use Quicken to help make your dreams come true. Its four chapters are:

Saving Money at Tax Time

In This Chapter:

- *Tax Planning Basics*

- *Including Tax Information in Accounts and Categories*

- *Tax Deduction Finder*

- *Quicken Tax Planner*

- *Tax Reports*

- *Quicken.com Tax Features*

Tax time is no fun. It can force you to spend hours sifting through financial records and filling out complex forms. When you're done with the hard part, you may be rewarded with the knowledge that you can expect a refund. But it is more likely that your reward will be the privilege of writing a check to the federal, state, or local government—or worse yet, all three.

Fortunately, Quicken can help. Its reporting features can save you time. Its planning features can save you money and help you make smarter financial decisions. By using the tax tools that are part of Quicken or available on Quicken.com, the next tax season may be a little less . . . well, *taxing*. In this chapter, I show you how.

The Importance of Tax Planning

Don't underestimate the importance of tax planning. Doing so can cost you time and money. In this section, I explain why tax planning is important and give you some tips on what you can do to plan for tax time.

Why Plan for Tax Time?

Use the following scenarios to get yourself thinking about how a little planning now can save you time and money later.

Mary's Interest Expense Lesson

Mary is a homeowner who has been using her credit cards a little more than she should. She decides to cut up most of the cards and is now reducing her debt by paying a little more than the minimum monthly payment on each credit card account. Mary never considered the tax benefit of using a home equity loan, with tax-deductible interest, to pay off her credit card debt. Silly Mary doesn't even realize that the home equity reserve's interest rate might even be half the rate she pays the credit card companies.

John's Capital Gains Lesson

John invests in the stock market. He's been holding shares in Company A for five years, in Company B for a year and a half, and in Company C for a few months. All three investments have been doing well. Now John wants to buy a new car. He needs to liquidate some of his investments for the down payment. Because selling all shares of Company C would give him just the right amount of money, he sells them. What John didn't consider is that the gain on the sale of Company C is recognized as a short-term capital gain. If he'd sold some shares of

Company A or B, he could have recorded a long-term capital gain, which is taxed at a lower rate.

Jean's Record-Keeping Lesson

Jean's young daughter has a serious medical problem that requires frequent trips to a big city hospital 50 miles away and other trips to doctors all over the state. Jean drives her there in the family car or, if her teenage son needs the car for work, she takes a cab. Her daughter's condition has improved greatly and the prognosis is good. But Jean's family health insurance doesn't cover all the transportation costs for the hospital and doctor visits. She was just told by a friend that she can deduct the cost of medical transportation from her income taxes. She's spent hours trying to compile a list of the dates of all those long drives and she wishes she'd asked for cab ride receipts.

Pete's Estimated Tax Lesson

Pete is a freelance writer who is having a very good year. By the end of June, he estimated that he'd already earned twice as much as he did the previous year. To celebrate, he bought a new car and took a two-week vacation in Peru. He also invested heavily in a mutual fund with good returns and a high front-end load. He feels great to have finally made the big time. But the estimated tax payments Pete has been making this year aren't nearly enough to cover his April 15 tax bill. He never considered increasing the payments to reduce his year-end tax bill, investing in a tax-deferred annuity or tax-free municipal bond to reduce his taxable income, or even saving some of his cash for April 15.

Learn from Their Mistakes, Not Yours

Mary, John, Jean, and Pete may as well be real people—I'm sure plenty of people find themselves in their situations every year. These examples illustrate the point: understanding the tax rules and planning ahead for tax time can save you time and money.

What You Can Do

Unless you're a tax accountant, you probably don't know all the tax laws. Fortunately, you don't need to know all the laws, just the ones that can affect you. Then, with the knowledge of what you can include on your tax returns, you can take steps to make smart decisions and keep track of items you can deduct.

Learning About Tax Rules

At tax time, people fall into two categories: those who do their own taxes and those who find (and probably pay) someone else to do their taxes for them.

If you do your own taxes, you can learn a lot about tax laws by reading the tax forms and publications for your return. If you pay a tax preparer, you can really get your money's worth by asking him or her about how you could save money. Any good tax preparer should be able to tell you.

Either way, you can also learn tax rules and get tips and advice by consulting the tax-related features within Quicken and the Taxes Department at Quicken.com. You learn about these resources throughout this chapter.

Saving Receipts and Recording Transactions

When you know what items are deductible, make a special effort to save receipts and record them in the proper Quicken categories. The receipts provide documentation for the expenditures, especially the date and amount. Recording them in the right account makes it possible to quickly generate reports of tax-deductible expenditures when it's time to fill out your tax returns.

Analyzing All Options Before Making a Decision

Many people make decisions based on limited information—or worse yet, no information at all. As a Quicken user, you have access to all kinds of information and decision-making tools. Use Quicken.com to learn about finance-related opportunities. Go the extra step to research how an opportunity could affect your tax bill. Finally, use Quicken's built-in tools—such as the Tax Planner and Deduction Finder (both of which are discussed in this chapter)—to help you make an informed decision.

Specifying Tax Information in Accounts and Categories

As discussed briefly in Chapter 2, Quicken accounts and categories can include information that will help you at tax time. In this section, I tell you more about this feature, including why you should use it and how you can set it up.

Why Enter Tax Information?

By including tax information in Quicken accounts and categories, you make it possible for Quicken to do several things:

- **Prepare tax reports.** These reports summarize information by tax category or schedule.

- **Save time using the Tax Planner.** This feature of Quicken Deluxe can import information from your Quicken data file based on tax information you enter.
- **Distinguish between taxable and non-taxable investments.** This enables you to create accurate reports on capital gains, interest, and dividends.

 SAVE TIME   By spending a few minutes setting up tax information for your accounts and categories, you can save hours compiling information for your returns.

Setting Portfolio Accounts as Taxable

Investments can be taxable or nontaxable. It's important to distinguish between these two types of investments if you want Quicken to generate accurate reports of taxable income and expenses.

To check or change the tax status of a portfolio account, open the Accounts window, select the account you want to work with, and click the Edit button at the bottom of the Accounts window. The Edit Account dialog box, which is shown next, appears. If the investment account is taxable, turn on the Taxable check box. Otherwise, turn it off. When you've finished, click Change.

Set the Taxable check box as desired.

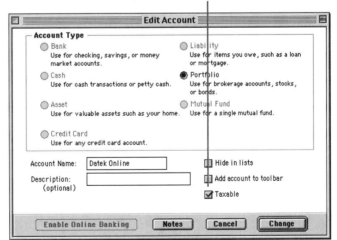

Setting Categories as Tax-Related

Quicken can automatically generate tax reports that include tax-related income and expenses. How does it know what categories are tax-related? You tell it.

Choose Lists | Categories & Transfers or press COMMAND-L to open the Categories & Transfers window. As you can see in Figure 14-1, some categories may have a diamond in the Tax column. These are categories that have been set as tax-related.

Shortcut *Quicken automatically sets tax information for many of the categories it creates automatically. Concentrate on the categories without the diamond in the Tax column; some of these may require tax information, depending on your situation.*

Select the category for which you want to change tax-related options. Then click the Edit button at the bottom of the window to display the Edit Category window, shown next. If the category's transactions should be included on your

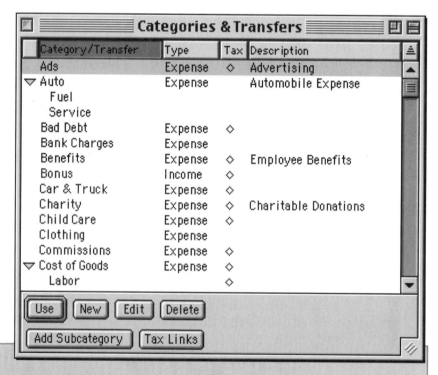

Figure 14-1 • Use the Categories & Transfers window to select categories and transfer accounts for which you want to set tax options.

tax return as either income or a deductible expense, turn on the Tax-related check box. Otherwise, turn it off. Then click the Change button.

Set the Tax-related check box as desired.

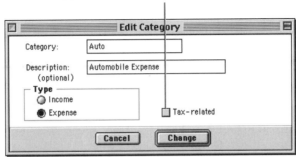

If you turned on the Tax-related check box, when you click the Change button, a dialog box like the one shown next may appear. It asks whether you want to assign a specific tax form line item to the category. To do so, click the Tax Links button to display the Assign Tax Links dialog box, which I discuss in the next section. To make the change without assigning a tax line, click Later.

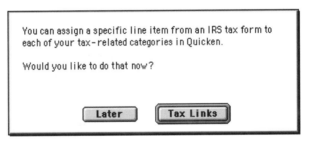

Repeat this process for all categories for which you want to change the tax-related status.

Assigning Tax Links

To get even more detail in your tax reports, you can assign specific tax form lines to the categories in your Quicken data file. Doing so summarizes your tax-related income and expenses in the same order they appear on your tax returns. As you can imagine, this can really save time at tax time!

SAVE TIME   Generating tax reports organized by tax form line item may save you time, but you can save even more time by exporting your Quicken data into MacinTax, Intuit's tax preparation software for Macintosh users. Just set up tax links as discussed in this section, and then follow the instructions within MacinTax to import the data. MacinTax is available separately from Intuit.

You assign tax form lines to categories with the Assign Tax Links dialog box. Click the Tax Links button in the Categories & Transfers window (see Figure 14-1) to display this dialog box. It should look something like this:

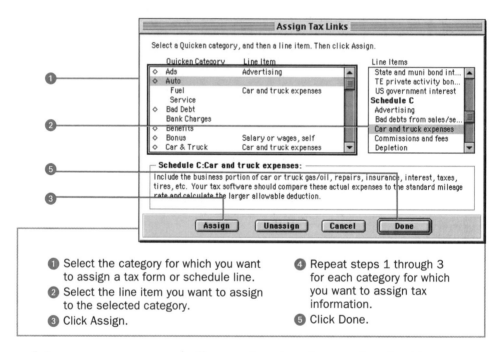

① Select the category for which you want to assign a tax form or schedule line.
② Select the line item you want to assign to the selected category.
③ Click Assign.
④ Repeat steps 1 through 3 for each category for which you want to assign tax information.
⑤ Click Done.

It is not necessary to match all categories—just the ones that should appear on your tax return. When you've finished, click Done to save your settings. The information is recorded for each category.

Tip   *You can also use this technique to assign tax line items to transfer accounts if necessary.*

Quicken Tax Tools

You don't have to wait until tax time to get tax help from Quicken. It's there all year long, helping you minimize your taxes and plan for tax day by offering two excellent tax planning tools:

- **Deduction Finder** asks you questions about expenditures to determine whether they may be tax-deductible.
- **Quicken Tax Planner** helps you estimate your federal income tax bill for 1999 and 2000.

Here's a closer look at these two features.

Tax Deduction Finder

One way to minimize taxes is to maximize your deductions. While Quicken can't help you spend money on tax-deductible items (that's up to you), it can help you identify expenses that may be tax-deductible—so you don't forget to include them on your tax returns.

The Tax Deduction Finder is a separate program, which comes with Quicken, that can help you learn which expenses are deductible. Its question-and-answer interface gathers information from you and then provides information about the deductibility of items based on your answers.

Getting Started

To open the Tax Deduction Finder, choose Activities | Financial Fitness | Tax Deduction Finder or click the Deduct button near the top of the Planning tab. The Tax Deduction Finder application launches and displays its main window. Read the information in the Getting Started screen and click the Next button at the bottom of the window to begin.

Next, the Tax Deduction Finder asks for some information about you. Enter your name, age, and annual income and click Next.

Answering Deduction Questions

The Deductions section is broken down into six types of deductions: Employee, Homeowner, Individual, Investor, Medical, and Self-employed. The Tax Deduction Finder will walk you through each section, one at a time. Click Next to move from one type of deduction to the next one. You can select a type of deduction in the left side of the window, and then answer questions about the deduction in the right side of the window. The answers to your questions will

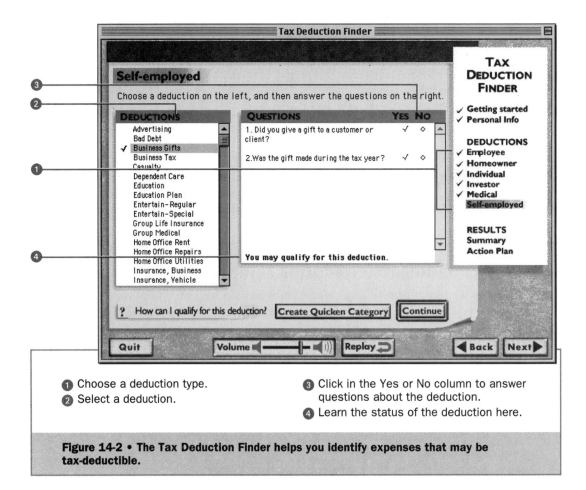

Figure 14-2 • The Tax Deduction Finder helps you identify expenses that may be tax-deductible.

determine whether your expense may be tax-deductible. Figure 14-2 shows an example of the screen for Self-employed deductions. (It looks like those Godiva chocolates I send my clients for the holidays every year may be tax-deductible.) You can click Continue to move from one deduction to the next one.

When you answer questions that may result in a deductible expense, the Tax Deduction Finder displays a window like the one shown next that you can use to add the category to your Quicken data file.

Turn on this check box to prevent this window from appearing automatically.   **Click Cancel to close the window without creating the category.**   **Click OK to create the new category.**

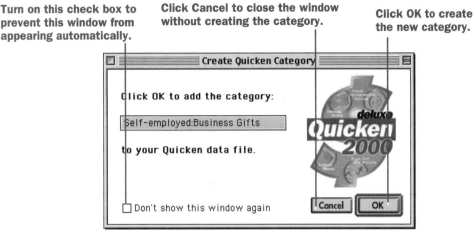

Tip   *You can also display the Create Quicken Category window by clicking the Create Quicken Category button in the Tax Deduction Finder window (see Figure 14-2).*

As you can see in Figure 14-2, answering questions in the Tax Deduction Finder is straightforward and easy. You don't have to answer questions about all the deductions—only the deductions you think may apply to you. When you've finished answering questions about a deduction, a green check mark or red X appears beside it. You can then move on to another deduction.

Finishing Up

The Results section of the Tax Deduction Finder (see Figure 14-3) summarizes all of the expenses that may be tax-deductible. It also includes an action plan, which explains the deductions and offers tips for tracking them with Quicken. Although you can read the Action Plan information onscreen, if you answered many questions, you may want to use the Print button within the window to print the information for future reference.

When you've finished using the Tax Deduction Finder, click the Quit button within its window. The information you entered is automatically saved and can be updated by launching the Tax Deduction Finder again. Any categories you created in the Tax Deduction Finder are automatically added to your Quicken data file.

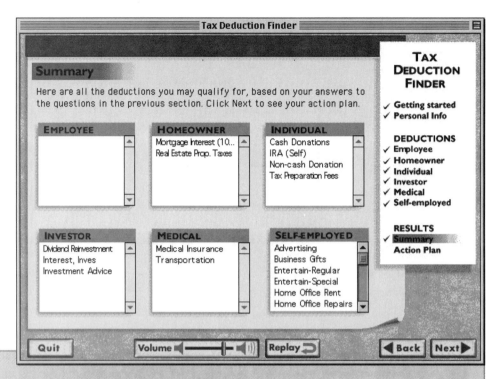

Figure 14-3 • The Results section of the Tax Deduction Finder summarizes the expenses that may be tax-deductible.

Quicken Tax Planner

One of the best reasons to think about taxes *before* tax time is to avoid surprises on April 15. Knowing what you'll owe before you owe it can help ensure that you pay just the right amount of taxes up front—through proper payroll deductions or estimated tax payments—so you don't get hit with a big tax bill or tax refund.

Quicken Tax Planner helps you estimate your federal income tax bill for 1999 and 2000. While this can help you avoid surprises, it can also help you see how various changes to income and expenses can affect your estimated tax bill.

SAVE MONEY You may think of a big tax refund as a gift from Uncle Sam. Well, it isn't. It's *your* money that Uncle Sam has been using, interest free, for months. When you overpay your taxes, you're giving up money that you could be using to reduce interest-bearing debt or earn interest or investment income. Make sure you don't overpay taxes throughout the year so you can keep your money where it'll do you the most good.

Getting Started

To open Quicken Tax Planner, choose Activities | Planning Calculators | Tax. Figure 14-4 shows what the Quicken Tax Planner window might look like with the Base scenario displayed.

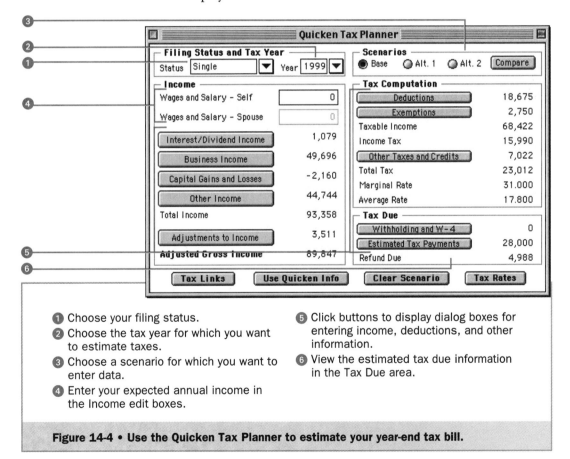

❶ Choose your filing status.
❷ Choose the tax year for which you want to estimate taxes.
❸ Choose a scenario for which you want to enter data.
❹ Enter your expected annual income in the Income edit boxes.
❺ Click buttons to display dialog boxes for entering income, deductions, and other information.
❻ View the estimated tax due information in the Tax Due area.

Figure 14-4 • Use the Quicken Tax Planner to estimate your year-end tax bill.

You can use buttons at the bottom of the window to work with window contents:

- **Tax Links** displays the Assign Tax Links dialog box discussed earlier in this chapter. You can use it to check or change your assignment of tax return line items.
- **Use Quicken Info** imports information from your Quicken data file into Quicken Tax Planner. This is a quick way to enter data based on actual amounts.
- **Clear Scenario** clears the entries in the current Quicken Tax Planner scenario.
- **Tax Rates** provides information about current tax rates. You can edit this information, if necessary, to account for changes in tax laws.

Entering Tax Planner Data

There are two ways to enter data into the Quicken Tax Planner: manually or automatically.

Manually Entering Income and Deductible Expenses   Manually entering data into the Quicken Tax Planner is pretty straightforward and easy to do. You can click buttons for various tax return categories and enter values into edit boxes. You might want to have some tax records on hand when you do this to help ensure accuracy. You can always reopen the Quicken Tax Planner window and make changes later if new information becomes available. All calculations are performed automatically for you based on your entries.

Automatically Entering Data from Your Quicken Data File   A quicker way to enter data is to click the Use Quicken Info button at the bottom of the Quicken Tax Planner window. This displays the Preview Information from Quicken dialog box, which is shown next. Quicken automatically annualizes the amounts entered into the data file, but you can override this option and use an actual amount by double-clicking a line item. For example, suppose it's October and you've already paid all your real estate taxes for the year. The actual amount in your Quicken data file is the amount that should be used in the Quicken Tax Planner, so you would set the annualize option to No for the Real Estate Taxes line item.

Click OK to import the data into Quicken Tax Planner.

Preview Information from Quicken				

Using items dated 1/1/99 thru 7/31/99
Double-click a line item to toggle between annualized or actual amounts

Tax Line Items	Quicken Amt	Destination	Ann.	Amt
Schedule A:Doctors, d...	396	Medical and Dental Expense	Yes	679
Schedule A:Real estate...	207	Real Estate Taxes	Yes	355
Schedule A:Other taxes	162	Real Estate Taxes	Yes	278
Schedule A:Home mort...	5,383	Mortgage Interest	Yes	9,227
Schedule B:Interest in...	338	Taxable Interest Income	Yes	579
Schedule B:Dividend i...	291	Dividends	Yes	500
Schedule C:Gross rece...	61,352	Revenue	Yes	105,175
Schedule C:Legal and p...	2,763	Other Allow – Expense & C...	Yes	4,736
Schedule C:Supplies (...	207	Other Allow – Expense & C...	Yes	355
Schedule C:Other busi...	11,675	Other Allow – Expense & C...	Yes	20,014
Schedule C:Advertising	455	Other Allow – Expense & C...	Yes	780
Schedule C:Insurance,...	4	Other Allow – Expense & C...	Yes	7

Double-click an item to toggle the Annualize setting.

[Annualize None]   [Annualize All]   [Cancel]   [OK]

Note *To make the most of this feature, you must properly set up all Tax Links before importing Quicken data into the Quicken Tax Planner.*

Using Scenarios

The scenarios feature of Quicken Tax Planner enables you to enter data for multiple scenarios—a "what-if" capability that you can use to see tax impacts based on various changes in entry data. For example, suppose you're planning to get married and want to see the impact of the additional income and deductions related to your new spouse. You can use a scenario to see the tax impact without changing your Base scenario.

To use this feature, select the Alt. 1 or Alt. 2 scenario radio button in the Scenarios area at the top of the Quicken Tax Planner window. A dialog box appears, asking if you want to copy the current scenario; click Yes or No as desired. Then change or enter values in the Quicken Tax Planner window for the scenario. You'll see the results immediately.

If you have created multiple scenarios, you can compare them by clicking the Compare button in the Scenarios area. Here's what it might look like with three scenarios set up:

Tax Scenario Comparisons			
	Base Case	**Alt. 1**	**Alt. 2**
Filing Status	Single	Married–Joint	Married–Separate
Tax Year	1999	1999	1999
Adjusted Gross Income	89,847	142,021	82,682
Deductions and Exemptions	21,425	23,962	21,093
Taxable Income	68,422	118,059	61,588
Total Tax	23,012	34,902	21,755
Marginal Rate	31.000	32.000	32.000
Average Rate	17.800	19.630	17.820

[Print Comparison]   [OK]

Acting on Quicken Tax Planner Results

The Tax Due area in the Quicken Tax Planner window estimates the amount of refund or tax due based on the information you entered. If the refund or amount due amount is large, you may want to adjust the amount of money you pay in taxes before the end of the year. There are two ways to do this:

- If you pay withholding taxes from your regular salary, submit a new W-4 form to adjust the amount of withholding you pay. You can usually get this form from your company's Human Resources department.
- If you pay estimated taxes, adjust the amount of quarterly estimated payments.

> **Tip** *In a few months, use the Quicken Tax Planner again to reassess the situation. You may find that another adjustment is necessary to make sure you minimize the amount of underpayment or overpayment.*

Finishing Up

When you've finished using the Quicken Tax Planner, click its Close button. This saves the information you entered so you can review or revise it in the future.

Tax Reports

Quicken offers several different tax reports that can make tax time easier by providing the information you need to prepare your taxes. All of these reports are based on the tax information settings for the accounts and categories in your Quicken file.

> **Note** *You can learn more about Quicken's reporting feature in Chapter 9.*

To create a report, begin by selecting Activities | Reports & Graphs | Reports or click the Reports button near the top of the Reporting tab. The Reports window, which is shown next, appears. It offers a number of reports you might find useful at tax time.

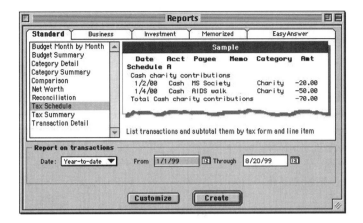

Standard Reports   Two reports on the Standard tab of the Reports window are specifically for taxes:

- **Tax Schedule** summarizes tax-related transactions, organized by tax form or schedule and line item.
- **Tax Summary** summarizes tax-related transactions, organized by category and date.

SAVE MONEY   If you pay a tax preparation specialist, be sure to furnish him or her with an accurate Tax Schedule report from Quicken. Doing so may save the preparer time and reduce your tax preparation bill.

Investment Reports   The Investment tab also offers two handy reports for tax time:

- **Capital Gains Report** summarizes gains and losses on the sales of investments, organized by the term of the investment (short or long) and the investment account.
- **Investment Income** summarizes investment cash inflows and outflows, usually due to dividends, interest earned, and investment expenses.

Quicken.com Resources

If you have access to the Internet, you also have access to the tax resources available at Quicken.com and other Web sites. To access Quicken.com tax resources, choose Online | To the Web | Tax Center. Figure 14-5 shows what the Quicken.com Taxes page looks like.

Note *Like all Web pages, the contents of the Quicken.com Taxes page can change daily. So don't be surprised if the features you find don't match the ones shown in Figure 14-5.*

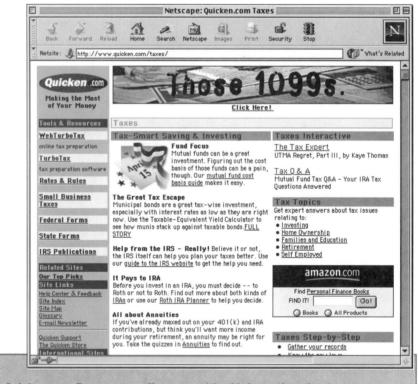

Figure 14-5 • The Quicken.com Taxes page offers a wealth of information about taxes.

Here are some of the features I find useful:

WebTurboTax   Imagine preparing your taxes by filling out interactive forms on a Web page. That's what WebTurboTax is all about. This new feature of Quicken.com brings the abilities of TurboTax to the Web. You can prepare your taxes for as little as $9.95, without buying any software or hiring a tax preparer. (Look out, H&R Block!)

Shortcut   *You can also access this feature by choosing Online | To the Web | WebTurboTax.*

Tip   *If you prefer to do your taxes on your computer (rather than on the Internet), be sure to check out MacInTax and MaxInTax State, Intuit's excellent tax return preparation programs for Macintosh users. I've been using these programs for years and can't imagine completing my tax returns without them!*

Forms and Publications   Although you can pick up tax forms at the local post office or library between January 1 and April 15 each year, what about the rest of the year? Or those obscure forms that no one seems to know about? Or the instructions for filling out those obscure forms that no one seems to know about? The Quicken.com Taxes page has you covered. It offers links to federal and state forms and IRS publications. You can get the forms and information you need any time of the day, any day of the year.

Tax Topics   The Tax Topics links on the Quicken.com Taxes page provide information about a variety of tax topics, including investing, home ownership, families and education, retirement, and self-employment. This is a great place to start researching any tax-related questions you may have.

SAVE TIME   Don't use Internet search engines to find sites to help with your taxes. Follow the links on the Quicken.com Taxes page instead. These sites are prescreened for value, so you don't waste time wading through information you can't use.

Minimizing Home, Car, and Insurance Expenses

Chapter 15

In This Chapter:

- *Types of Loans*

- *Loan Considerations*

- *Preparing for a Major Purchase*

- *Insurance Basics*

- *Quicken.com Resources*

- *Loan and Insurance Worksheets*

Possibly the biggest purchase you'll ever make is the purchase of a new home or car. These aren't the kinds of things you buy on a whim. They require research and planning. It's not only important to find the right living space or vehicle, it's important to get the right financing. You want the best deal on a loan, with a low interest rate and monthly payments that won't stretch your budget.

As your assets, family, and responsibilities grow, so does your need for insurance. Insurance can protect you from financial loss in the event of loss, theft, or damage to your assets. It can help you cover medical costs and make ends meet if illness or injury requires extensive medical care or prevents you from working. It can provide for your family if something happens to you.

In this chapter, I tell you about the tools within Quicken and on Quicken.com that you can use to learn more about financing a home or car and obtaining the insurance you need to protect your possessions and family. Along the way, I provide useful information about loans and insurance to give you a good idea of what's available. As you'll see in this chapter, Quicken can help you get the information you need to make informed decisions that can save you money.

Mortgage and Loan Basics

Before you start shopping for a loan—or for a home or car, for that matter—it's a good idea to have an understanding of loan basics. What kinds of loans are there? What are their benefits and drawbacks? Which is the right one for your purchase? What things are important when comparing one loan to another? In this section, I answer all of these questions and more.

Types of Loans

There are several types of loans, some of which are designed for specific purposes. Here's a quick summary of what's available, along with their pros and cons.

Mortgage

A *mortgage* is a long-term loan secured by real estate. Most mortgages require a 10% or higher down payment on the property. Monthly payments are based on the term of the loan and the interest rate applied to the principal. The interest you pay on a mortgage for a first or second home is tax-deductible. If you fail to make mortgage payments, your house could be sold to pay back the mortgage.

A *balloon* mortgage is a special type of short-term mortgage. Rather than make monthly payments over the full typical mortgage term, at the end of the fifth, seventh, or tenth year, you pay the balance of the mortgage in one big "balloon" payment. Some balloon mortgages offer the option of refinancing when the balloon payment is due.

Home Equity Loans or Lines of Credit

A *home equity loan* or *second mortgage* is a line of credit secured by the equity in your home—the difference between its market value and the amount of outstanding debt. Your equity rises when you make mortgage payments or property values increase. It declines when you borrow against your equity or property values decrease. A home equity loan lets you borrow against this equity.

There are two benefits to a home equity loan: interest rates are usually lower than other credit, and interest may be tax-deductible. For these reasons, many people use home equity loans to pay off credit card debt; renovate their homes; or buy cars, boats, or other recreational vehicles. But, like a mortgage, if you fail to pay a home equity reserve, your house could be sold to satisfy the debt.

Reverse Equity Loans

A *reverse equity loan* provides homeowners who own their homes in full with a regular monthly income. Instead of you paying the lender, the lender pays you. This type of loan is attractive to retirees who live on a fixed income. The loan is paid back when the home is sold—often after the death of the homeowner. (You can imagine how the next of kin feel about that.)

Car Loans

A *car loan* is a loan secured by a vehicle such as a car, truck, or motor home. Normally, you make a down payment and use the loan to pay the balance of the car's purchase price. Monthly payments are based on the term of the loan and the interest rate applied to the principal. Interest on car loans is not tax-deductible.

Personal Loans

A *personal loan* is an unsecured loan—a loan that requires no collateral. Monthly payments are based on the term of the loan and the interest rate applied to the principal. You can use a personal loan for just about anything. Some people use them to pay off multiple smaller debts so they have only one monthly payment. Interest on personal loans is not tax-deductible.

Loan Considerations

When applying for a loan, a number of variables have a direct impact on what the loan costs you now and in the future. Be sure to ask about all these things before applying for any loan.

GET SMARTER   The Loan Comparison Worksheet and Mortgage Comparison Worksheet at the end of this chapter enable you to take notes about the loans and mortgages you research. Use them to compare options before you make a decision.

Interest Rate

The *interest rate* is the annual percentage applied to the loan principal. Several factors affect the interest rate you may be offered:

- **Your credit record.** A borrower with a good credit record can usually get a better rate than one with a bad credit record. Of course, if your credit record is really bad, you might not be able to borrow money at any rate.
- **The type of loan.** Generally speaking, personal loans have the highest interest rates, whereas mortgages have the lowest. From highest to lowest between these two types are a used car loan, a new car loan, and a home equity reserve or line of credit.
- **The loan term.** The length of a loan can vary the interest within a specific loan type. For example, for car loans, the longer the term, the lower the rate.
- **The amount of the down payment.** The more money you put down on the purchase, the lower the rate may be.
- **Your location.** Rates vary from one area of the country to another.
- **The lender.** Rates also vary from one lender to another. Certain types of lenders have lower rates than others.

SAVE MONEY   When we purchased our current home, we used a mortgage company, rather than a bank, and got a considerably lower rate than what the local banks were offering.

Two kinds of interest rates can apply to a loan: fixed and variable.

- **Fixed rate** applies the same rate to the principal throughout the loan term.
- **Variable rate** applies a different rate to the loan throughout the loan term. For example, the loan may start with one rate and, each year, switch to a different rate. The rate is usually established by adding a certain number of percentage points to a national index, such as treasury bill rates. A cap limits the amount the rate can change. Mortgages with this type of rate are referred to as *adjustable rate mortgages,* or *ARMs.*

SAVE MONEY   When we purchased our first home, in the mid-1980s when interest rates were high, we selected an ARM. When interest rates dropped, so did the rate on our mortgage. If we'd selected a fixed-rate mortgage when we bought that home, we would have had to refinance to get the same savings. But because rates were much lower when we bought our current home, we selected a fixed rate to protect us from possible rate increases in the future.

Term

A loan's *term* is the period of time between the loan date and the date payment is due in full. Loan terms vary depending on the type of loan.

- Mortgage loan and home equity reserve loan terms are typically 10, 15, 20, or 30 years.
- Balloon mortgage loan terms are typically 5, 7, or 10 years.
- Car loan terms are typically 3, 4, or 5 years.

Down Payment

A *down payment* is an up-front payment toward the purchase of a home or car. Most mortgages require at least 10% down; 20% down is preferred.

SAVE MONEY   If you make only a 10% down payment on a home, you may be required to pay for the cost of private mortgage insurance. This protects the lender from loss if you fail to pay your mortgage, but increases your monthly mortgage payments.

GET SMARTER The Real Estate Settlement Procedures Act of 1974 requires that your lender provide a Good Faith Estimate of closing costs. This document summarizes all of the costs of closing on a home based on the mortgage the lender is offering. If you're not sure what a fee is for, check the Mortgage Glossary available in the Home & Mortgage Department on Quicken.com, which I tell you about later in this chapter.

Application Fees

Most lenders require you to pay an application fee to process your loan application. This usually includes the cost of obtaining a property appraisal and credit report. These fees are usually not refundable—even if you are turned down.

Mortgage Closing Costs

In addition to the application fee and down payment, many other costs are involved in securing a mortgage and purchasing a home. These are known as *closing costs*. Here's a brief list of the types of costs you may encounter. Because they vary from lender to lender, they could be a deciding factor when shopping for a mortgage. Note that most of these fees are not negotiable.

- **Origination fee** covers the administrative costs of processing a loan.
- **Discount (or "points")** is a fee based on a percentage rate applied to the loan amount. For example, 1 point on a $150,000 mortgage is $1,500.
- **Appraisal fee** covers the cost of a market-value appraisal of the property by a licensed, certified appraiser.
- **Credit report fee** covers the cost of obtaining a credit history of the prospective borrower(s) to determine credit worthiness.
- **Underwriting fee** covers the cost of underwriting the loan. This is the process of determining loan risks and establishing terms and conditions.
- **Document preparation fee** covers the cost of preparing legal and other documents required to process the loan.
- **Title insurance fee** covers the cost of title insurance, which protects the lender and buyer against loss due to disputes over ownership and possession of the property.

- **Recording fee** covers the cost of entering the sale of a property into public records.
- **Prepaid items** are taxes, insurance, and assessments paid in advance of their due dates. These expenses are not paid to the lender but are due at the closing date.

Preparing for a Major Purchase

Whether you're buying a home, car, or recreational vehicle, you'll need to do some planning before you make your purchase. In this section, I tell you what information a lender wants to know about you, as well as how you can determine what a loan will cost you.

Gathering Financial Fitness Information

Before anyone lends you money (except maybe Big Louie, who works out of the back room of a bar on the bad side of town), you'll need to provide some assurance that you can pay it back, with interest, within the allotted time. Before a potential lender starts examining your financial fitness, you should. Then you'll know in advance what the lender will discover, and if there are problems, you can fix them.

Your Net Worth

Start by taking a look at your net worth. If you've been faithfully recording all of your financial information in Quicken, this is easy. Choose Activities | Reports & Graphs | Reports, or click the Reports button near the top of the Reporting tab to display the Reports window. Click the Standard tab to display its options. Then select the Net Worth report and click Create. Quicken creates a Net Worth Report, which shows all of your assets and liabilities. The difference between these two is your net worth. The bigger this number is, the better off you are.

> **Tip**   *You can customize the Net Worth report to include only the accounts you specify. I tell you more about creating reports in Chapter 9.*

Not all of the numbers on your Net Worth report will interest a lender. They're interested primarily in cash, cars, real estate, investments, credit card balances, and other debt. If your home inventory values your T-shirt collection at $5,000, so what? T-shirts aren't easily exchanged for cash to make mortgage payments.

Debt Reduction

If all of your assets and liabilities have been recorded in Quicken and your net worth is a negative number, stop right here! No one (except maybe Big Louie) will loan you money, because too many others already have. Turn to Chapter 17, "Planning for the Future," where I cover saving money and reducing debt. You'll need to follow the advice and instructions there before you can even think about applying for a loan. You might also find Chapter 10, "Budgeting and Forecasting," helpful to get your spending under control.

Credit Report

A lender is also going to be very interested in your credit history. Credit reports are created and maintained by third-party credit monitoring organizations such as Experian, Equifax, and Trans Union. They know everything about your finances—sometimes even things that aren't true. Before you apply for a loan, you may want to see what a credit report says about you. If there are errors, you can get them fixed before someone uses them to form a bad opinion of you.

Quicken Deluxe users who have access to the Internet can obtain a free credit report as part of a trial offer from CreditCheck. Choose Online | To the Web | Credit Report to connect to the Internet and display a Web page that provides basic information about credit reports available to you and how you can obtain them (see Figure 15-1). Follow links to sign up for the trial program and get your credit report.

Getting Current Interest Rates

Before you can estimate the monthly payments on a loan, you need a good idea of what the current interest rates are. You have three ways to research this information: check the newspaper, call banks, or look it up on Quicken.com.

Caution   *Interest rates change often, sometimes on a daily basis. Although short-term variations are usually small, rates over a few weeks or months old usually aren't very accurate.*

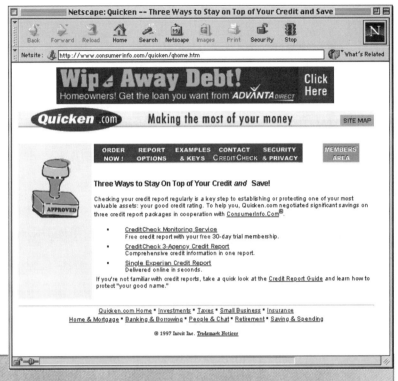

Figure 15-1 • This Web page provides information and links for getting a free credit report.

Checking a Recent Newspaper

Many banks and other lenders advertise their rates in the financial pages of the newspaper. Some newspapers summarize this information for you. For example, the big paper in my area, *The Arizona Republic*, has a weekly listing of organizations offering mortgages, complete with rates and phone numbers.

Checking with Local Banks

Get out the phone book and call a few banks in your area. Ask them what their rates are. Most banks will provide this information over the phone.

Looking Up Rates on Quicken.com

Quicken.com offers up-to-date rates on all kinds of loans. All you need is an Internet connection to check them for yourself.

Choose Online | To the Web | Bank Rates. Your computer connects to the Internet and displays the Banking & Credit Department main page (see Figure 15-2). You can find average rates for home equity, car, and personal loans right on that page.

For mortgage rates, click the Mortgages link on the left side of the Banking & Credit Department main page or, in Quicken, choose Online | To the Web | Mortgage Center. The QuickenMortgage home page appears (see Figure 15-3). Click the Quick Rates link on the left side of the page. Use the form that appears

Figure 15-2 • The Banking & Credit Department main page displays rates for many types of loans.

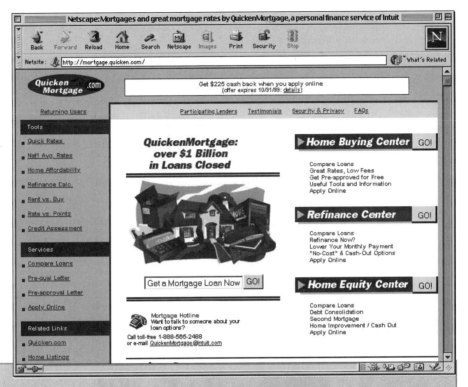

Figure 15-3 • The QuickenMortgage home page is a great place to visit when you want to buy or refinance a home.

to enter information about the home you plan to buy and the mortgage you will need. When you click the Calculate button, a list of lenders and loan terms, including the monthly mortgage payment amount, appears.

Calculating the Cost of a Loan

Once you have an idea of what the interest rate for a loan will be, you can use one of two different tools within Quicken to determine how much the loan will cost you.

Loan Calculator

Quicken's Loan Calculator can quickly calculate the principal or periodic payment for a loan. Choose Activities | Planning Calculators | Loan, or choose

Loan from the PlnClc button's menu near the top of the Planning tab. The Loan Calculator window appears:

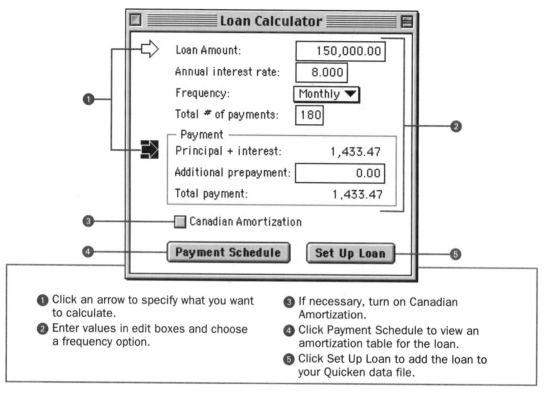

① Click an arrow to specify what you want to calculate.

② Enter values in edit boxes and choose a frequency option.

③ If necessary, turn on Canadian Amortization.

④ Click Payment Schedule to view an amortization table for the loan.

⑤ Click Set Up Loan to add the loan to your Quicken data file.

Begin by selecting one of the two calculation options:

- To calculate the amount of loan you can afford, click the arrow beside Loan Amount. Then you can enter an affordable monthly payment in the "Principal + interest" edit box.

- To calculate the periodic payment, click the arrow beside "Principal + interest." Then you can enter the amount of the loan in the Loan Amount edit box.

Enter values in the edit boxes. Be sure to choose the correct payment frequency from the Frequency pop-up menu. As you tab from field to field, the loan is calculated and recalculated. You can try different values to play "what-if" until you have a good idea of how the loan could work for you. With the information this provides, you should be able to tell whether you can afford the home or car you have your eye on; or, if you haven't started looking yet, it can tell you how much you can afford to spend.

You can use the two buttons at the bottom of the window to work with the loan entries:

- **Payment Schedule** displays an amortization table for the loan. It shows the amount of principal and interest paid for each payment, as well as the ending balance and accumulated interest paid. Here's an example:

	Principal	Interest	Prepayment	Balance	Total Interest
	8.000%			149,999.15	
1	433.48	999.99	0.00	149,565.67	999.99
2	436.37	997.10	0.00	149,129.30	1,997.09
3	439.27	994.20	0.00	148,690.03	2,991.29
4	442.20	991.27	0.00	148,247.83	3,982.56
5	445.15	988.32	0.00	147,802.68	4,970.88
6	448.12	985.35	0.00	147,354.56	5,956.23
7	451.11	982.36	0.00	146,903.45	6,938.59
8	454.11	979.36	0.00	146,449.34	7,917.95
9	457.14	976.33	0.00	145,992.20	8,894.28
10	460.19	973.28	0.00	145,532.01	9,867.56
11	463.26	970.21	0.00	145,068.75	10,837.77

- **Set Up Loan** displays the Set Up Loan window, which you can use to add the loan to your Quicken data file. I tell you how to use this window in Chapter 6.

SAVE MONEY   You can use the "Additional prepayment" edit box and Payment Schedule button to see how the loan's payment schedule would change if you made additional principal payments as part of each loan payment. To use this feature, enter a value in the "Additional prepayment" edit box; then click the Payment Schedule button. Scroll to the end of the payment schedule that appears to see the new last payment number and total interest paid. With the example used here, an additional $100 per month prepayment would reduce the loan's term by ten months and reduce total interest paid by $15,000.

Refinance Calculator

If you already own a home and are thinking about refinancing, you can try the Refinance Calculator. Choose Activities | Planning Calculators | Refinance, or choose Refinance from the PlnClc button's menu near the top of the Planning tab. The Refinance Calculator window appears:

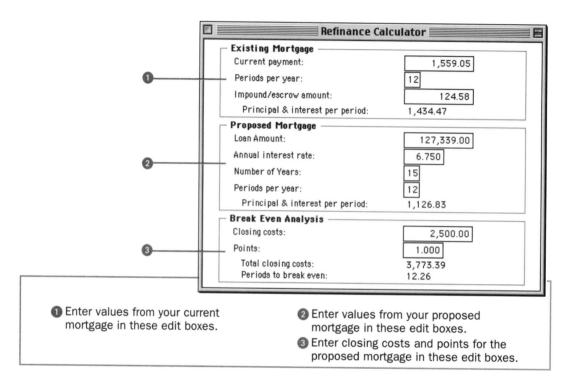

❶ Enter values from your current mortgage in these edit boxes.

❷ Enter values from your proposed mortgage in these edit boxes.

❸ Enter closing costs and points for the proposed mortgage in these edit boxes.

Enter values for your current mortgage and proposed mortgage in the edit boxes to calculate your monthly savings with the new mortgage. As you tab from field to field, Quicken calculates the results. If you enter closing costs and points for the proposed mortgage, you can even calculate how many months it will take to break even after paying these fees.

For example, in the previous illustration, refinancing the mortgage would save just over $300 a month. It would take just over a year to save enough to cover the refinancing costs. Based on this information, refinancing looks like a good idea.

Insurance Basics

Buying insurance can be baffling. Not only do you need to know what kinds of insurance are available, but you need to know which type you need, how much coverage you should have, and where you can get it.

In this section, I provide some basic information about insurance types and some of the terminology you need to know to understand what a policy covers.

Tip   *If you have access to the Internet, you can learn everything you need to know about insurance at the Insurance Basics pages of Quicken InsureMarket. Use your Web browser to visit* **http://www.insuremarket.com/basics/**.

GET SMARTER   Before you start shopping for insurance—whether you shop online via Quicken.com or by phone with a phone book—be sure you know the basic information about the type of insurance you want to buy. Understanding insurance options is the only way to be sure you are purchasing all the insurance coverage you need, without being sold extra coverage for the benefit of an insurance company or commissioned salesperson.

Types of Insurance

If you think insurance is limited to home, life, and auto, think again. Here's a quick rundown of the different types of insurance available today.

Auto Insurance

Auto insurance covers specific auto-related losses you may incur during the term of the insurance policy. Auto insurance can be broken down into several parts:

- **Liability insurance**, which is required by law in most states, covers injuries or damage to others or their property. Many insurance advisors recommend that you carry enough liability insurance to protect all of your assets in the event of a lawsuit. This is usually much more than the minimum required by law.

- **Collision insurance** covers damage to your car when the damage results from colliding with another car or object or overturning your car. Although this coverage is not required by law, it is usually required by a lender if the car is purchased with an auto loan.

- **Comprehensive insurance** covers damage to your car when the damage results from causes other than a collision—for example, theft, hail, fire, flood, or vandalism. Although this coverage is not required by law, it is usually required by a lender if the car is purchased with an auto loan.
- **Uninsured and underinsured motorist insurance** covers injury or damage to you, your passengers, and your car in the event that your car is hit by someone who either doesn't have any insurance or doesn't have enough insurance to cover the cost of the accident.
- **Medical payments insurance** covers you and your passengers for reasonable medical (and funeral) expenses incurred as a result of an accident.

Auto insurance rates are affected by where you live, drive, and park your car; the make and model of your car; your age; and your driving record. Many insurance companies offer discounts for good drivers and multiple policies within the same household.

Home Insurance

Home insurance covers financial losses caused by theft, storms, fires, and other similar occurrences that could cause loss or damage to your home and property. It also covers damages resulting from injuries to other people for which you are held legally responsible.

There are different types of home insurance:

- **Homeowner's insurance** covers a house and the homeowner's property, including the house itself, other structures on the property, personal property within the house or on the property, and liability lawsuits brought against the homeowner for injuries sustained on the property.
- **Renters insurance** covers the personal property of someone renting a home or apartment.
- **Condo or co-op insurance** covers the homeowner's personal property and liability lawsuits brought against the homeowner for injuries sustained within the condo or co-op.

Home insurance rates are affected by the value of your home, the location of your home, the year your home was built, and the proximity of your home to a fire hydrant or fire station.

Life Insurance

Life insurance is money that an insurance company pays to your named beneficiary when you die. There are several types of life insurance:

- **Term life** pays a specific lump-sum amount to your beneficiary when you die. A term life policy is designed specifically to protect your family by providing money to replace your salary and cover the cost of your funeral.
- **Cash value policies**, such as whole life, variable life, universal life, and universal variable life pay a specific lump-sum amount to your beneficiary when you die. But they also build a cash value account that you can use for noninsurance purposes while you're alive.

Annuities

An *annuity* is a contract between you and an insurance company in which you pay a premium and, in return, the insurance company promises to make benefit payments to you or to another named beneficiary. This is usually done through the use of investments managed by the insurance company.

Annuities can be classified by the timing of the benefit payments and how the annuity earnings accumulate:

Immediate Versus Deferred Annuities   An *immediate* annuity begins paying you benefits within one month to one year of its purchase. A *deferred* annuity accumulates earnings over a period of time, and then begins paying you benefits after a specific date—typically a retirement date.

Fixed Versus Variable Annuities   A *fixed* annuity guarantees a fixed rate of return for a specific time period. A *variable* annuity pays a return that varies based on the performance of the investments you select.

Business Continuation Insurance

Business continuation insurance protects your company from financial loss caused by the death or the long-term disability of a key employee. There are three types:

- **Business overhead expense (BOE) insurance** pays business overhead expenses, such as rent, salaries, and utilities, while a business owner is disabled.
- **Key person disability insurance** protects your company while a key employee is disabled.
- **Key person life insurance** covers the cost of losses due to the death of a key employee.

Disability Income Insurance

Disability income insurance covers a percentage of your lost income if you cannot work or perform the duties required by your occupation because you are disabled. The coverage and rates for disability income insurance vary depending on the broadness of the coverage and the amount of benefits to be paid.

Long-Term Care Insurance

Long-term care insurance covers the cost of long-term care, which includes custodial care, to help with the activities of daily life, whether at home or in a nursing home.

Medical Insurance

Medical or health insurance covers the cost of medical care. There are three different types:

- **Employer-provided medical insurance** is usually subsidized by your employer, making it more cost-effective than individual medical insurance. Medical plans vary from one provider and company to another.
- **Individual medical insurance** is available directly from insurance companies for individuals. This is often the only option for nonworking or self-employed individuals and their families.
- **Medicare** Part A coverage provides mandatory basic hospitalization for all U.S. citizens over the age of 65. An additional voluntary program (Part B) provides coverage for doctor bills at a monthly cost. Medicare usually covers only 50% of the average senior citizen's health care bills and can be supplemented with Medigap insurance.

Umbrella Liability Insurance

Umbrella liability insurance may indeed cover you for injuring someone with your umbrella. But that's not its only purpose. It covers injuries to other people or damage to their property for which you are legally responsible. It's an expansion of the basic liability coverage of your auto and home insurance.

Insurance Terminology

Part of what makes buying insurance so tough sometimes is the terminology used to describe policy terms. Here are a few of the terms you should know when researching insurance policies.

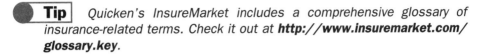

Tip *Quicken's InsureMarket includes a comprehensive glossary of insurance-related terms. Check it out at **http://www.insuremarket.com/ glossary.key**.*

Premium A *premium* is the amount paid for an insurance policy. Premiums may be paid annually, semi-annually, quarterly, or on some other payment plan.

Binder A *binder* is a temporary insurance policy issued while the paperwork on the permanent policy is being processed.

Renewal A *renewal* is either a new policy or a document from the insurance company stating that the terms and conditions of your old policy remain in effect for a specific period of time.

Claim A *claim* is your request for reimbursement at the loss of insured property. You file a claim with your insurance company after a loss has occurred.

Floater A *floater* is a type of insurance policy that covers moveable property, such as jewelry.

Endorsement An *endorsement* is an amendment to an insurance policy that changes its terms.

Named Perils *Named perils* are specific dangers that a policy insures you against. These dangers are named in the insurance policy. For example, a homeowner's policy might include the following named perils: fire, hail, and wind.

Exclusion An *exclusion* is an insurance policy provision that denies coverage for a certain type of loss. For example, flood damage is often excluded from homeowner's insurance policies. (If you live in an area prone to flooding, you can get flood insurance through the U.S. government.)

Limit A *limit* is the maximum amount a policy will pay on a covered loss. For example, if you have a $3,000 limit and the loss is $5,000, your insurance company will pay only $3,000.

Deductible A *deductible* is the amount of out-of-pocket expenses you have to pay before an insurance company begins paying on a covered loss. For example, if your car has $1,500 worth of covered damages and your deductible is $500, you pay $500 and the insurance company pays $1,000. If you have only $300 worth of covered damages, you pay the whole thing. In most cases, raising your deductible will lower your insurance premium.

Appraisal   An *appraisal* is an evaluation of the value of the property you want to insure when you buy insurance or the amount of loss when you file a claim for covered property.

Depreciation   *Depreciation* is the amount of money deducted from the value of an item to account for age and use. For example, if you paid $15,000 for your car four years ago, it may be worth only $9,000 today. The $6,000 difference is depreciation.

Replacement Value   *Replacement value* is the amount it would cost to replace or rebuild a covered item based on current market prices. For example, the replacement cost of a three-year-old stereo system would be the amount it would cost to buy a comparable stereo system today.

Actual Cash Value   *Actual cash value* is the amount you originally paid for an item minus the item's depreciation.

No-Fault Insurance   *No-fault insurance* covers the cost of repairs and medical expenses for minor accidents, regardless of who caused the accident. No-fault insurance helps speed up the insurance process and lowers insurance costs, but may limit the right to sue for damages.

Quicken.com Resources

The mother lode of information about buying a home, car, or insurance is the Quicken.com Web site. You can find links to useful tools and information in at least three departments: Home & Mortgage (or QuickenMortgage.com), Banking & Credit, and Insurance.

Here's a brief overview of some of the things I think are useful in these three departments.

> **Note** | *Like everything else on the Internet, the contents of Quicken.com Web pages can change daily. Don't be surprised if the features you find don't match the ones shown in the figures throughout this chapter.*

 SAVE TIME   Don't use Internet search engines to find sites for loan and insurance information. Instead, follow the links on the Quicken.com Home & Mortgage, Banking & Credit, and Insurance Department pages. These sites are prescreened for value so you don't waste time.

Home & Mortgage

The Home & Mortgage Department, which is also known as QuickenMortgage.com (refer to Figure 15-3), offers a wealth of information about buying or refinancing a home or obtaining a home equity loan for the home you already own. To go to this page, click the Home & Mortgage link on the Quicken.com home page or, within Quicken, choose Online | To the Web | Mortgage Center.

Here are the links I find most useful:

Tools   In addition to the Quick Rates feature, which I discuss earlier in this chapter, the Tools area on the left side of the page includes links you can use to evaluate the affordability of a home, make a rent versus buy decision, and understand how rates and points work.

Loan Services   A number of loan services, also listed along the left side of the page, make it possible to compare loan terms, get a pre-approval letter, and apply for a loan online.

Home Listings   The Home Listings link takes you to Realtor.com, where you can find real estate listings for any part of the country. Use this feature to start your search for a new home.

Mortgage Glossary   The Mortgage Glossary link takes you to a glossary of mortgage terms. Use this link to decipher the information you get when you shop for a mortgage online or call a lender.

Banking & Credit

The Banking & Credit Department (refer to Figure 15-2) offers links to information about the world of banking and borrowing money. This area is especially useful for learning about auto loans and other types of financing. To open this window, click the Banking & Credit link in the Quicken home page or, within Quicken, choose Online | To the Web | Bank Rates.

Here are a few of the links I find very helpful:

Loans   The Loans link displays national average loan rates as well as links to articles and other information about borrowing money.

QuickAnswers   The QuickAnswers area offers links that answer questions you may have about banking and borrowing money. Click a question to learn its answer. In some cases, you'll be prompted to enter information about your financial situation so Quicken.com can calculate an exact answer for you.

Interactive Tools   The Interactive Tools area offers links to a number of Quicken.com tools you can use to learn more about applying for a loan, working with credit reports, and reducing your debt.

Insurance

The Insurance Department offers links to tools and information on Quicken InsureMarket that you can use to research and shop for insurance. To open the Insurance Department's main page (see Figure 15-4), click the Insurance link in the Quicken.com home page. To open InsureMarket's main page (see Figure 15-5), from within Quicken, choose Online | Go to Web | Insurance Center.

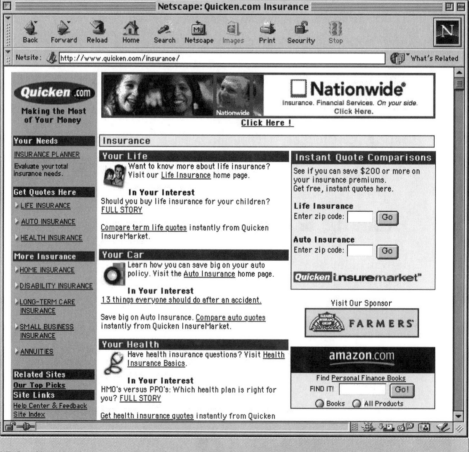

Figure 15-4 • Use the Insurance Department on Quicken.com to learn more about and shop for insurance.

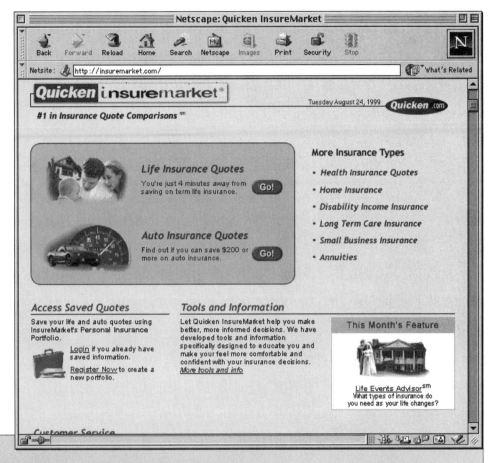

Figure 15-5 • Use InsureMarket's main page to learn more about insurance and get insurance rate quotes.

Here are some links on the Insurance Department's main page that I find very useful:

Insurance Planner   The Insurance Planner link takes you to InsureMarket's interactive Insurance Planner. This feature asks questions about you and your health, job, home, and automobiles. You'll spend about ten minutes answering questions, and then learn about the types of insurance you need.

Get Quotes Here   The Get Quotes Here area offers links to Quicken InsureMarket for obtaining rate quotes on life, auto, and health insurance. Use this feature to start shopping for insurance online.

GET SMARTER Two worksheets at the end of this chapter help you compare the costs and benefits of insurance policies: the Term Life Insurance Worksheet and the Auto Insurance Worksheet. Use these worksheets to take notes about the policies you research. They'll help you compare apples to apples to see which policy comes out on top.

Planning Tools   Links in the Planning Tools area display interactive features for learning more about insurance and your insurance needs. These tools include the Insurance Planner, Auto Risk Evaluator, Life Events Advisor, Family Needs Planner, and Annuities.

Worksheets

Use the following worksheets to help you compare and evaluate different loans, mortgages, and insurance policies.

Loan Comparison Worksheet			
Basic Information			
Instructions: Enter information for each loan, one per column.			
Lender Name			
Contact Name			
Phone Number			
Comments			
Amount of Loan			
Rates and Fees			
Instructions: Enter rate and fee values for each loan.			
Application Fee			
Other Fees			
Term (in months)			
Annual Interest Rate			
Payment Calculations			
Instructions: Calculate the monthly payments. Use the Loan Calculator within Quicken for accuracy (choose Activities I Planning Calculators I Loan). Then calculate the total of all payments and fees.			
Monthly Payment			
Total Payments (monthly payment × number of months)			
Total Payments Plus Fees			

Mortgage Comparison Worksheet (page 1)

Basic Information

Instructions: Enter information for each mortgage, one per column. Note: You can get most of this information from the Good Faith Estimate the lender should provide.

Lender Name			
Contact Name			
Phone Number			
Comments			

Purchase Price and Down Payment Information

Instructions: Enter the purchase price, down payment, and loan amount for each mortgage. For the best comparison, these should be the same.

Purchase Price						
Down Payment	%	$	%	$	%	$

Basic Loan Information

Instructions: Enter values for each mortgage. Then calculate monthly payments. Use the Loan Calculator within Quicken for accuracy (choose Activities I Planning Calculators I Loan). Total the monthly payments for the life of the mortgage.

Annual Interest Rate						
Term (in years)						
Fixed or Variable						
If Variable, Adjustment Period and Cap	Period	Cap	Period	Cap	Period	Cap
Monthly Payments						
Total Monthly Payments (Term × 12 × Monthly Payments)						

Mortgage Comparison Worksheet (page 2)						

Closing Costs

Instructions: Enter expected closing costs for each loan. Do not include prepaid amounts that are due at closing. Not all of these fees may apply; use space at the bottom of this section to enter other fees not listed here.

Origination Fee	%	$		%	$		%	$
Discount Fee (Points)	%	$		%	$		%	$
Credit Report Fee						
Lenders Inspection Fee						
Tax Service Fee						
Application Fee						
Underwriting Fee						
Courier Fee						
Settlement Fee						
Document Preparation Fee						
Notary Fee						
Administration Fee						
Title Insurance Fee						
Recording Fee						
City/County Tax Stamps						
State Tax Stamps						
Recordation Tax						

Mortgage Comparison Worksheet (page 3)			
Loan Program Fee			
Pest Inspection Fee			
Final Inspection Fee			
Total Closing Costs	$	$	$

Total Mortgage Costs

Instructions: Add the Total Monthly Payments to the Total Closing Costs to arrive at the total cost of each mortgage.

Total Mortgage Costs	$	$	$

Term Life Insurance Worksheet			

Basic Information

Instructions: Enter information and values for each policy, one per column.

Company Name			
Agent Name			
Phone Number			
Policy Name			
Coverage Amount			
Annual Premium			
Comments			

Features and Options

Instructions: Check off the features and options included with each policy. If a feature or option is not included, leave the space blank. If it is available as an option for which you must pay more, enter an O (for option) or the additional amount you must pay. You can enter additional features and options at the bottom of the form.

Guaranteed Level Premium			
Guaranteed Renewable			
Guaranteed Convertible			
Accelerated Death Benefit			
Disability Waiver Option			
Accidental Death Option			
Child Rider			
Other Insured Option			

Auto Insurance Worksheet (page 1)					

Basic Information

Instructions: Enter information for each policy, one per column.

Company Name			
Agent Name			
Phone Number			
Comments			

Coverage and Cost

Instructions: Enter the limits and/or deductibles for each category of coverage in one column and the corresponding premium cost in the other. You can enter additional coverage options at the bottom of the section. Be sure to subtotal the Premiums column.

Standard Coverage	Limits or Deductibles	Premiums	Limits or Deductibles	Premiums	Limits or Deductibles	Premiums
Bodily Injury Liability		$		$		$
Property Damage Liability						
Medical Payments						
Personal Injury Protection						
Uninsured/ Underinsured Motorist: • Bodily Injury • Property Damage						
Comprehensive						
Collision						

Auto Insurance Worksheet (page 2)						
Additional Coverage Options	Limits or Deductibles	Premiums	Limits or Deductibles	Premiums	Limits or Deductibles	Premiums
Rental Reimbursement		$		$		$
Towing/ Labor						
Emergency Road Service						
Electronic Equipment Protection						
Sound Reproducing/ Tapes and Compact Disks						
Auto Loan/ Lease Gap						
Premium Total	$		$		$	

Auto Insurance Worksheet (page 3)			

Discounts

Instructions: Enter discounts offered by each insurance company. You can enter additional discounts at the bottom of the section. Be sure to total the discounts.

Multi-policy	$	$	$
Multi-car Coverage			
Safety Equipment			
Good Driver			
Anti-Lock Brakes			
Anti-Theft System			
Driver Training			
Discount Total	$	$	

Policy Cost

Instructions: Subtract the discount total from the premium total to arrive at the total cost of the policy with the options you selected.

Policy Cost	$	$	$

Maximizing Investment Returns

In This Chapter:

- *Types of Investments*

- *Investment Considerations*

- *Tips for Getting Started*

- *Researching Securities Online*

- *Quicken.com Resources*

If you're good at managing your finances, you probably have a little left over every month. If you're concerned about risk and don't mind relatively low returns, the savings accounts and certificates of deposit offered by your local bank may be just the place for your money. But if you don't mind a little risk for the possibility of greater financial rewards, there's a good chance you've discovered Wall Street and investing.

In this chapter, I provide some basic information about investing, as well as what you can do to get started. I also tell you about the tools within Quicken and on Quicken.com that can help you research your investments to make smart financial decisions.

Tip   *If you think Wall Street and its risks are just for high rollers, skip this chapter for now and move ahead to Chapter 17. That's where I tell you about savings and the types of low-risk accounts you can open with your local bank.*

Investment Basics

An investment is a security you purchase with the hope that it rises in value, and pays you interest or a dividend, or both. Investments differ from savings in several ways:

- An investment is somewhat more difficult to redeem for cash, thus making it less liquid.
- An investment's value varies depending on the market—what another investor is willing to pay for it—thus giving it the potential to be worth far more (or less) than you paid for it.
- An investment is not insured against loss, thus making it more risky.

In this section, I provide the information you need to understand what investments are available, what you need to know before deciding on a specific investment type, and the things you can do to get started as an investor.

Types of Investments

There are many types of investments and each one has its pros and cons. Following is a summary of the most common types of investments.

Money Market Funds

A *money market fund* or *account* is an investment in short-term debt instruments such as certificates of deposit, commercial paper, banker's acceptances, treasury bills, and discount notes. Although you can open a money market account with your local bank, it is not insured by the FDIC (Federal Deposit Insurance Corporation) as are most other bank accounts. The rate of return and value is not guaranteed. Money market funds earn income for investors by paying dividends.

Treasury Bills

A *Treasury bill* (or *T-bill*) is a short-term government security, sold through the Federal Reserve Bank by competitive bidding. T-bills are the most widely used of all government debt securities. They are backed by the full faith and credit of the U.S. government. T-bills earn money for investors by paying interest.

Stocks

A *stock* is part ownership of a corporation. Sold as shares through stock exchanges throughout the world (as well as privately, in the case of private corporations), their market values fluctuate daily. Thousands or millions of shares of any given stock can change hands each day. Stocks earn money for investors by paying dividends or rising in value.

Bonds

A *bond* is essentially a loan made by the investor to a company or government entity. Bonds earn money for investors by paying interest. The actual interest rate paid often depends on the stated interest rate and the purchase price of the bond.

Mutual Funds

A *mutual fund* is a group of securities held by a group of investors. When you invest in a mutual fund, your investment dollars are pooled with other investors. A fund manager buys and sells securities to maximize the fund's return. Mutual funds earn money for investors by paying dividends (which can often be automatically reinvested in the fund) or rising in value. In return for his or her services, the fund manager is paid a fee. Other fees may include *loads,* which can be applied when you invest or sell mutual fund shares.

There are thousands of mutual funds, each with its own "mix" of investment types. Investors—especially novice investors—find mutual funds attractive because an investment professional can make decisions for them.

Investment Considerations

When evaluating an investment, you should consider several important factors: return, risk, goal, and taxability.

Return

An investment's *return* is what it earns for the investor. Most investments earn money by paying interest, paying dividends, or rising in value.

Interest   *Interest* is a rate applied to the face or par value of a security that is then paid to the investor in cash. Treasury bills and bonds pay interest. Money market accounts pay dividends, although amounts are calculated like interest and often referred to as interest on bank statements.

Dividends   *Dividends* are per-share payments to shareholders. There are two types: cash and stock.

- **Cash dividends** pay a certain cash amount per share to each stockholder. For example, a $1 per share cash dividend pays each stockholder $1 for each share held. Cash dividends are normally paid by large companies; smaller companies need cash to grow.
- **Stock dividends** pay a certain number of stock shares per share to each stockholder. A stock split is a type of stock dividend. For example, a 2-for-1 stock split doubles the number of shares each stockholder owns. Although this cuts the per-share value in half, the value is expected to rise again over time.

Capital Gains   A stock's price indicates what another investor is willing to pay for it. When the stock's price is higher than what you paid, you have a gain on your investment. When the stock's price is lower than what you paid, you have a loss on your investment. A capital gain (or loss) can be realized or unrealized:

- **Realized gains (or losses)** are the gains or losses you can record when you sell an investment. If an investment is taxable, the realized gain or loss must be reported on your tax return.
- **Unrealized gains (or losses)** are the gains or losses based on your purchase price and the current market value for investments you have not yet sold. Because the investment has not been sold, the gain is not realized and does not have to be reported on your tax return.

Risk

Risk is your chance of making or losing money on an investment. Although all investments have some element of risk involved, some investments are more conservative (less risky) than others.

There is a direct relationship between risk and return. The higher the potential return, the higher the risk. The lower the risk, the lower the potential return. For example, money market accounts and one-year T-bills are considered relatively conservative investments. On June 29, 1999, they earned an average of 3.05% and 5.5%, respectively. Stocks, on the other hand, are considered more risky. On June 29, 1999, the rates of return for a one-year investment in Intuit, Compaq, and Apple were 43.86%, 20.04%, and 58.17%, respectively. As these examples show, you can make more money in the stock market, but you can also lose some.

Caution *These examples are for illustrative purposes only. Exact accuracy is not guaranteed. I am neither recommending nor advising against an investment in any of these securities.*

Goal

Goal refers to your goal as an investor. You should choose an investment based on its ability to meet your goals. There are two main goals: income and growth.

- **Income investments** generate income for investors in the form of dividends and interest. Investors get regular cash payments. Income investments are popular with investors who are retired and living on fixed incomes. Income investments include money market accounts, T-bills, bonds, stocks of larger ("blue chip") companies, and some mutual funds.
- **Growth investments** grow in market value. Growth investments are popular with younger people who want to build a "nest egg" for their later years. Growth investments include stocks of smaller companies and some mutual funds.

Taxability

The *taxability* of an investment refers to how it is taxed. This matters most to individuals in high tax brackets. Generally speaking, investments fall into three categories: taxable, nontaxable, and tax-deferred:

- **Taxable investments** are fully taxed by the federal and local government. You must report and pay taxes on interest and dividend income, as well as capital gains. Capital losses can be deducted from income (within certain limitations) to reduce your tax bill. Visit the Taxes Department on Quicken.com or talk to your tax advisor for more information.

- **Nontaxable investments** are not taxed by the federal government. They may, however, be taxed by local governments such as your state government. Examples of nontaxable investments include municipal bonds.

- **Tax-deferred investments** are investments for which income is not taxed until it is withdrawn. An example is an investment set up as a tax-deferred annuity. In this case, you invest as much as you like. Income, when earned, is automatically reinvested into the account but is not taxed at that time. The value of the account continues to grow. When you're 59½ years old, you can begin withdrawing money from the account. Income on the investment is taxed then, when you're likely to be in a lower tax bracket.

Getting Started

If you've never invested money before, the following sections outline some things you might want to consider doing to get started on the right track.

Doing Your Research

Would you go grocery shopping blindfolded? Groping around on the shelves for beef stew, only to wind up with dog food? Poking meat packages for porterhouse steak, only to wind up with bacon ends?

Investing without research is like shopping blindfolded. You spend money but don't know what you've purchased until it's paid for. Even then, you may not know—until it's too late and you've lost money.

The Research Security feature and Investments Department on Quicken.com offers literally hundreds of resources you can tap into to get almost any information you can imagine about a company. Even if you don't know where to start, these features can help you search for stocks and mutual funds that meet criteria you specify. You can get news, price histories, and ratings. You can get financial results. You can even participate in message boards to see what other investors think is hot.

If you're not sure what you should be looking for, the Research Security feature and Investments Department can help, too. They offer links to basic information that goes far beyond the basics I provided at the beginning of this chapter. Spend a few hours learning about the types of investments that interest you. Then check out the individual investments themselves. Gather information before you make a decision.

Remember, it's your money. Put it where it'll work hardest for you.

Finding a Broker

If you decide to invest in stocks and bonds, you need a broker. (It's a lot cheaper than buying a seat on the stock exchange.) A stockbroker or brokerage firm can handle the purchases and sales of securities. Nowadays, there are three kinds of brokers:

- **Full-service brokers** can buy and sell securities for you, based on your instructions. But these people also research investments for you and tell you about the ones they think are hot. They also keep an eye on the securities you own and tell you when they think one of them may lose value. Based on their recommendations, you can buy or sell. Fees for full-service brokers are higher than any other—a typical stock purchase or sale could cost well over $100 in commissions. But you're getting more service for your money—you're paying someone to do investment research for you. If you decide to use a full-service broker, track his or her performance carefully; if your broker is not meeting your expectations, you might want to find another broker.
- **Discount brokers** can buy and sell securities for you, too. They usually don't offer any advice, though. They're much cheaper than full-service brokers—a typical stock purchase or sale could be $25 to $60.
- **Deep discount brokers** can also buy and sell securities for you. They don't offer advice either. They're dirt cheap—I've seen fees as low as $8 per trade.

You have two main ways to contact your broker to buy or sell stock:

- **Telephone trading** enables you to give buy or sell instructions by phone, either by speaking to someone at the brokerage firm or by entering information using your telephone keypad.
- **Online trading** enables you to enter buy or sell instructions using your computer and Internet connection. This is fast, convenient, and cheap. In fact, companies that offer both telephone and online trading usually offer online trading for less money.

Tip   *I've been using online trading for over two years now and I'm very happy with it. I can do more trades for less money. My brokerage firm can process orders within 60 seconds of receiving them. They even allow me to trade on margin—that's the brokerage term for "credit"—and pay interest on any cash balance in my account!*

If you're interested in telephone trading, you can find a broker the same way you'd find a bank: ask your friends or check your local phone book. Or ask your bank—some banks offer brokerage services or are connected with brokerage firms. You can also find broker information on Quicken.com.

If you're interested in online trading, your first stop should be Quicken.com. It provides information and links to a number of online brokerage firms. See what each one has to offer and select the one with the best deal for you.

 GET SMARTER   When shopping for a broker, use the Broker Comparison Worksheet at the end of this chapter to take notes about and compare different services and fees.

Getting Advice from a Pro

If you don't want a full-service broker but you do want investment advice, find a financial advisor. Many banks have financial advisors on staff and they can usually provide good, objective advice about investing. They often even handle investment transactions for you (which really makes them a full-service broker).

The trick (I think) is finding an advisor who is objective. Most of the ones I've spoken to deal only with certain types of investments or certain fund families. While these might be great investments, the fact that the advisor doesn't even deal with others makes me wonder how objective he or she can be.

Quicken.com also offers information and links for finding a financial advisor. If you can't get a good recommendation from a knowledgeable friend, be sure to tap into Quicken.com's online resources to see what's out there.

Remember to Diversify!

I'm not a financial planner and, in this lawsuit-crazy era we live in, I don't like to give advice. But here's a one-word piece of advice I must share, one that can help minimize your investment risks: *diversify*.

I can explain with my version of an old story. Farmer Joe has chickens. Every day, he takes a wicker basket to the hen house and collects the eggs. One day, on his way back from the hen house, the basket breaks, dropping the eggs all over the farmyard. As you can imagine, almost every egg breaks. That day, Farmer Joe learned the hard way that he should never put all of his eggs in one basket.

The eggs and basket story applies to your finances, too. If all your investment dollars are in one security and that security fails, you're liable to lose a lot of money. Now take that a step further. If all your investment dollars are in the stock market and the stock market takes a turn for the worse, you're also liable to lose money.

I'm not saying that you shouldn't have "favorite" investments or that you shouldn't invest in the stock market. I'm saying that you should spread your investment dollars among multiple securities and types of investments. If you don't put your eggs in one basket, you can't lose them all.

Checking Investment Performance

Quicken offers a number of reports and graphs you can use to check on the performance of your investments. Although I cover reports and graphs in Chapter 9, here's a closer look at the reports and graphs that you can use to monitor your investment performance and become a better investor.

Reports

To create an investment report, begin by opening the Reports window. Choose Activities | Reports & Graphs | Reports, or click the Reports button near the top of the Reporting tab. In the Reports window that appears, click the Investment tab to display its options:

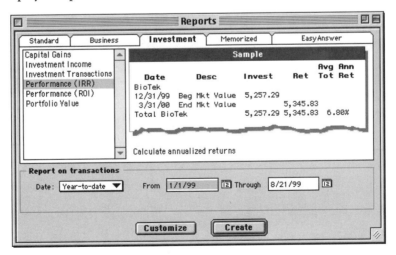

Here's a quick rundown of the reports you can access from this window:

- **Capital Gains** reports capital gains (and losses) from the sale of investment securities for a specific period. The report includes the security name, number of shares, purchase and sale dates, selling price, basis, and gain or loss.
- **Investment Income** displays the income and expenses from investments during a specific period.
- **Investment Transactions** provides a summary of all investment-related transactions for a specific period. The report includes the date, account, action, security name, category, price, number of shares, commission, cash amount, investment value, and net transaction value for each transaction.
- **Performance (IRR)** (see Figure 16-1) provides the internal rate of return of investments during a specific period. The report includes dates, actions, transaction descriptions, investments, returns, and average annual return on

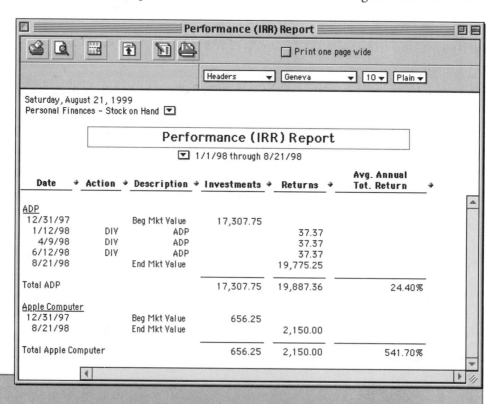

Figure 16-1 • A Performance (IRR) Report shows investment performance with an annualized internal rate of return.

investment. This report offers a good way to compare the performance of one security to another.

- **Performance (ROI)** provides the return on investment during a specific period. The report includes dates, accounts, actions, transaction descriptions, investments, returns, and total return on investment.

- **Portfolio Value Report** provides the value of your investment portfolio on a specific date. The report includes the security name, number of shares, current price, cost basis, unrealized gain or loss, and balance for each security in your portfolio.

Graphs

You can create an investment graph from within the Graphs window. Choose Activities | Reports & Graphs | Graphs, or click the Graphs button near the top of the Reporting tab. The window looks like this:

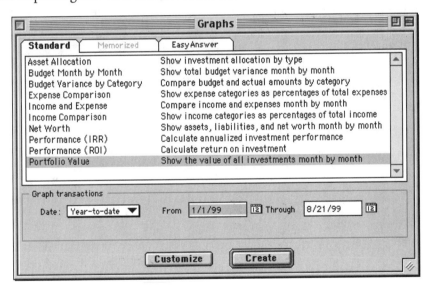

There are three investment graphs to choose from:

- **Performance (IRR)** shows the annualized internal rate of return for each of the securities in your portfolio during a period you specify.

- **Performance (ROI)** shows the return on investment for each of the securities in your portfolio during the period you specify.
- **Portfolio Value** (see Figure 16-2) uses a stacked column chart to show the total value of your portfolio's investments for each month in the period you specify.

Research Security

The Research Security feature offers quick access to information about stocks and mutual funds. This information is on Quicken.com, so you need Internet access to use this feature.

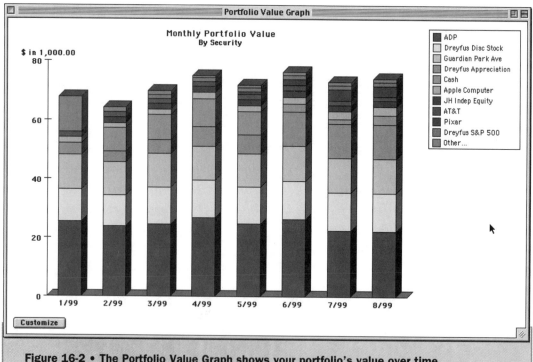

Figure 16-2 • The Portfolio Value Graph shows your portfolio's value over time.

Getting Started

Choose Online | Research Security, or click the Research button near the top of the Investing tab. The tiny Research Security dialog box appears:

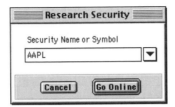

Enter a security name or ticker symbol in the edit box, or choose one of the securities in your Quicken data file from the menu. Then click Go Online. Quicken connects to the Internet and displays the Quotes page for the security (see Figure 16-3).

Viewing Security Information

As shown in Figure 16-3, the Research Security feature displays the Full Quote screen for the security you are researching. You can click links along the left side of the Web page to view other information:

- **Quote** (see Figure 16-3) shows current price information (delayed approximately 20 minutes), trading volume, a number of ratios, and recent headline links.
- **Chart** displays a one-year chart of closing prices for the security. You can use menus in the chart window to modify the chart's display.
- **Intraday Chart** displays a chart of security prices for the current day.
- **News** displays news headlines for the security. Click a headline to read the story.
- **Evaluator** displays a wide variety of performance and other evaluation information for the security.

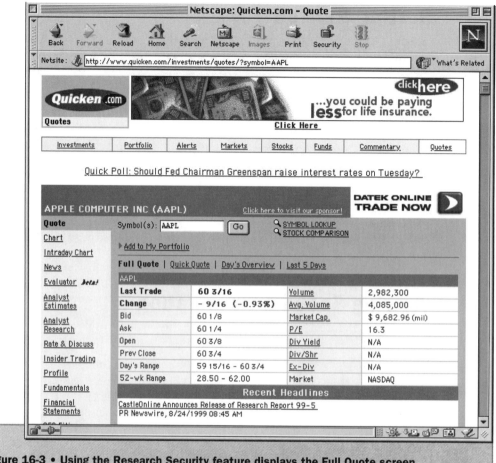

Figure 16-3 • Using the Research Security feature displays the Full Quote screen for a security.

- **Analyst Estimates** displays analysts' ratings and estimates of earnings per share for the security.
- **Analyst Research** displays links to free and for-purchase reports prepared by analysts about the security.
- **Rate & Discuss** displays ratings and recent message board subjects for the security. These ratings and messages are submitted by Quicken.com Investment Department message board participants. Click a message board subject to read the messages.
- **Insider Trading** displays a list of the security trades conducted by company insiders.

- **Profile** displays a concise summary of the security, including contact information, exchange, sector, and business description.
- **Fundamentals** displays share information, valuation, growth rates, financial strength, and management effectiveness ratios. You may find this information helpful when evaluating the security or comparing it to a similar security.
- **Financial Statements** displays four years' worth of annual financial statement summaries for the security.
- **SEC Filings** displays a list of forms filed with the SEC by the company.

Quicken.com Resources

The Research Security feature is part of Quicken.com's investment resources. A small part. There's a lot more where that came from in the Investments Department.

Choose Online | To the Web | Investing Center. If necessary, Quicken launches your Web browser and connects to the Internet. The Investments Department main page appears, as shown in Figure 16-4.

Here's a quick look at some of the features I think are very useful in the Investments Department.

Note *Like everything else on the Internet, the contents of the Quicken.com Web pages can change daily. Don't be surprised if the features you find don't match the ones shown in this chapter.*

Quotes and Research   The Quotes and Research form on the Investments main page offers another way to get to the information available in the Research Security feature discussed earlier in this chapter. Enter a ticker symbol in the text box, select a view option, and click Go. The requested information for the security you specified appears in the Web browser window.

Mutual Fund Finder   There are thousands of mutual funds out there. How do you find the one that's best for you? The Mutual Fund Finder (see Figure 16-5) is a good start. It offers a variety of ways you can search for funds that match your criteria. To access this feature, click the Find Top Funds link in the Investments Department main page (see Figure 16-4). From within Quicken, you can choose Online | To the Web | Mutual Fund Finder or click the MutFund button near the top of the Investing tab. Follow instructions within the window to perform your search and get information about funds.

Your Portfolio and Mini Portfolio   These two features display your portfolio on the Quicken.com Web site so you can monitor it when you're away from

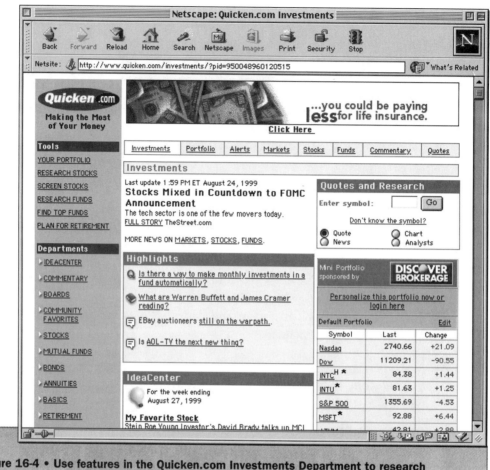

Figure 16-4 • Use features in the Quicken.com Investments Department to research investments.

Quicken. I like this feature because it automatically updates the prices of my stocks throughout the day, so I can see current values any time I like. The Mini Portfolio appears on the Investments main page (see Figure 16-4); you must click the Your Portfolio link in the navigation bar on that page to view the full portfolio page. To customize the portfolios so they show your investments (rather than the default investments), click the "Personalize this portfolio now or login here" link. Follow the instructions to set up a free Quicken.com account. Then click the Edit link in the Your Portfolio area of the Portfolio page to customize the portfolio.

QuickAnswers   QuickAnswers provides just that: quick answers to questions. For example, clicking the question "How much can I invest before taxes each year?"

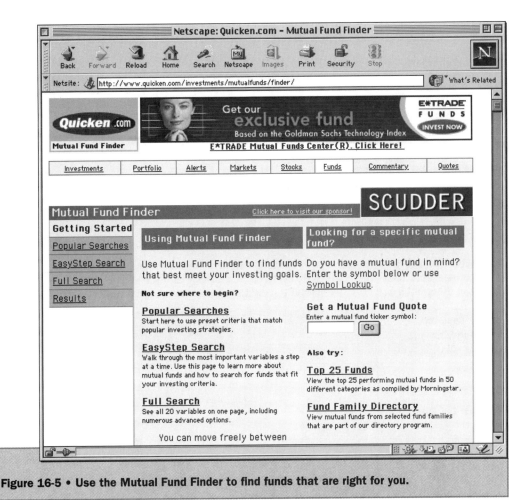

Figure 16-5 • Use the Mutual Fund Finder to find funds that are right for you.

provides information about IRAs, 401(k) plans, and other retirement accounts. It also provides links to related Quicken.com features and other questions.

Find a Broker   If you're looking for a stock broker, this link is a great place to start. It not only provides links to a number of online brokerage firms, but it offers information you might find useful when selecting a broker.

Worksheets

Use the following two worksheets to help you compare and evaluate brokerage firms and mutual funds.

Broker Comparison Worksheet (page 1)		
Basic Information		
Instructions: Enter information for each brokerage firm, one per column.		
Company Name			
Agent Name			
Phone Number			
Type of Brokerage Firm (circle one)	Full / Discount	Full / Discount	Full / Discount
Comments			
Trading Fees		
Instructions: Enter fees for each of the services listed. If fees vary based on the number of shares in the transaction, base the fee on 1,000 shares. If a service is not available, enter N/A. If a service is free, enter $0. Enter additional trading fees at the end of each section if necessary.		
Broker-assisted telephone trading		
Market Orders			
Limit Orders			
Options (per trade)			
Options (per contract)			
Bonds			
Treasury Bills			
Mutual Funds			
Touch-tone telephone trading		
Market Orders			
Limit Orders			
Options (per trade)			
Options (per contract)			
Bonds			
Treasury Bills			
Mutual Funds			

Broker Comparison Worksheet (page 2)			
Online Trading			
Market Orders			
Limit Orders			
Options (per trade)			
Options (per contract)			
Bonds			
Treasury Bills			
Mutual Funds			

Other Fees

Instructions: Enter fees for each of the services listed. Enter additional fees at the end of this section if necessary.

Real-time Quotes			
Return Check Fee			
Wire Transfer Fee			
Stock Certificate Issuance Fee			
Check Writing Fee			
Stock Transfer Fee			
Cash Transfer Fee			

Interest Rates

Instructions: Enter the interest rate charged or paid for the following items.

Margin Rates (for <$50,000)			
Account Cash Balance Rates			

Mutual Funds Comparison Worksheet			
Basic Information			
Instructions: Enter information for each fund, one per column.			
Family Name			
Phone Number			
Fund Name			
Ticker Symbol			
Manager Name			
Manager Tenure			
Category			
Goal			
Minimum Initial Purchase			
Comments			
Ratings			
Instructions: Enter ratings information from the fund's Morningstar profile.			
Stars			
Return			
Risk			
Returns			
Instructions: Enter the current average returns for each period listed. You can get this information from the fund's profile.			
3 Months			
Year to Date			
1 Year			
3 Years			
5 Years			
10 Years			
Fees			
Instructions: Enter values for the expense ratio and each of the fees charged by the fund.			
Expense Ratio			
Front Load			
Deferred Sales Charge			
Redemption Fee			
12b-1 Fee			

Planning for the Future

Chapter 17

To many people, the future is an unknown, a mystery. After all, who can say what will happen tomorrow, next year, or ten years from now? But if you think about your future, you can usually come up with a few events that you can plan for: your marriage, the purchase of a new home, the birth of your children (and their education years later), and your retirement. (These are just examples—everyone's life runs a slightly different course.) These events, as well as many unforeseen events, all have one thing in common: they affect your finances.

The best way to prepare for life events is to build up your savings. Saving money is an important part of financial management. Savings enable you to take vacations and make major purchases without increasing debt, help your kids through college, handle emergencies, and have a comfortable retirement.

In this chapter, I tell you about planning for future events and how tools within Quicken and on Quicken.com can help. I provide plenty of information about various savings and retirement accounts so you can learn about your savings options. If you're in debt and can't even think about saving until you dig your way out, this chapter can help you, too. It also covers Quicken tools for reducing your debt.

Tip *If you don't mind risk and want to earn higher income on your savings, consult Chapter 16. It discusses investments, including stocks, bonds, and mutual funds.*

Saving Basics

Remember when you got your first "piggy bank"? It may not have looked like a pig, but it had a slot for slipping in coins and, if you were lucky, a removable rubber plug on the bottom that made it easy to get the coins out when you needed them. Whoever gave you the bank was trying to teach you your first financial management lesson: saving money.

As an adult, things are a little more complex. In this section, I explain why you should save, provide some saving strategies, and tell you about the types of savings accounts that make your old piggy bank obsolete.

Why Save?

Most people save money so there's money to spend when they need it. Others save for a particular purpose. Still others save because they have so much they can't spend it all. Here's a closer look at why saving makes sense.

Saving for "Rainy Days"

When people say they are saving for a rainy day, they probably aren't talking about the weather. They're talking about bad times or emergencies—situations when they need extra cash.

For example, suppose the family car needs a new transmission. Or your beloved dog needs eye surgery. Or your daughter manages to break her violin three days before the big recital. In the "rainy day" scheme of things, these might be light drizzles. But your savings can help keep you dry.

Here are a few other examples. Suppose your employer goes bankrupt and closes up shop. Or after a three-martini lunch with a customer, you get back to the office, tell your boss what you really think of him, and quit on the spot. Or after being poked one too many times in the butt by a bull, you find it impossible to continue your career as a rodeo clown. If your paychecks stop coming, do you have enough savings to support yourself or your family until you can get another source of income? On the "rainy day" scale, this could be a torrential downpour. Your savings can be a good umbrella.

Saving for a Goal

Planning for your future often includes planning for events that affect your life—and your wallet. Saving money for specific events can help make these events memorable for what they are, rather than what they cost.

For example, take a recently engaged couple, Sally and Joe. They plan to marry within a year and buy a house right away. Within five years, they plan to have their first child. That's when Sally will leave her job to start the more demanding job of mother and homemaker. Someday, they hope their children will go to college and they want to help cover the expenses. They also want to be able to help pay for their children's weddings. Eventually, they'll retire. And throughout their lives, they want to be able to take annual family vacations, buy a new car every six years or so, and get season tickets for the Arizona Diamondbacks.

All of these things are major events in Sally and Joe's lives. Saving in advance for each of these events will make them possible—without going into debt.

Saving for Peace of Mind

Some people save money because events in their lives showed them the importance of having savings. Children who lived through the Depression or bad financial times for their families grew up to be adults who understand the value of money and try hard to keep some available. They don't want to repeat the hard times they went through. Having healthy savings accounts gives them peace of mind.

Saving Strategies

There are two main ways to save: when you can or regularly.

Saving When You Can   When money is tight, saving can be difficult. People who are serious about saving, however, will force themselves to save as much as possible when they can. Saving when you can is better than not saving at all.

Saving Regularly   A better way to save money is to save a set amount periodically. For example, save $25 every week or $200 every month. Timing this with your paycheck makes sense; you can make a split deposit for the check. A savings like this is called an *annuity,* and you'd be surprised at how quickly the money can accumulate. Table 17-1 shows some examples based on a 4.5% annual interest rate.

Types of Savings Accounts

There are different types of savings accounts, each with its own benefits and drawbacks.

 **Tip**   *All the accounts discussed in this chapter (except when noted) should be insured by the FDIC (Federal Deposit Insurance Corporation). This organization covers savings deposits up to $100,000 per entity (person or company) per bank, thus protecting you from loss in the event of a bank failure.*

	Weekly Contributions				Monthly Contributions				
Month	$25	$50	$75	$100	$50	$100	$200	$300	$400
1	$100	$200	$300	$401	$50	$100	$200	$300	$400
2	$226	$452	$677	$903	$100	$200	$401	$601	$801
3	$327	$653	$980	$1,307	$151	$301	$602	$903	$1,205
4	$428	$856	$1,284	$1,712	$201	$402	$805	$1,207	$1,609
5	$555	$1,110	$1,665	$2,220	$252	$504	$1,008	$1,511	$2,015
6	$657	$1,314	$1,971	$2,628	$303	$606	$1,211	$1,817	$2,423
7	$759	$1,519	$2,278	$3,038	$354	$708	$1,416	$2,124	$2,832
8	$888	$1,776	$2,664	$3,552	$405	$811	$1,621	$2,432	$3,242
9	$991	$1,982	$2,974	$3,965	$457	$914	$1,827	$2,741	$3,654
10	$1,095	$2,190	$3,284	$4,379	$509	$1,017	$2,034	$3,051	$4,068
11	$1,225	$2,449	$3,674	$4,899	$560	$1,121	$2,242	$3,363	$4,483
12	$1,329	$2,658	$3,987	$5,316	$613	$1,225	$2,450	$3,675	$4,900

Table 17-1 • Saving Regularly Is the Best Way to Save Money

Standard Savings Accounts   All banks offer savings accounts and most accommodate any balance. Savings accounts pay interest on your balance and allow you to deposit or withdraw funds at any time.

Holiday Clubs   A "holiday club" account is a savings account into which you make regular, equal deposits, usually on a weekly basis. Many banks offer these accounts, along with an option to automatically withdraw the deposit funds from your regular savings or checking account. The money stays in the account, earning interest until the club ends in October or November. The idea behind these accounts is to provide you with cash for the holidays, but there are variations on this theme, such as vacation club accounts that end in May or June.

Credit Union Payroll Savings   A bank isn't the only place where you can open a savings account. If your company has a credit union, it also offers a number of accounts. These accounts often offer the option of payroll savings deductions. This is a great feature for people who have trouble saving money, because the money comes out of their paycheck before they see (and can spend) it. It's as if the money never existed, when in reality it's accumulating in an interest-bearing account. In case you're wondering, the withdrawn funds are included in your taxable income.

Tip   I had a payroll savings account with the credit union of my last employer. Every time I got a raise, I increased the amount of the savings withdrawal so my take-home pay was almost the same. Before I left that job, I was saving $100 a week and I didn't miss a penny of it. Not bad!

Certificates of Deposit   A certificate of deposit, or CD, is an account, normally with a bank, that requires you to keep the money on deposit for a specific length of time. As a reward for your patience, your earnings are based on a higher, fixed interest rate than what is available for a regular savings account. The longer the term of the deposit and the more money deposited, the higher the rate. At the CD's maturity date, you can "roll over" the deposit to a new account that may have a different interest rate, or you can take back the cash. If you withdraw the money before the CD's maturity date, you pay a penalty, which can sometimes exceed the amount of the interest earned.

Money Market Accounts   A money market account is actually a form of investment, but it should be included here because it is offered by many banks. It has a higher rate of return than a regular savings account but is not insured by the FDIC. It is considered a conservative investment and can be treated just like a savings account for depositing and withdrawing money.

Interest-Bearing Checking Accounts   Many banks offer interest-bearing checking accounts. They usually have minimum balance requirements, however, forcing you to keep a certain amount of money in the account at all times. Although it's nice to earn money on checking account funds, the interest rate is usually so low that it's better to have a regular checking account and keep your savings in a savings account or money market account.

Reducing Your Debt

It's not easy to save money if most of your income is spent paying credit card bills and loan payments. If you're heavily in debt, you might even be having trouble keeping up with all your payments. If that's the case, stop thinking about saving for a moment and start thinking about reducing your debt.

Consumer credit is a huge industry. It's easy to get credit cards—sometimes too easy. And it's a lot easier to pay for something with a piece of plastic than with cold, hard cash. The "buy now, pay later" attitude has become an acceptable way of life. It's no wonder that many Americans are deeply in debt.

Those credit card bills can add up, however. And paying just the minimum payment on each one only helps the credit card company keep you in debt—and paying interest—as long as possible. I've been there, so I know. Unfortunately, it took two experiences to set me straight. I hope you can learn your lesson the first time.

Don't despair. There is hope. Here are a few things you can do to dig yourself out of debt.

 GET SMARTER   Use the Debt Reduction Planner on Quicken.com to develop a complete plan for reducing your debt. I tell you about it later in this chapter.

Breaking the Pattern

Your first step in reducing debt must be to break the pattern of spending that got you where you are. For most people, that means cutting up credit cards. After all, it's tough to use a credit card if you can't hand it to a cashier at the check-out counter.

Before you take out the scissors, however, read this: You don't have to cut up *all* of your credit cards. Leave yourself one or two major credit cards for emergencies like car trouble or unexpected visits to the doctor. The cards that should go are the store and gas credit cards. They can increase your debt, but they can only be used in a few places.

Here's the logic behind this strategy. If you have 15 credit cards, each with a credit limit of $2,000, you can get yourself into $30,000 of debt. The minimum monthly payment for each card may be $50. That's $750 a month in minimum credit card payments. If you have only two credit cards, each with a credit limit of $2,000, you can only get yourself into $4,000 of debt. Your monthly minimum payment may be only $100. This reduces your monthly obligation, enabling you to pay more than the minimum so you can further reduce your debt.

Shopping for Cards with Better Interest Rates

Yes, it's nice to have a credit card with your picture on it. Or one that's gold, platinum, or titanium. Or one with your college, team, club, or association name on it. A friend of mine who breeds horses showed off a new Visa card with a picture of a horse on it. She told me it was her favorite. I asked her what the interest rate was and she didn't know.

The purpose of a credit card is to purchase things on credit. When you maintain a balance on the account, you pay interest on it. The balance and interest rate determine how much it costs you to have that special picture or name on a plastic card in your wallet. Is it worth 19.8% a year? Or 21%? Not to me!

Tip   *Here's a reality check exercise: Gather together all of your credit card bills for the most recent month. Now add up all the monthly finance fees and interest charges. Multiply that number by 12. The result is an approximation of what you pay in interest each year. Now imagine how nice it would be to have that money in your hands the next time you went on vacation or needed a down payment on a new car or home.*

Low-interest credit cards are widely available. Sometimes you don't even have to look for them—offers arrive in the mail all the time. They promise low rates—usually under 10% a year. But you must read these offers carefully before you apply for one of these cards. Most offer the low rates for a short, introductory period—usually no longer than six months. (I got one once that offered 0% for the first 25 days. Big deal.) Some offer the low rate only on new purchases, while others offer the low rate only on balance transfers or cash advances. Be sure to find out what the rate is after the introductory period.

Here are two strategies for using a low-interest card:

- Consolidate your debt by transferring the balances of other credit cards to the new card. For this strategy, select a card that offers a low rate on balance transfers. When you transfer the balances, be sure to cut up the old cards so you don't use them to add more to your debt.
- Make purchases with the low-interest card. Make the new card your emergency credit card. Be sure to cut up your old emergency card so you don't wind up using both of them.

Tip *If you really like that special picture or name on the card in your wallet, call the credit card company and ask if they can give you a better interest rate. In many instances, they can—especially when you tell them you want to close your account.*

Consolidating Your Debt

Consolidating your debt is one of the best ways to dig yourself out. By combining balances into one debt, whether through balance transfers to a single credit card or a debt consolidation loan, you're better able to pay off the balances without causing financial hardship. This is sometimes the only option when things have gotten completely out of control and you can't meet your debt obligations.

Tip *If you own a home, consider a home equity loan to consolidate your debt. The interest rate is usually lower than any credit card or debt consolidation loan and the interest may be tax-deductible. I tell you more about home equity loans in Chapter 15.*

Using Charge Cards, Not Credit Cards

There's a difference between a credit card and a charge card:

- **Credit cards** enable you to buy things on credit. If each month you pay less than what you owe, you are charged interest on your account balance. Most major "credit cards" are true credit cards. MasterCard, Visa, and Discover are three examples. Most store "charge cards" are also credit cards.

- **Charge cards** enable you to buy things on credit, too. But when the bill comes, you're expected to pay the entire balance. You don't have to pay any interest, but if you don't pay the entire balance on time, you may have to pay late fees and finance charges. American Express is an example of a charge card.

The benefit of charge cards is that they make it impossible to get into debt. How can you owe the charge card company money if you must pay the balance in full every month? Using these cards prevents you from overspending. Every time you use the card to make a purchase, a little accountant in the back of your head should be adding the charge to a running total. You should stop spending when that total reaches the limit of your ability to pay.

Tip   *Chapters 4 and 12 explain how you can use Quicken to track credit card balances manually or online. This includes charge cards. If you use Quicken to keep track of expenditures, you won't need that little accountant in the back of your head.*

If you don't want an American Express card (for whatever reason), use another major credit card as a charge card. Just pay the entire balance each time you get a bill. If you don't carry a balance you won't be charged interest.

If You Can't Stop Spending, Get Help

Many people who are deeply in debt may have a spending problem. They can't resist buying that fifth pair of running shoes or that trendy new outdoor furniture. They don't need the things they buy, but they buy them anyway. There's nothing wrong with that if your income can support your spending habits, but if your net worth is less than $0, it's a real problem—one that might require counseling to resolve.

The next time you make a purchase, stop for a moment and think about what you're buying. Is it something you need? Something you can use? Something you can justify spending the money on? If you can't answer yes to these questions, don't buy it. If you have to buy it anyway, it's time to seek professional help.

Living Debt-Free

It is possible to live debt-free—and you don't have to be rich to do it. Just learn to stop relying on credit cards to make your purchases and to spend only what you can afford to.

With the exception of my mortgage, I've been debt-free for the past three years. I do have major credit and charge cards, but I pay their balances in full every month, along with the bills I get for utilities and other living expenses. My trick: I only spend what I can afford to. I'm able to save whatever money I don't spend, and I don't pay a penny of nondeductible interest. Compared to the feeling I had (twice) when I was drowning in debt, being debt-free feels great! Try it sometime and see for yourself.

Planning for Retirement

Throughout your life, you work and earn money to pay your bills, buy the things you and your family need or want, and help your kids get started with their own lives. But there comes a day when it's time to retire. Those regular paychecks stop coming and you find yourself relying on the money you put away for retirement.

Retirement planning is one of the most important financial planning jobs facing individuals and couples. In this section I tell you about the importance of planning, and offer some planning steps and a word of advice based on personal experience.

The Importance of Planning

Retired people live on fixed incomes. That's not a problem—*if* the income is fixed high enough to support a comfortable lifestyle. You can help ensure that there's enough money to finance your retirement years by planning and saving now.

Poor retirement planning can lead to catastrophic results—imagine running out of money when you turn 75. Or having to make a lifestyle change when you're 65 just to accommodate a much lower income.

Planning is even more important these days as longevity increases. People are living longer than ever. Your retirement dollars may need to support you for 20 years or more, at a time when the cost of living will likely be much higher than it is today.

With proper planning, it's possible to properly finance your retirement years without putting a strain on your working years. By closely monitoring the status of your retirement funds and periodically adjusting your plan and acting accordingly, your retirement years can be the golden years they're supposed to be.

Planning Steps

Retirement planning is much more than deciding to put $2,000 in an IRA every year. It requires careful consideration of what you have, what you'll need, and how you can make those two numbers the same.

Tip *Quicken's Retirement Calculator and Quicken.com's Retirement Planner, which I discuss later in this chapter, can help you perform many of the calculations you need to come up with a good retirement plan.*

Assess What You Have

Take a good look at your current financial situation. What tax-deferred retirement savings do you already have? A pension? An IRA? Something else? What regular savings do you have? What taxable investments do you have? The numbers you come up with will form the basis of your final retirement funds—like a seed you'll grow.

Be sure to consider property that can be liquidated to contribute to retirement savings. For example, if you currently live in a large home to accommodate your family, you may eventually want to live in a smaller home. The proceeds from the sale of your current home may exceed the cost of your retirement home. Also consider any income-generating property that may continue to generate income in your retirement years or can be liquidated to contribute to retirement savings.

Tip *Your savings, investments, and other assets are part of your net worth. If you use Quicken to track all of your assets, you can use its reporting feature to generate a Net Worth report. I explain how in Chapter 9.*

Determine What You'll Need

What you'll need depends on many things. One simple calculation suggests you'll need 80% of your current gross income to maintain your current lifestyle in your retirement years. You may find a calculation like this handy if retirement is still many years in the future and you don't really know what things will cost.

Time is an important factor in calculating the total amount you should have saved by retirement day. Ask yourself two questions:

- **How long do you have to save?** Take your current age and subtract it from the age at which you plan to retire. That's the number of years you have left to save.

- **How long will you be in retirement?** Take the age at which you plan to retire and subtract it from the current life expectancy for someone your age and gender. That's the number of years you have to save for.

When I did this math, I learned that I have only 22 years left to save for a 28-year retirement. I'm glad I've been saving!

Develop an Action Plan

Once you know how much you need, it's time to think seriously about how you can save it. This requires putting money away in one or more savings or investment accounts. I tell you about your options a little later in this chapter.

Stick to the Plan!

The most important part of any plan is sticking to it. For example, if you plan to save $5,000 a year, don't think you can just save $2,000 this year and make up the $3,000 next year. There are two reasons: First, you can't "make up" the interest lost on the $3,000 you didn't save this year. Second, you're only kidding yourself if you think you'll manage to put away $8,000 next year.

If you consider deviating from your plan, just think about the alternative: making ends meet with a burger-flipping job in the local fast food joint when you're 68 years old.

Don't Wait! Act Now!

I remember when I first began thinking about retirement. I was 30 or 31 and had been self-employed for about three years. I didn't have a pension or 401(k) plan with my former employer. I didn't have much saved. I only had $2,000 in an IRA. Up until that point, I never worried about retirement. But one day, something just clicked and retirement became something to think about.

I've done a lot of retirement planning and saving since then. While I admit that I don't have a perfect plan (yet), I've certainly come a long way in six years. But when I consider how much more I could have saved if I'd begun five years earlier, I could kick myself for waiting.

See for yourself. Table 17-2 shows how $1,000, $2,000, and $5,000 per year contributions to a tax-deferred retirement account earning 8% a year can grow. (These calculations do not take into consideration tax benefits or inflation.)

Start Age	Years of Saving	Savings at Age 62		
		$1,000/year	$2,000/year	$5,000/year
60	2	$2,080	$4,160	$10,400
55	7	$8,923	$17,846	$44,614
50	12	$18,977	$37,954	$94,886
45	17	$33,750	$67,500	$168,751
40	22	$55,457	$110,914	$277,284
35	27	$87,351	$174,702	$436,754
30	32	$134,214	$268,427	$671,068
25	37	$203,070	$406,141	$1,015,352
20	42	$304,244	$608,487	$1,521,218

Table 17-2 • Your Savings Can Grow Over Time

Retirement Funds

There are many different kinds of retirement funds. In this section, I tell you about the most common: social security, pension plans, tax-deferred savings and investments, and other savings and investments.

Social Security

Social security is the government's way of helping us fund our retirement. If you work, you make mandatory contributions to the social security system. When you reach age 62, you can begin to collect benefits in the form of a monthly check. You don't have to collect social security until you reach the age of 70½; the longer you wait, the more your monthly benefit will be. One thing is relatively certain, however: your monthly benefit will probably not be enough to fund your retirement.

Tip   *You can find out how much you'll get from social security when you retire by obtaining a Personal Earnings and Benefit Estimate Statement (PEBES) from the Social Security Administration. Call 800-772-1213 to request your free copy.*

Pension Plans

Pension plans are among the most common—and most traditional—methods of retirement funding. They reward loyal employees by guaranteeing benefits upon retirement. There are several types of pension plans, including company pension plans and 401(k) and 403(b) plans.

Company Pension Plan

In a company pension plan you and your employer contribute regularly to a pension fund. This is commonly referred to as a *defined benefit plan,* because the final benefit can always be calculated using a formula that usually includes your years of service, final salary, and a fixed percentage rate. Benefits are usually paid monthly from your retirement date, for the rest of your life.

Most pension funds are insured by the Pension Benefit Guaranty Corporation (PBGC), a government agency that protects employer-sponsored defined benefit plans. That means the money will be there when you retire.

Company pension plans cannot be transferred from one employer to another. If you leave a job where you had a pension plan, your benefits stay with the plan until you turn 65, when you can start collecting benefits.

401(k) and 403(b) Plans

A 401(k) plan is a tax-deferred investment and savings plan that works like a personal pension fund for employees. It allows a company's employees to save and invest for their own retirement. The employee authorizes a pre-tax payroll deduction that is invested in one of the investment options offered by the plan. Some companies may match the employee's contribution by paying 25% to 100% into the plan.

There are two tax benefits to a 401(k) plan:

- **Reduction in taxable income.** Because the contribution comes from pre-tax earnings, it reduces the amount of taxable income, thus reducing the employee's income tax.
- **Taxes are deferred until money is withdrawn.** The contributions and earnings grow tax-deferred until withdrawal, when they are taxed as ordinary income. Because funds are normally withdrawn at retirement when the employee is in a lower tax bracket, the tax hit is reduced.

One of the benefits of a 401(k) plan over a company pension plan is portability. If you leave your job, you can take your 401(k) plan's funds to your new employer's plan or roll it over into an IRA.

A 403(b) plan is basically the same as a 401(k) plan, but it is designed for the employees of certain types of tax-exempt organizations.

Tax-Deferred Savings and Investments

You can take advantage of a number of tax-deferred savings and investments if you don't have a pension or want to supplement one. These plans all have one thing in common: they enable you to save money for retirement without paying taxes on interest or investment earnings until they are withdrawn.

IRAs

The most well-known type of tax-deferred savings is an Individual Retirement Account (IRA). An IRA is a tax-deferred investment and savings account that acts as a personal retirement fund for people with employment income. You hear a lot about these accounts around tax time because the government allows you to deduct contributions for many types of IRAs from your taxable income, thus reducing your taxes. Here's a summary of the different types of IRAs currently available:

- **IRA** contributions (up to $2,000) can be deductible or nondeductible; earnings are tax-deferred until withdrawn after the age of 59½, when they are taxed as ordinary income. There are two types of IRAs: regular and spousal. A regular IRA is designed for an individual, whereas a spousal IRA is designed for married couples in which only one person has employment income.

- **Roth IRA** contributions (up to $2,000) are not tax-deductible. The contributions and earnings, however, can be withdrawn *tax-free* after the age of 59½. The idea is to provide an alternative for people who expect to be in a high tax bracket when they retire. You can contribute to a Roth IRA for as long as you like.

- **SEP-IRA, or Simplified Employee Pension IRA,** is provided by sole proprietors of small businesses to employees (including themselves). The employer can contribute up to 15% of the employee's compensation, up to $24,000. The SEP-IRA is subject to the same other rules as an IRA. Employees with SEP-IRAs can also contribute to regular IRAs.

- **SARSEP-IRA, or Salary Reduction SEP-IRA,** is provided by sole proprietors of businesses with less than 25 employees. Contributions, which can be made by both employer and employee, are tax-deductible. The SARSEP-IRA is subject to the same other rules as an IRA. New SARSEP-IRA accounts can no longer be started; this type of savings and investment plan has been replaced by the SIMPLE-IRA.

- **SIMPLE-IRA or Savings Incentive Match Plan for Employees-IRA** replaced the SARSEP-IRA in 1997. It's basically the same as the SARSEP-IRA, but can be used by companies with up to 100 employees, and allows maximum contributions of $6,000 for the employee plus the employer share. The SIMPLE-IRA is subject to the same other rules as an IRA. Employees with SIMPLE-IRAs can also contribute to regular IRAs.

Keoghs

A Keogh plan is a tax-deferred retirement plan for self-employed individuals, including sole proprietors who report income on Schedule C, and partners who report income on Schedule E. Contributions and earnings are tax-deferred until withdrawn after the age of 59½. There are two kinds of Keogh plans:

- **Profit-Sharing Keogh** plans allow contributions of up to 13.04% of your self-employment income, with a maximum of $30,000. The contribution percentage can be adjusted annually.
- **Money-Purchase Keogh** plans allow contributions of up to 20% of your self-employment income, with a maximum of $30,000. The contribution percentage you select must be the same from year to year.

Tax-Deferred Annuities

A tax-deferred annuity enables you to make contributions (that are not tax-deductible) toward an investment for which the earnings are tax-deferred until withdrawal, after the age of 59½. Annuities are sponsored by insurance companies and other financial institutions and are commonly available through agents, banks, stockbrokers, and financial planners. There are two types of annuities:

- **Fixed annuities** have a guaranteed rate of return.
- **Variable annuities** have a rate of return that varies based on the performance of the securities in which annuity funds are invested.

Other Savings and Investments

Any type of savings or investment can be used to fund your retirement: stocks, bonds, mutual funds, savings accounts, certificates of deposit, money market accounts, and so on. I tell you about these things in Chapter 16.

Unlike the tax-deferred savings and investments discussed in this chapter, taxable savings and investments can be liquidated or withdrawn and spent at any time. This is a two-edged sword. Although the money will always be available in the event of an emergency, you may find it a tough source of funds to resist when a new car or boat is on your mind. To me, the main benefit of retirement funds is that they're almost untouchable. In my mind, my retirement funds don't even belong to me right now—I'm not tempted to spend them.

You shouldn't overlook the tax benefits of tax-deferred retirement funds, either. Your money will grow more quickly when earnings aren't taxed.

Quicken Planning Calculators

Quicken includes three planning calculators that you can use to help yourself save money: the Investment Calculator, College Calculator, and Retirement Calculator. These calculators are very similar in appearance and functionality, but each is designed for a specific purpose.

Investment Calculator

The Investment Calculator enables you to calculate savings annuities. Choose Activities | Planning Calculators | Investment & Savings. The Investment Calculator appears:

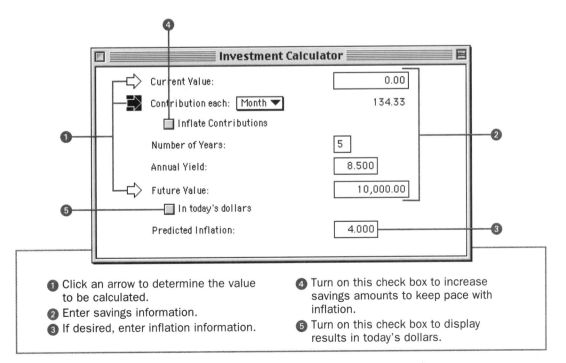

Begin by clicking one of the arrows to determine what should be calculated by Quicken:

- **Current Value** calculates the amount of money you should currently have saved based on the values you enter.
- **Contribution** calculates the minimum amount you should regularly contribute to savings based on the values you enter.
- **Future Value** calculates the total amount saved at the end of the savings period based on the values you enter.

Enter values throughout the window. Be sure to choose the appropriate contribution frequency from the pop-up menu. Most options are pretty straightforward and easy to understand. The Inflation options enable you to enter a predicted inflation rate, and then apply that rate to the calculation of the result. As you tab from field to field, Quicken calculates a result.

College Calculator

The College Calculator enables you to calculate savings for the cost of a college education. Choose Activities | Planning Calculators | College. The College Calculator appears:

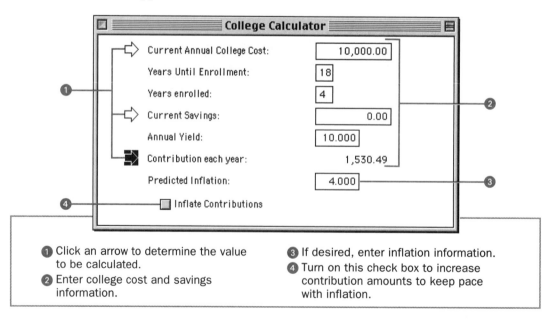

① Click an arrow to determine the value to be calculated.

② Enter college cost and savings information.

③ If desired, enter inflation information.

④ Turn on this check box to increase contribution amounts to keep pace with inflation.

First, click one of the arrows to determine which value Quicken should calculate:

- **Current Annual College Costs** calculates the annual tuition you'll be able to afford based on the values you enter.
- **Current Savings** calculates the amount of money you should currently have saved based on the values you enter.
- **Contribution Each Year** calculates the minimum amount you should contribute to college savings based on the values you enter.

Enter or select values throughout the window. Most options are pretty straightforward and easy to understand. The Inflate Contributions check box tells Quicken to increase your contributions to keep pace with inflation. When you tab from field to field, Quicken automatically recalculates the result.

Retirement Calculator

The Retirement Calculator can help you calculate some of the numbers you need to plan for your retirement. To open it, choose Activities | Planning Calculators | Retirement. The Retirement Calculator appears:

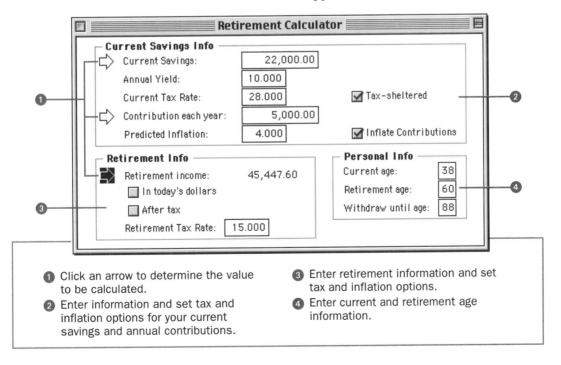

❶ Click an arrow to determine the value to be calculated.

❷ Enter information and set tax and inflation options for your current savings and annual contributions.

❸ Enter retirement information and set tax and inflation options.

❹ Enter current and retirement age information.

Begin by clicking the arrow for the value you want Quicken to calculate:

- **Current Savings** calculates the amount of money you should currently have saved based on the values you enter.
- **Contribution Each Year** calculates the minimum amount you should contribute to a retirement account based on the values you enter.
- **Retirement Income** calculates the annual amount of retirement income you'll have based on the values you enter.

Enter values and set options throughout the window. Most options are pretty straightforward and easy to understand. Tax and inflation options make complex calculations to account for the effect of taxes and inflation on your savings dollars. As you tab from field to field, Quicken calculates the result for you.

Quicken.com Resources

The Quicken.com Web site also offers resources for saving money and planning for the future. You can find them in three different Quicken.com departments: Life Events, Saving & Spending, and Retirement.

Tip *The Banking & Borrowing Department's main page also offers saving- and debt-related information—including current rates on savings accounts, money market accounts, and CDs. Open it by clicking the Banking & Credit link on the left side of the Quicken.com home page window. I tell you about its resources in Chapter 15, so consult that chapter to learn more about what you can find there.*

This section provides a quick summary of some of my favorite resources in these three Quicken.com departments.

Note *Like everything else on the Internet, the contents of the Quicken.com Web pages can change daily. Don't be surprised if the features you find don't match the ones shown in the figures throughout the rest of this chapter.*

Life Events Department

The Life Events Department (see Figure 17-1) is full of links you can use to help you plan for major events in your life, such as college, weddings, parenting, and retirement. You can view this page by clicking the Life Events link on the Quicken.com home page, or from within Quicken, by choosing Online | To the Web | Life Events.

Here are a few of my favorite links:

Tools & Resources   The Tools & Resources area offers several links to interactive tools you can use to plan for events and check your finances. The Life Events Planner (see Figure 17-2) is especially useful—it helps you plan for all kinds of major events. The quick Financial Fitness Quiz and longer Financial Health Checkup can help you understand the condition of your finances.

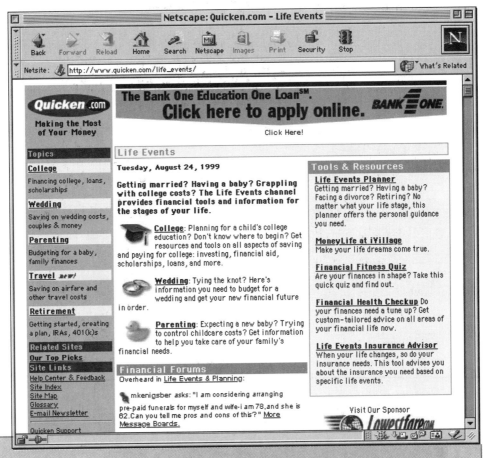

Figure 17-1 • The Life Events Department on Quicken.com offers links for planning.

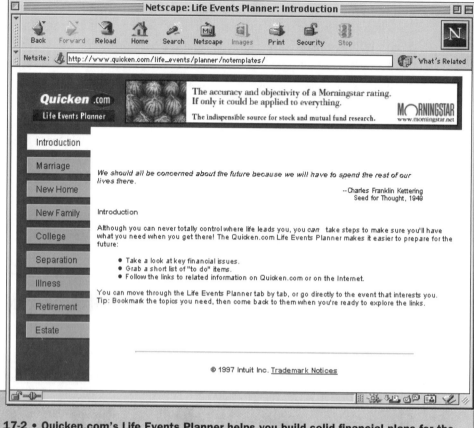

Figure 17-2 • Quicken.com's Life Events Planner helps you build solid financial plans for the events in your life.

Expert Advice   The Expert Advice area offers articles you can read to learn more about planning for major events in your life. Click an article title to read the article.

Our Top Picks   Click the Our Top Picks link to view a page full of links to high-quality Web sites where you can get more information about specific life events.

 SAVE TIME   Top Picks links on Quicken.com offer the best way to find valuable Web sites that are chock-full of information you can use. Using these links is a lot quicker and easier than using Internet search engines and wading through hundreds or thousands of matches.

Saving & Spending Department

The Saving & Spending Department (see Figure 17-3) is all about saving and spending money. You'll find links to articles, Web sites, and tools for doing just that. To open this page, click the Saving & Spending link on the Quicken.com home page.

Here are a few of the features I like:

Debt Reduction Planner   The Debt Reduction Planner is an interactive tool for helping you reduce your debt. You enter information about your financial situation and Quicken develops a debt reduction plan for you. As you'll see when you use the planner, Quicken's plan can save you hundreds (if not thousands) of

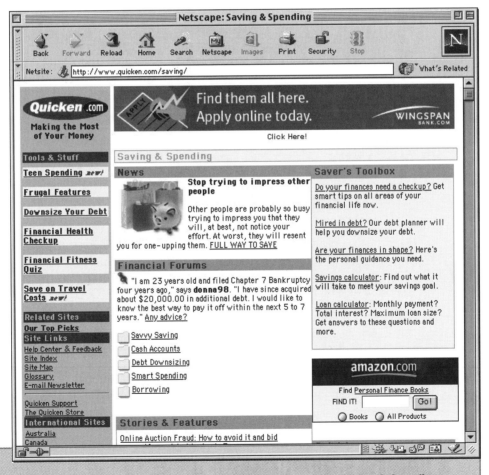

Figure 17-3 • Need help saving and spending money? Check out the Saving & Spending Department on Quicken.com.

dollars by reducing your debt as quickly as possible. To use this feature, click the Mired in Debt link on the Saving & Spending Department main page; or, from within Quicken, choose Online | To the Web | Debt Reduction Planner.

Frugal Features   Frugal Features has regularly updated articles about saving money by being frugal, as well as links to tools and resources for saving wisely. It's a great place to start if you want to save money but don't know how to begin.

QuickAnswers   The QuickAnswers area offers answers to questions you might have about saving and spending money. Many of these questions include interactive features where you can enter information about your financial situation and have Quicken.com calculate the results for you. For example, when you click the "How long will it take to reach your savings goal?" link, Quicken.com displays a Web page with a form for you to provide information. When you click the Calculate button on the page, the answer appears.

Stories & Features   The Stories and Features area offers links to articles related to saving and spending money. You'll find plenty of ideas that can really make a difference in your finances.

Retirement Department

The Retirement Department (see Figure 17-4) offers a wealth of information for retirement planning. To open the Retirement Department's main page, click the Retirement link on the Quicken.com home page.

Here are some links I find useful:

Retirement Planner   Quicken.com's Retirement Planner helps you build a complete plan for funding your retirement. It walks you, step by step, through the entry of information about your financial situation, and then provides you with instructions for implementing its plan. To use this feature, click the Retirement Planner link on the Retirement Department's main page; or, from within Quicken, choose Online | To the Web | Retirement Planner.

Areas   The Areas links on the left side of the Retirement Department's main page provide basic information about a number of retirement-related topics that should interest you, as well as interactive tools (like the Retirement Planner) that you can use to plan for your retirement.

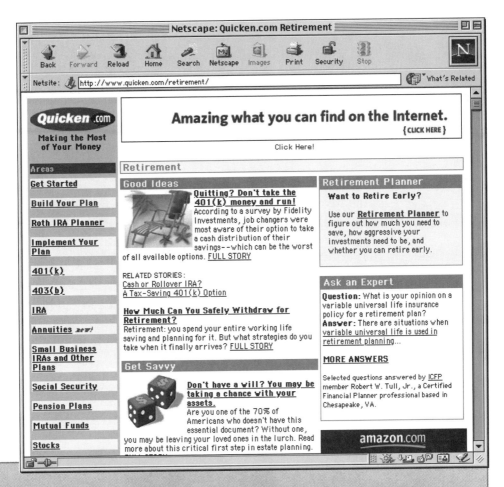

Figure 17-4 • Make the Retirement Department a regular place to visit if you're interested in planning for retirement.

Good Ideas   The Good Ideas area is full of just that: good ideas for retirement. Articles change regularly, so be sure to check in often to see what new ideas you can get.

Retirement QuickAnswers   This area provides links to specific questions and answers about retirement and retirement funds.

Index

D